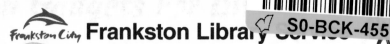

Green ... *Sh...*

BESTSELLING BOOK SERIES

Ten Gree...

- ✔ Replace sir... the dead o... ...dispose of
- ✔ Turn down...
- ✔ Unplug the... plug all cha... ...harged, or
- ✔ Disable you... when you'r... ...display ...ode after you're awa... ...for more than a fifteen minutes.
- ✔ Turn off any energy-wasting features you aren't using on mobile phones, computers, and other gadgets, including wireless (WiFi) networking, Bluetooth, and GPS.
- ✔ On portable gadgets with backlit screens, reduce brightness to the lowest comfortable level, and turn on autolock, screen dimming, and shutoff options if available.
- ✔ Read and review documents on the screen rather than print them on paper.
- ✔ If you must print, reduce your printer's quality setting to 300 dots per inch (dpi), print on both sides of the page, and refill inkjet and toner cartridges rather than buy new ones.
- ✔ Reduce fuel consumption and auto emissions by shopping and banking online and by renting or buying downloadable and streaming movies and TV programs rather than rent DVDs at your local video store or by mail.
- ✔ If your home's thermostat isn't programmable, buy one and set it to heat and cool only when you're at home.
- ✔ When purchasing new gadgets, research the most energy-efficient models by visiting mygreen electronics.org or energystar.gov.
- ✔ Consider selling unwanted gadgets locally on Craigslist or trading them in for cash or credit toward a new product by visiting EZTradein.com.

The Best Green Gadget Web Sites

- ✔ **CNET Green Tech:** news.cnet.com/greentech
- ✔ **EcoGeek:** ecogeek.org
- ✔ **Electronic House:** electronichouse.com
- ✔ **The Fun Times Guide to Living Green:** green.thefuntimesguide.com
- ✔ **Green Daily:** greendaily.com/category/gadgets-and-tech
- ✔ **Greenpeace:** greenpeace.org/electronics
- ✔ **Inhabitat:** inhabitat.com/category/green-gadgets
- ✔ **Mother Nature Network:** www.mnn.com/technology
- ✔ **PC magazine Green Tech:** pcmag.com/category2/0,2806,2256470,00.asp
- ✔ **TreeHugger:** treehugger.com

For Dummies: Bestselling Book Series for Beginners

Green Gadgets For Dummies®

Cheat Sheet

Implementing the 4 Rs in Your Life

Unplug chargers and other energy vampires.

Install sight sensors that turn lights on and off whenever you enter and exit a room.

Map your trip with a GPS navigator so that you arrive as quickly and efficiently as possible.

Shop, bank, and rent downloadable movies and TV shows online rather than drive around in your car.

Refill your printer's ink or toner cartridges.

Donate, sell, or give away unwanted gadgets.

Upgrade your existing computer rather than buy a new one.

Choose rewriteable CD and DVD discs over single-use discs.

REDUCE

REUSE

RECYCLE

RETHINK

Contact computer manufacturers to see whether they offer take-back recycling programs.

Remove usable memory chips, hard disks, and other components before recycling your computer.

Enter your zip code at the Call2Recycle Web site at www.rbrc.org and then drop off dead mobile phone batteries at wireless stores or nearby locations.

Coordinate a gadget recycling day with friends and family.

After your current computer is ready to be replaced, buy a more efficient notebook computer rather than a desktop.

Choose a mobile phone whose housing is made of recycled plastic bottles.

Select an ecofriendly HDTV that can turn itself off whenever you specify or when it senses you've left the room.

Connect to an ecofriendly WiFi home network router that cuts power to Ethernet ports when connected devices are turned off or are not accessing the network.

For Dummies: Bestselling Book Series for Beginners

Green Gadgets

FOR

DUMMIES®

Green Gadgets FOR DUMMIES®

by Joe Hutsko

Foreword by Tom Zeller Jr.
Editor, Green Inc.
The New York Times

WILEY

Wiley Publishing, Inc.

Green Gadgets For Dummies®

Published by
Wiley Publishing, Inc.
111 River Street
Hoboken, NJ 07030-5774
www.wiley.com

WILEY

About the Author

Joe Hutsko lives in Ocean City, New Jersey and blogs about green gadgets for the Green Inc. section of the *New York Times*. For more than two decades, he has written about computers, gadgets, video games, trends, and high-tech movers and shakers for numerous publications and Web sites, including *Macworld, PC World, Fortune, Newsweek, Popular Science, TV Guide, The Washington Post, Wired,* Gamespot, MSNBC, and Salon.com. You can find links to Joe's stories on his tech blog, JOEyGADGET.com, and on his green gadgets blog, gGadget.org.

As a kid, Joe built a shortwave radio, played with electronic project kits, and learned the basics of the BASIC programming language on his first computer, the Commodore Vic 20. In his teens, he picked strawberries to buy his first Apple II computer. Four years after that purchase (in 1984), he wound up working for Apple, where he became the personal technology guru for the company's chairman and CEO. Joe left Apple in 1988 to become a writer and worked on and off for other high-tech companies, including Steve Jobs' one-time NeXT. He authored a number of video game strategy guides, including the best sellers *Donkey Kong Country Game Secrets: The Unauthorized Edition,* and *Rebel Assault: The Official Insiders Guide.*

Joe's first novel, *The Deal,* was published in 1999, and he recently rereleased a trade paperback edition of it with a new foreword by the author (`tinyurl.com/hutskodeal`).

Dedication

This book is lovingly dedicated to my closest friend, considerate neighbor, and frequent dog walker and supper-supplying feeder, Frances Hutsko. Thank you, Mom, for being you.

Author's Acknowledgments

This book wouldn't have my name on its cover if my literary agent, Carole Jelen, hadn't reached out on LinkedIn.com last summer to say hello after we had fallen out of contact since meeting in the 1980s, when I was working at Apple. Thank you, Carole, for pitching me to Wiley acquisition editor Amy Fandrei — and thank you, Amy, for saying yes!

Kudos to copy editor Rebecca Whitney for minding my words, grammatically speaking.

I'm enormously grateful to Tom Zeller, Jr., the editor of the Green. Inc. section of the *New York Times,* for his insightful eye when helping me shape and edit my contributions on green gadgets. Special thanks to technology editor Damon Darlin, for making introductions — and for his first-rate guidance on features I've written for the newspaper's Personal Technology section.

Special thanks to the people and companies who provided the "greener" notebook computer loaners used to write this book, including Janette Barrios, Bill Evans, and Keri Walker of Apple; Jeffrey Witt of Lenovo; Kelly Odle of Gateway; and Debby Lee of ASUS.

Major thanks to every one of my ever-encouraging dear friends, especially Drew Davidson and Sue Godfrey, and to Ric Firmino, Katherine Etzel and Robert Pascale, David Unruh, David Baron, my cousin Chip McDermott, my brothers Steve and John, and my sister, Janice.

I'm deeply indebted to five close friends, without whose generous support and faith this book could not have been written (literally!): Lisa Napoli, Linda Williams, Randee Mia Berman, Val Petrosian, and the person to whom this book is dedicated.

Last but not least, I'm hugely grateful for having the cosmically good fortune of being assigned to project editor Nicole Sholly, for her gently worded yet enormously intelligent guidance, brilliant organization, incisive editing, well-honed instinct, and, above all, tremendous wit and generous sense of humor. Nicole, you were this first-time *For Dummies* author's dream-come-true-editor as we worked together to turn what was initially a nightmarishly over-whelming big-picture subject into 20 keenly focused, easy-to-understand chapters, from which I hope readers benefit as much from reading as I did from writing them.

Publisher's Acknowledgments

We're proud of this book; please send us your comments through our online registration form located at http://dummies.custhelp.com. For other comments, please contact our Customer Care Department within the U.S. at 877-762-2974, outside the U.S. at 317-572-3993, or fax 317-572-4002.

Some of the people who helped bring this book to market include the following:

Acquisitions, Editorial, and Media Development

Project Editor: Nicole Sholly

Acquisitions Editor: Amy Fandrei

Copy Editor: Rebecca Whitney

Technical Editor: Lee Musick

Editorial Manager: Kevin Kirschner

Media Development Project Manager: Laura Moss-Hollister

Media Development Assistant Project Manager: Jenny Swisher

Media Development Assistant Producers: Josh Frank, Marilyn Hummel, and Shawn Patrick

Editorial Assistant: Amanda Foxworth

Sr. Editorial Assistant: Cherie Case

Cartoons: Rich Tennant (www.the5thwave.com)

Composition Services

Project Coordinator: Lynsey Stanford

Layout and Graphics: Reuben W. Davis, Christine Williams

Proofreaders: Cynthia Fields, Amanda Graham

Indexer: Sharon Shock

Special Help: Brian Walls, Barry Childs-Helton, and Jennifer Riggs

---

Publishing and Editorial for Technology Dummies

    Richard Swadley, Vice President and Executive Group Publisher

    Andy Cummings, Vice President and Publisher

    Mary Bednarek, Executive Acquisitions Director

    Mary C. Corder, Editorial Director

Publishing for Consumer Dummies

    Diane Graves Steele, Vice President and Publisher

Composition Services

    Debbie Stailey, Director of Composition Services

Contents at a Glance

Table of Contents

Foreword

· ·

*T*he very idea of "green gadgets," to many, might seem an oxymoron. After all, it is a fundamental tenet of the environmental movement that less stuff is better, and that consumerism — the thing that makes us want to have that snazzy new cell phone, or to covet that nifty new digital camera — is at odds with maxims like "reduce, reuse, recycle."

There's some truth to this paradox — but it is hardly the only way to frame the contribution that technology can make to a greener, cleaner world. Setting aside the efforts underway to develop large-scale, clean-energy technologies like wind and solar power, which promise to address the steady march of climate change, there remain myriad ways for ordinary consumers to make simple adjustments in how they live — and what they buy — to generate substantial environmental gains.

In many cases, gadgets can help. Sure, we could all do better to manage our electricity consumption at home — but what if there were a product that could provide detailed data on when and where we were being most wasteful? What if there were "greener" versions of the technologies — like computers and cell phones — that we use frequently, and upgrade regularly?

Of course, such technologies do exist, and that's part of what Joe Hutsko has assembled here: A guide to green gadgetry and how you can best deploy it to your own personal environmental advantage.

But this is not just a buying guide, and there's a key point in that: Making better, less wasteful use of the gadgets you already own, and finding sensible ways to reduce, reuse and recycle those things you no longer need, are first-order strategies for consumers seeking to limit their overall footprint.

So, too, is learning to understand the increasingly complex eco-friendly and energy-efficent labeling systems used to keep consumers informed. You'll find guidance on these matters here as well.

There is no magic wand — no magic gadget — that will neutralize consumers' impact on the planet. But I think few green advocates would quibble with the idea that every consumer can make simple, informed choices about the technologies they buy and the energy they use — and that these decisions, factored collectively, are an indispensable part of any environmental movement.

Tom Zeller Jr.
Editor, Green Inc.
the *New York Times*

Introduction

*I*f you're in interested in finding out all about the latest environmentally and economically friendly gadgets and computers, if you want to use more efficiently the gadgets you already own, and if you want to know how to get rid of those gadgets in a responsible way, *Green Gadgets For Dummies* is the book for you.

Whether you're reading this book to get greener with gadgets to help save the planet — or just to save some green in your wallet — one thing is certain: Reading this book can help you achieve both goals at the same time. But this book can't cover everything there is to know about green gadgets the world over. Even the most ardent green gadget activist, thinker, blogger, designer, or enthusiast would be hard pressed to tell you everything there is to know about green gadgets. (There's just that much to know.) *Green Gadgets For Dummies*, however, gives you a running start along a much greener path.

About Green Gadgets For Dummies

Technology moves at the speed of light, and although high-tech companies were comparatively slow to jump on the get-green bandwagon, they're now falling all over each other in an effort to claim the title of World's Greenest Company that created the World's Greenest <insert gadget name here>.

I climbed aboard that get-green wagon 25 years ago as a household recycler when I lived in California. Though I'm a little older now, I'm also a lot wiser, but I'm as passionate as ever about finding, figuring out, using, and writing about green gadgets, gizmos, and high-tech gear. I've written this book to share that passion. Here are some of the things you can do with this book:

- ✔ Understand the role that gadgets play in affecting the environment
- ✔ Instantly take action to begin living a greener lifestyle with the gadgets and electronics you own
- ✔ Get a handle on green gadget factors to make the most energy-efficient choices possible when buying new mobile phones, computers, and other electronic devices

- ✔ Find ways to "do the right thing" by donating, gifting, trading, or selling working and useful but unwanted computers and other gadgets

- ✔ Properly dispose of broken or hopelessly useless gadgets and electronics with the smallest impact on the planet

- ✔ Protect your identity by securely erasing your personal information from gadgets and computers before getting rid of them

Foolish Assumptions

In writing this book, I made a few assumptions about you, dear reader. To make sure we're on the same page, I assume that

- ✔ You give a darn about the planet.

- ✔ You don't think we should live in caves, but you do believe we should be conscious about how we use energy to power our gadgets.

- ✔ You know your way around your Web browser.

- ✔ You're comfortable turning your gadgets and computers on and off, and you use them for the basic purposes for which they were intended.

- ✔ You want practical advice on making green gadget purchases and using the gadgets you own so as to save energy and a little money, too.

- ✔ You know that following that practical advice and saving energy will make a difference in the world but that you and your gadgets can't (unfortunately) completely save it overnight.

- ✔ You understand that products used to illustrate green (or not-so-green) gadget qualities don't constitute endorsements, unless otherwise explicitly stated, of said products and the companies that manufacture and sell them.

- ✔ You appreciate the speed at which technology-based products change, with newer, sleeker, better, faster models replacing previous versions in as little as a few months. (Which is to say, the products used to illustrate green gadget features, qualities, and behaviors might be replaced by newer models by the time you read this book.)

- ✔ You realize that it's therefore up to you to go online to find updated information about the companies and products described throughout this book.

✔ You know that keeping up with the topic of green gadgets and green technologies and trends (even as a full-time job, as it is for me) still can't make a guy the Ghandi of Green Gadgets. You will, accordingly, alert me to cool stuff you discover in your green gadget odyssey so that I can consider including it in the next edition of this book.

✔ You don't expect general green living advice, especially because you can buy, or might already own, the best book on the subject — *Green Living For Dummies,* by Yvonne Jeffery, Liz Barclay, and Michael Grosvenor (Wiley Publishing).

Conventions Used in This Book

To help you navigate this book as efficiently as the green gadgets it helps you get the most from, I use a few style conventions:

✔ Terms or words that I *truly* want to emphasize are *italicized* (and defined).

✔ Web site addresses, or URLs, are shown in a special monofont typeface, `like this`.

✔ Numbered steps that you need to follow and characters you need to type are set in **bold**.

What You Don't Have to Read

You don't have to read anything that doesn't pertain to what you're interested in. In fact, you can even skip a chapter entirely. I hope you don't, though, because I believe that reading all chapters can make your overall reading experience more efficient and (dare I say it?) enjoyable.

As for sidebars you encounter throughout this book, feel free to ignore them because they contain, for the most part, tangential thoughts, miniature essays, or otherwise forgettable blathering that you're just as likely to forget anyway after you read them. Ditto for any of the text you see alongside the Technical Stuff icon.

How This Book Is Organized

Because all *For Dummies* books are structured in a modular way, you're free to remove your seatbelt and roam about this one in whatever way you like. *Green Gadgets For Dummies* is split into six parts, and the book's table of contents can help you find the topic you're looking for. From there, you can go directly to the part, chapter, or section you're interested in and skip all the rest. You'll find no required reading here. In this section, however, I briefly describe which green-gadget-related information you'll find in each part.

Part I: Settling into a Green Gadget Mindset

In this part, I explain what green gadgets are (and aren't), describe the effect they can have on the planet, and tell you about the mostly good, though sometimes bad or ugly, effects they can have on the environment when they're improperly disposed of. I also give you a bunch of instant-action tips and steps you can take to get greener with the gadgets, gizmos, and other consumer electronics devices you tote on your person or use in your home or at work.

Part II: Getting Green with Gadgets You Own

Making the most of the gadgets you already own by using them more efficiently — and saving money by using less energy — is what it's all about in Part II, Alfie. From tweaking your mobile phone settings to turning off features you aren't using, this part is where you can find out how to do your part in reducing the toll your gadgets take on the environment.

Part III: Minimizing Your Computer's Carbon Footprint

Lowering your system's consumption can shave as much as $75 from your yearly electricity expense. You don't do it by using a screen saver to save energy (that's the type of myth I debunk in this part), but you can make adjustments to your Windows or Mac computer's power-saving settings to save energy for real. I also give you tips and tricks for reducing the number of energy-consuming things you connect to your computer, such as printers and mobile phones.

Part IV: Acquiring Green Gadgets and Gear

There's no other way to say it, so I'll just say it: Let's go shopping! Maybe you're looking for a super-efficient HDTV to replace that conked-out tube TV that finally gave up the ghost. Or, you might be in the market for the most environmentally friendly mobile phone (and wireless provider) money can buy. Chances are good that you'll find what you're looking for in these chapters.

Part V: Ridding Yourself of Gadgets the Green Way

You need to know all your options when the time comes to get rid of gadgets you no longer use. In this part, I cover organizations and take-back programs that can find grateful homes for your working but unwanted computer or mobile phone. I help you find the closest drop-off location for your fried note-book, and I also describe the many ways to properly dispose of your digital stuff.

Part VI: The Part of Tens

Here's where things start out a little kooky — in a good way. The first two chapters in Part VI contain a total of 20 cool green gadgets. The first 10 are green add-ons and accessories for your computer. The items in the second set — with the exception of one — aren't real products that you can acquire. Not yet, anyway. They represent the ten design finalists from the 2009 Greener Gadgets Conference, which I attended a week before finishing this book. The last two chapters are where you'll find ten green gadget buying tips and answers to ten frequently asked questions about green gadgets.

The companion Web site

Throughout this book, I provide several Web site URLs where you can go to find more information about companies, gadgets, and general green issues. To help you navigate to some of these places more easily, I have provided a list of links on the companion Web site. Just go to `www.dummies.com/go/greengadgetsfd` and click the link for whatever site you want to peruse.

Icons Used in This Book

What's a *For Dummies* book without icons pointing you in the direction of focused information that's sure to help you along your way? The icons you encounter throughout *Green Gadgets For Dummies* are tiny road signs to attract or steer your attention to particularly useful information — or, in rare instances, potential trouble.

The Tip icon points out useful nuggets of information that can help you get things done more efficiently or direct you to something helpful that you might not know about.

When you spot this icon, it grabs your attention so that I don't have to say something like "Remember: Unplug your cellphone charger when your phone is fully charged so that it doesn't continue to draw and waste electricity."

Danger, Will Robinson! When you see the Warning icon, you know to proceed with caution in regard to a topic, an issue, or a series of steps that it's cozying up next to.

This icon highlights actions you can take — now or in the future — to make you an especially greener person.

Techie types, such as me, wouldn't dream of missing these byte-size bits of nerdiness. Everyone else, feel free to skip them.

Where to Go from Here

If you want to know what defines a green gadget and how you can instantly take action on the ones you own, without a lot of preamble, Part I is the starting point for you. If you're looking to spend some green on a green smartphone, computer, or wind-up charger so that you can keep your gadgets alive when you hit that remote campground, by all means step right up to Part III. If you aren't quite sure what your carbon footprint is, dive in at the beginning to wrap your brain around the basics, which can help you understand the sum of the other parts contained in all the other chapters that await you in *Green Gadgets For Dummies*.

Welcome to the world of green gadget living!

Part I

Settling into a Green Gadget Mindset

The 5th Wave   By Rich Tennant

"Russell! Do you remember last month when I told you to order 150 <u>SMART</u> phones for the sales department?"

In this part . . .

Understanding what makes a gadget green (or not so green) and how it affects the planet can give you a greater appreciation and confidence regarding your relationship with the gadgets in your life.

The first chapter in this part provides insight into how electronics products are manufactured, distributed, used, reused, and eventually recycled when they're no longer useful — and how all those tasks affect the planet. You find that the three Rs of green gadgets — reduce, reuse, and recycle — join forces with a fourth: rethink.

The second chapter lists numerous ways you can instantly get greener with the gadgets you own by taking steps to decrease energy consumption while increasing savings. The chapter also includes ways to reuse, repurpose, and properly recycle the gadgets you want to get rid of.

Chapter 1

Mother Nature's Green-Eyed View of Gadgets

In This Chapter

▶ Spelling out the meaning of green gadgets

▶ Understanding the effect of the three Rs — plus one — on the environment

▶ Discovering what makes the "greenest" gadgets green

▶ Getting acquainted with green gadget standards and ratings

▶ Calculating your gadgets' carbon footprints and taking steps to reduce them

▶ Keeping up on green gadget news

This is Chapter 1, so I start the chapter from the green beginning, as it were, and describe exactly what green gadgets are. A *green gadget* is one that's ecofriendlier, or greener, than products that have a greater negative impact on the environment in Mother Nature's eyes. You might already know about the three Rs of the environment — reduce, reuse, recycle — but you might not know about a fourth R: rethink. I tell you how all four Rs relate to gadgets and their relationship with the planet.

I take you on a tour of the greenest notebook available (at the time I wrote this book), to illustrate exactly how green gadget factors look and feel in terms of a product you can hold in your hands. I also show you a couple of other notably greener gadgets, explain the role that your existing gadgets play in the big-planet picture, and show you how you can calculate your gadgets' energy consumption to figure out — and reduce — their contribution to the carbon footprint you generate by using them.

Finally, I introduce you to the terms and green labels you should look for when shopping for new greener gadgets, and I explain what each one means.

A disclaimer

You know that voice that talks *really* fast at the end of a drug commercial? It's the one that says "talk to your doctor first" or "your mileage may vary." Herewith, my own speedy disclaimer of sorts (read as quickly as possible to simulate the full end-of-the-commercial effect):

"All mobile phones, PDAs, desktop computers, notebooks, TVs, and other gadgets described in this chapter and throughout this book were chosen to illustrate unique, greener-computing innovations and advances and are not meant to represent your only green choices, nor does their inclusion here represent an endorsement of one particular brand or model over others that aren't covered in these pages."

Hey, Joe, Where You Goin' with That Green Gadget in Your Hand?

Green gadget? What green gadget?

Do you mean the silver aluminum notebook I'm typing this chapter on, which Apple calls its "greenest MacBook ever?"

Or, do you mean the black, solar-powered Iqua SUN Bluetooth headset, stuck in my ear, that charged itself in the morning sunlight as I walked my dog, Nick, on the beach and answered a call from my mom?

Maybe you're referring to The Energy Detective (TED) sitting on my kitchen counter. It displays in real-time exactly how much electricity my house is consuming in kilowatts — and in dollars and cents. Is *that* the green gadget you're talking about? (I probably should mention that The Energy Detective is housed in white plastic.)

Ohhh, now I get you. You mean *that* green gadget — the big, round, pulsating ecobutton, sitting next to my Eee PC 1000HE, that with a single touch can instantly make the mini-notebook go to sleep by switching it to ecofriendlier Suspend mode. And yes, although the photo of the gadget in Figure 1-1 is in black and white, I can attest to the fact that the ecobutton's base is green and the pulsating lights inside are absolutely, positively, 100 percent green-green-green or my name isn't Joe.

Figure 1-1:
A snooze
button to
put your
computer to
sleep.

But my name would be Pinocchio if I told you that the ecobutton is, in spite of its green color and light, a green gadget.

It's not.

Neither is the MacBook, a solar Bluetooth headset, or a home energy monitor.

But all four represent considerably ecofriendlier, or *greener,* gadgets (what I refer to simply as green gadgets throughout the book) than products that are less sensitive to the planet.

So what *is* a green gadget?

Nothing. Because there's no such thing.

Wait! Before you double-check this book's cover to make sure that you're reading the book you thought you were reading (assuming that you didn't fling it across the room), let me explain what I mean.

Before I do, however, I want to take a bigger-picture view of how the gadgets and electronics in your life affect the planet in a number of ways, as calculated by the article "How to Go Green: Home Electronics" at The Discovery Channel Planet Green site (http://planetgreen.discovery.com/go-green/home-electronics):

- ✔ **15 percent:** The percentage of money spent on powering computers worldwide; the rest of the $250 billion is spent on energy wasted from idling.

- ✔ **70 percent:** The percentage of all hazardous waste that's composed of discarded electronics.

- ✔ **529 pounds:** The amount of fossil fuels needed to manufacture a 53-pound computer system (including the monitor), along with 49 pounds of chemicals and 1.5 tons of water.

- ✔ **15 billion:** The number of batteries produced annually worldwide.

- ✔ **40 percent:** The percentage of energy used for electronics in your home while the devices are turned off.

- ✔ **1 billion:** The number of kilowatt hours of power each year that can be saved by using energy-efficient battery chargers in the United States. This in turn would save more than $100 million each year and prevent the release of more than a million tons of greenhouse gases.

Assessing "green" companies

Just because a company says that it and its products are green doesn't necessarily make them so, as I explain further in Chapter 9, the chapter that dispels the myths of greenwash hype. In a 2008 Consumer Electronics Association (CEA) survey, 74 percent of consumers polled said that companies should do more to protect the environment. Yet only 17 percent of consumers said they felt familiar with the policies and reputations of companies that manufacture consumer electronics. What's more, more than half of the people polled said they felt that companies overstate the environmental friendliness of their products in order to sell more of them.

To quote the environmental organization Greenpeace (`http://greenpeace.org/electronics`) about the findings of its 2008 Green Electronics Survey, it found "no products that could claim the title of a truly green product."

However, both Greenpeace and the CEA report that companies manufacturing gadgets are increasingly eliminating toxic chemicals from their products while making them more energy-efficient and easier to recycle.

Here are some of the choice nuggets uncovered by the 2008 Greenpeace survey:

- ✔ **Manufacturers continue to phase out the use of hazardous chemicals, and more products are PVC-free than in the previous year's findings.** Notebooks that use LED-type LCD displays that draw less power and are free of mercury are becoming more popular.

- ✔ **Larger consumer electronics, such as TVs and computer monitors, are being manufactured with significant amounts of postconsumer recycled plastic.** Most mobile phones and desktop and notebook computers, however, are lagging in this regard.

- ✔ **Manufacturers have adapted quickly to new Energy Star requirements.** Even so, a small number of products that Greenpeace evaluated don't yet meet the most recent Energy Star specifications.

- ✔ **More manufacturers track the amount of energy used to produce their electronic products.** Without an international standard (none currently exists) for comparing how the products stack up against each other, this information means little to consumers.

- ✔ **Computer manufacturers are more forthcoming with in-use power consumption data and comparisons for their products.** Monitor and TV manufacturers are lagging behind in this area.

- ✔ **Many companies have special "green" sections on their Web sites.** These sections are meant to help consumers learn about a company's ecofriendly features and benefits. That's a good thing, but most of these green sections weren't prominently advertised to promote greener electronic products as major purchasing decisions.

The survey assessed more than 50 consumer electronics products, scoring each on a number of factors. With a maximum of 100 attainable points, the total points for each product in the survey was adjusted to a possible top score of 10. (See Chapter 9 for more about the survey results.)

Of all products that were evaluated (desktop computers, notebook computers, mobile phones, smartphones, PDAs, televisions, and computer monitors), the highest-ranking product was the Lenovo L2440 wide display, shown in Figure 1-2, which scored 6.90 points.

The Acer TravelMate 6293 notebook landed at the bottom of the scale with a score of 3.44, and topping the category was the Toshiba Portégé R600. I introduce you to the Portégé in the later section "Following a Green Gadget's Carbon Footprint."

Although you can see that no single absolutely, positively, 100 percent supergreen gadget exists, increasingly *greener* mobile phones, notebook computers, wireless network routers, Blu-ray DVD players, high-definition TVs (HDTVs), and other consumer electronics products do exist. That's what I talk about in this book.

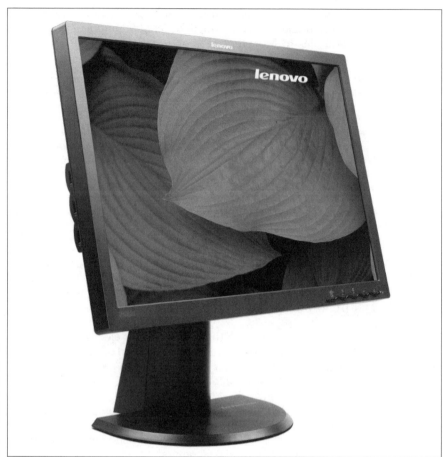

Figure 1-2:
Displaying
the high-
est level
of gadget
greenness.

Defining gadgets

You may want to ask, "Since when, Mr. *Green Gadgets For Dummies,* is some-thing that's too big to fit in my pocket — such as a humongous high-def TV — considered a gadget, green or otherwise?"

Well, it's not.

Okay, an HDTV isn't a gadget per se, but it incorporates many elements that gadgets such as mobile phones and MP3 players have — for example, inte-grated circuits, speakers, and liquid crystal displays (LCD), albeit on a gigan-tically bigger, and wider scale.

At the annual Greener Gadgets Conference (`http://greenergadgets.com`), see Figure 1-3, people gather to learn about and discuss the environmental impact of manufacturing, distributing, efficiently using, reusing, and properly recycling consumer electronics. It's fair to say that in this book, the term *green gadgets* is all-encompassing. Besides, doesn't this book's title have a nicer ring than *Green Consumer Electronics For Dummies*?

Figure 1-3: They don't call it the Greener *Consumer Electronics* Conference.

Defining green gadgets

Just to be sure that we're on the same page, let me say that *green gadgets* are consumer electronic products that strive to be ecofriendlier. They have a few or all of these characteristics:

- They contain little or no toxic chemicals or materials.
- They are manufactured as efficiently as possible, using the fewest materials possible, by companies that practice environmentally friendlier policies and processes.
- They are built with highly recyclable materials, such as aluminum, arsenic-free glass, or recycled plastic bottles, for as many parts as possible.
- They draw as little power as possible — and uses that energy as efficiently as possible.
- They can power down to Standby mode or shut off (and shut off other gadgets that are plugged into them) if they detect that you aren't using them or after a certain amount of time has passed.
- They use a rechargeable battery pack, or batteries, rather than disposable ones.

✔ They can be recharged (or can recharge other gadgets) from sources other than electricity, such as by absorbing sunlight with solar panels or by winding a crank to generate power.

✔ They can help you save gas and produce fewer carbon emissions by plotting the most efficient route to your destination or by monitoring and analyzing your driving style and then offering tips to help you drive more efficiently.

✔ They are packaged as efficiently as possible in packaging made of partially to 100 percent recycled materials.

✔ They can be easily recycled — ideally through hassle-free take-back or trade-in programs offered by the manufacturer.

Relating the Four Rs to Green Gadgets

Most people are probably familiar with the eco-aware mantra known as the three Rs of green gadgets: Reduce, reuse, recycle. I now introduce you to what the Consumer Electronics Association Web site at MyGreenElectronics. org refers to as the fourth R — rethink — to help you make green gadget purchases. I discuss the four Rs in detail in Chapter 2, but this list sums them up:

✔ **Reduce:** Less is more. Using less energy by turning off gadgets and devices when you aren't using them, as well as adjusting their power settings to run more efficiently when they're on, can provide more savings in both kilowatts and in the amount of money you pay for them.

✔ **Reuse:** If it ain't broke, don't nix it. Refilling your printer's inkjet or laser toner cartridges, donating to charity an older but still usable mobile phone, or upgrading an older PC with faster components rather than buying a new computer are all examples of applying the second R to the gadgets in your life.

✔ **Recycle:** This R can make more of a difference to the planet than any of the others. Every year, hundreds of thousands of old or broken computers and cellphones wind up in landfills or incinerators. Tossing unwanted or broken electronics into town or city municipal trash collection streams is ignorant, irresponsible, lazy, and offensive. It can even be potentially life threatening if the discarded digital items wind up in an incinerator, where they eventually reach the air we breathe, or in a landfill, where they break down and seep into the ground and contaminate the water we drink.

Adding to the problem are the thousands more discarded electronics that wind up as electronic waste, or e-waste, that are often illegally exported to Asia from the U.S. and other industrialized countries. The e-waste wind up in scrap yards that expose workers to toxic chemicals and poisons.

✔ **Rethink:** To help minimize the disastrous long-term effects of e-waste, picture the life cycles of future purchases all the way to the recycling bin. Consider this: In a 2008 survey conducted by the CEA, nearly 90 percent of consumers said energy efficiency will be a determining factor in choosing and purchasing their next televisions. Yet less than half of the people polled said that they understand the ecofriendlier attributes associated with consumer electronics and gadgets.

How do some or all of these factors tie together cleaner-living, cleaner-breathing green gadgets in the real world? Let me show you.

Following a Green Gadget's Carbon Footprint

Visualizing how a gadget's carbon footprint affects the environment is easier to understand by taking a closer look at how a real product that you can hold in your hand relates to the four Rs as it moves from the stage of raw materials and components to being

✔ Manufactured and packaged in a factory

✔ Shipped to resellers or directly to you, the consumer

✔ Used by the consumer

✔ Given away or repurposed by the consumer

✔ Discarded by you or someone you gave it to

✔ Recycled

So that you can follow a gadget's carbon footprint, I take you on a guided tour of the Toshiba Portégé R600 ultralight notebook computer, shown in Figure 1-4. This notebook earned the coveted title of Greenest Notebook in the 2008 Greenpeace Green Electronics Survey.

Figure 1-4:
The Toshiba
Portégé
R600.

Toshiba's "green procurement" initiative in all aspects of the Portégé series development means that the company works in collaboration with component and parts suppliers to help it achieve its targeted carbon footprint — a term I define in the following sidebar, "Sticking your carbon footprint in your mouth," in case you're not exactly sure what it stands for.

What's more, the factory in which the Portégé series is manufactured recovers and recycles waste generated during the manufacturing process, including silver, copper, and tin.

To quote Greenpeace, "Toshiba is ahead of everyone else when it comes to the elimination of toxic chemicals."

To browse a fuller menu of unappetizing hazardous chemical substances and find out why they're so upsetting to the planet's stomach (and ours), check out the Chapter 16 sidebar "An e-waste recipe for disaster."

Thoughtful manufacturing

Beginning with the raw materials that go into giving "birth" to the notebook, Toshiba lessens the carbon footprint of the Portégé R600 during the manufacturing process by eliminating hazardous substances — including cadmium, mercury, and lead from batteries and other components. The elimination of those substances directly affects the notebook's carbon footprint and impact on the planet when the notebook "dies" and is recycled at the end of its lifecycle.

Choices like the ones in the following list reduce a gadget's carbon footprint before it reaches your hands and you then use it:

✔ **The R600 LED-type LCD display helps eliminate additional mercury.**
More and more computer makers are offering this type of mercury-free
display in their products. Less mercury means less potential harm to the
environment when the display reaches its end of life and is broken down
and disposed of or recycled.

✔ **The notebook is packaged in the smallest (yet still protective) box.**
Smaller packaging means that more boxes can be packed into fewer
shipping containers.

✔ **The entire unit is packed in antishock cushioning made from partially
or completely recycled materials.** Using recycled materials in the packaging translates to fewer new resources taken from the planet to box the
computer. It also means that the packaging can be more easily broken
down and recycled, either after receiving the computer or by someone
you later give the computer to.

In addition to the Greenpeace assessment, the R600 ranks high in other green
terms, including its

✔ Energy Star 4.0 compliance

✔ Number-one ranking in the Electronic Product Environmental Assessment
Tool (EPEAT) Gold category (at the time this book was written)

✔ Compliance with the Restriction of Hazardous Substances Directive
(RoHS)

These kudos translate to better energy efficiency when you use a notebook
like the R600, which means a further reduction of its carbon footprint's
impact on the environment throughout its usable lifecycle.

In the later section "Understanding Energy Star and EPEAT Green Gadget
Labels," I explain these and other assessment standards or ratings to look for
when considering new gadget purchases.

Ecofriendly features

The following list describes some of the other green features that help lessen
the carbon footprint of the R600 and its impact on the environment:

✔ **Thin, lightweight (2.4 lb) design:** This translates to less stress when lug-
ging it in your shoulder bag and less resources taken from the planet.

✔ **Rechargeable battery:** The battery can last more than $7^1/_2$ hours. Finally,
you can leave the charger at home!

- ✔ **Transreflective display:** You can see and use the display outdoors with the backlight turned off. Who says that a park bench isn't a truly greener home office?

- ✔ **Solid-state drive (SSD) option:** Say goodbye to moving parts and typical hard drive crashes. Think of it as the same kind of memory that's in your mobile phone.

The R600 also boasts James Bond-like features, such as a fingerprint scanner for securing your identity and passwords, as shown in Figure 1-5, and a built-in webcam with face recognition for added protection. Okay, these features aren't exactly green, but they sure are cool — say "Cheese!"

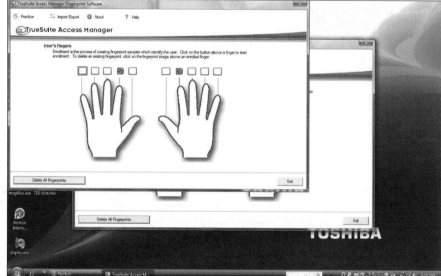

Figure 1-5:
Personal
security
that's
uniquely
you.

Other green electronics

The following list describes three more green consumer electronics products that illustrate what Greenpeace calls "the race to the top to produce truly green products":

- ✔ **Samsung solar-powered Blue Earth mobile phone:** Designed to look like a flat, well-rounded, shiny pebble, it's the world's first solar-powered touch-screen phone. A solar panel on the back of the phone can generate enough power to make calls and charge the battery.

Sticking your carbon footprint in your mouth

It's a term that rolls off tongues whenever there's talk about the environment and being green, as pervasively present in print, radio, and TV advertisements as fleas on a junkyard dog (for which I don't blame the dog, mind you). It's a phrase that I personally bandy about in every chapter of this book: *carbon footprint*.

Knowing what the term *carbon footprint* means can help you gain a better appreciation of why it matters so much to Mother Nature and the planet she oversees, and on which she must wish we would responsibly dwell. Simply put, a *carbon footprint* is the total amount of carbon dioxide (CO_2) — or *greenhouse gases* — produced by humans as we live our lives. For instance, when you drive to the store to pick up some ecofriendly dish soap, your car's engine burns gasoline, which in turn produces CO_2 emissions from the muffler and into the air. More efficient cars produce fewer emissions than gas guzzlers, whereas walking or riding your bike instead produces none. And, although your bicycle or walking shoes don't contribute to your carbon footprint when you're using them, the mining and harvesting of materials for manufacturing, and the manufacturing process itself, play a part in increasing the world's greenhouse gases.

Manufacturing, packaging, shipping, shelving, buying, using, maintaining, and eventually disposing of gadgets all contribute to the total carbon footprint over the life of the product. Adding each of your gadget's individual carbon footprints to the others in your life that you generate — when you drive, fly to on an airplane, ride the roller coaster at an amusement park, flush the toilet, make coffee, pray in church or a nondenominational meeting hall, and rest your head on a pillow and curl up with a paperback thriller at the end of the day — total the personal carbon footprint, which doesn't stop growing until the day you die.

Come to think of it, your carbon footprint doesn't quite come to a complete halt when you die, because firing up a crematorium or digging your grave and conducting your funeral service — not to mention all the travel and energy expended by those who attend — all contribute to your grand-total carbon footprint after all is said and done (so to speak).

The gadget is made from recycled plastic extracted from water bottles, and both the phone and its charger — which draws fewer than 0.03 watts after it charges the phone — are free from toxic substances, including brominated flame retardants (BFRs), beryllium, and phthalates.

The Eco mode feature adjusts the brightness, backlight duration, and Bluetooth energy efficiency settings — they're a single touch away. The Eco Walk function counts your steps with a built-in pedometer and calculates how much CO_2 emissions have been reduced by hoofing it rather than driving.

✔ **HYmini wind-powered charger:** Cranking or winding rechargers turns your energy into power you can use to charge your gadgets. Relying on the wind, rather than on you, is how the HYMini wind-powered charger (at www.hymini.com) generates power to juice up your MP3 player, digital camera, mobile phone, and other gadgets.

What, no wind today? No worries. Connect the HYMini to your bicycle's handlebars or strap it to your upper arm with optional accessories and start peddling or running to make a little wind as you go about your merry, ecofriendlier way.

✔ **Sony Bravia VE5:** Sensing when you're no longer in the room and watching, the Sony Bravia VE5 Series (`www.sonystyle.com`) can turn itself off to save energy. Come back in, and the HDTV turns itself on again. Sony says that the set draws 40 percent less power than other LCD models — and almost zero watts when it's powered off in Standby mode. What's more, a light sensor can automatically adjust the picture brightness to match the room's "mood," drawing even less energy when the lights go down and it's time to start the show.

Understanding Energy Star and EPEAT Green Gadget Labels

Energy Star defines energy efficiency standards for a variety of products and services and qualifies specific products that meet those standards. The EPEAT system helps buyers evaluate, compare, and select desktop computers, laptops, and monitors based on their environmental attributes. All EPEAT-registered products are automatically Energy Star qualified. You can find more information by visiting these Web sites:

✔ **Energy Star:** Consumers can use the Energy Star standards to shop for products and services that meet those standards. See `www.energystar.gov`. For instance, computers bearing the Energy Star logo must, at a minimum, offer three distinct operating modes — Standby, Active, and Sleep — to ensure energy savings when computers are being used, as well as when they're in Standby or Sleep mode. Energy Star-approved computers must also use more efficient internal power supplies.

✔ **EPEAT:** This system, at `http://epeat.net`, helps purchasers evaluate, compare, and select desktop computers, laptops, and monitors based on their environmental attributes. As I describe earlier in "Following a Green Gadget's Carbon Footprint," Toshiba's Portégé R600 was ranked the "Greenest Notebook" by Greenpeace because of EPEAT criteria it met, such as these:

- Is made from green materials
- Is highly recyclable
- Is energy efficient
- Is packaged using a minimum of recycled (and recyclable) materials

✔ **Restriction of Hazardous Substances (RoHS):** This European directive restricts the use of six hazardous materials in the manufacturing of electronics. Banned from the EU market are new electrical and electronic equipment containing more than agreed-upon levels of lead, cadmium, mercury, hexavalent chromium, polybrominated biphenyl (PBB) and polybrominated diphenyl ether (PBDE) flame retardants. Check out www.rohs.gov.uk.

Initially, computers and monitors (the worst offenders) were the first products to wear the Energy Star logo. Since partnering with the Department of Energy in 1996 for additional product categories, the label can now be found on everything from major appliances and office equipment to DVD players and set-top cable TV boxes.

Earning one of the three EPEAT ratings is sort of like winning an Olympic medal — which is exactly how the three levels of accomplishment are named:

✔ **Bronze:** Products meet all required criteria.

✔ **Silver:** Products meet all required criteria plus 50 percent of optional criteria.

✔ **Gold:** Products meet all required criteria plus 75 percent of optional criteria.

Here are a few fun facts provided by the CEA about the badges of green gadget ecoconsciousness awarded by Energy Star and EPEAT:

✔ Sales of Energy Star televisions, monitors, audio, and video products in the U.S. reached nearly 35 million units in 2006.

✔ Seven million of those products were sold by Best Buy, which, according to EPA calculations:

- Saved consumers $100 million dollars on their utility bills
- Eliminated 1.4 billion pounds of carbon emissions — or the equivalent of removing 128,000 cars from the road

✔ The savings gained from purchases of EPEAT-certified products in 2007 equaled

- 75.5 million metric tons of primary materials — equivalent to the weight of more than 585 million refrigerators
- 3,220 metric tons of toxic materials, which equal a stack of 1.6 million bricks
- 42.2 billion kilowatt-hours, which is enough energy to power 3.7 million U.S. homes for an entire year

Implementing Green Living Habits with Gadgets You Already Own

Thinking about past purchases that may not have been labeled as greener when you bought them plays just as important a role in Mother Nature's view of gadgets as choosing and using new greener gadgets in your future.

Getting into a greener gadget lifestyle can be as simple as making a few changes to the electronics in your life or as complex as installing a home control system that can monitor and remotely or automatically operate every powered item in your house, from automatically turning lights on and off to regulating the climate to save energy when you aren't home.

Taking a bite out of "energy vampires"

Forty percent of the energy used for electronics in your home is consumed while devices known as *energy vampires* are turned off. They suck power the way the eponymous mythical creatures suck blood. But energy vampires are no myth. You don't need garlic or a stake to fight energy vampires, though, because these simple actions can be your weapons:

✔ Unplug your mobile phone's charger.

✔ Turn off your computer monitor or set it to shut off itself and the computer after you haven't used it for a few minutes.

✔ Program your thermostat to turn up the heat or cool things down only when you're in the house.

You can do all these tasks immediately to reduce energy consumption and extend the life of your gadgets. Cutting off several energy vampire gadgets can be a heck of lot easier when you plug them into a *smart* power strip, one that cuts the power when your devices are turned off.

My favorite is the Belkin Conserve because its remote control lets you instantly shut off eight of its outlets all at one time while leaving two on all the time. I can use the Conserve to reduce the amount of energy being wasted by my Xbox 360, HDTV, Vudu movie box, notebook computer, mobile phone and PlayStation Portable rechargers, and laser printer. Plugging devices that are on all the time, such as my Wi-Fi router and cable broadband modem, into the pair of always-on outlets means that I can surf the Web and take care of my e-mail on the sofa. To further reduce my gadgets' total carbon footprint, I can plug the Conserve power strip into a wall outlet timer that cuts the juice at bedtime every night and then turns it back on just before my usual waking time of 6:30 a.m.

Calculating your gadgets' carbon footprints

You can gauge your gadgets' individual power consumption by plugging them into products that feed useful information back to you. The Kill A Watt energy monitor monitors individual gadgets, or you can monitor your entire home's energy consumption with a product such as The Energy Detective (TED), shown in Figure 1-6. Using one of these products can help you better understand — and reduce — your gadgets' carbon footprints.

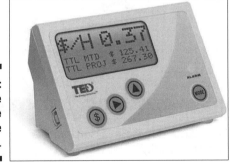

Figure 1-6:
Home energy: The complete picture.

Calculating the estimated carbon footprint of your household or individual gadgets by using one of these Web-based calculators can also help you minimize their negative effect on the planet:

- **MyGreenElectronics.org:** `http://mygreenelectronics.org/EnergyCalculator.aspx`
- **Home Energy Saver:** `http://hes.lbl.gov`
- **Energy Star HomeCalc and Home Energy Yardstick:** `www.energystar.gov/index.cfm?c=bulk_purchasing.bus_purchasing`
- **Carbon Footprint:** `www.carbonfootprint.com/calculator.aspx`
- **UC Berkeley carbon footprint:** `http://coolclimate.berkeley.edu`
- **WattzOn:** From `www.wattzon.com`, shown in Figure 1-7

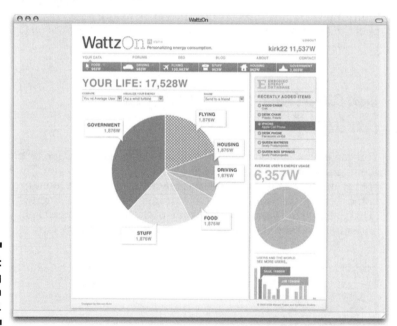

Figure 1-7:
Visualizing your carbon footprint.

Taking other simple green gadget steps

Here are some actions you can take with your existing gadgets to help you live a greener life with your electronics right away:

✔ Replace single-use disposable batteries in your gadgets with rechargeable ones that you can reuse again and again. Check out Chapter 3 for the lowdown on all things battery-related.

✔ Adjust your mobile phone's autolock and display timeout settings to lock or black out the screen after several seconds of inactivity. Chapter 4 has the details.

✔ Adjust your computer's power-saving settings to turn off the monitor when you're away for more than a few minutes, and then switch the PC to either Standby or Hibernate mode if you haven't returned a little while later. Part III covers just about anything you can do to reduce your computer's carbon footprint.

Staying Informed about Green Gadget Developments

No single source can tell you everything there is to know about green gadgets — not even this book!

By visiting Web sites and blogs that cover the topic of green gadgets, or that have sections that cover them, you can

✔ Find out about the latest ecofriendly efforts and products being made by consumer electronics companies.

✔ Read reviews and features of those products so that you can make more informed purchase decisions.

✔ Find out how to get the most from the gadgets and gear you already own.

✔ Communicate with other people who are also interested in living a green gadget lifestyle.

I include, on the Cheat Sheet in the front of this book, ten useful Web sites focused on green gadgets and environmentally friendly technologies. Don't forget that you can always get the latest green gadget words of wisdom, brought to you by yours truly, at these fine worldwide Web locations:

✔ **NYTimes.com Green Inc:** `http://greeninc.blogs.nytimes.com`

✔ **My own blogs:** gGadget.org and JoeyGadget.com, as shown in Figure 1-8

Figure 1-8:
Hey, Joe,
now where
you goin'
with that
green gad-
get in your
hand?

Chapter 2

Practicing Green Gadget Living

• •

In This Chapter

▶ Taking stock of how much energy you use

▶ Turning off gadgets to reduce their carbon footprints

▶ Giving your gadgets and gear another go-round

▶ Recycling your unwanted or useless gadgets

▶ Weighing whether to make new gadget purchases

▶ Relating ecofriendly electronics concepts to others

• •

A green-gadget lifestyle should be pursued incrementally. You implement a few green practices to start out, and then as they become part of your routine, you implement a few more. I predict that the more you do, the more you'll be motivated to do. But where do you begin? In this chapter, I show you that evaluating how much energy you use (and how much you unwittingly waste) will likely be an eye-opening experience. It's a vital first step.

Knowing how you use your gadgets might then motivate you to take steps to apply the standard "three Rs" of green living — reduce, reuse, and recycle. In this chapter, however, I expand on the concept of the fourth R, which I mention in Chapter 1, and tell you how to *rethink* the way you view gadgets. Rethinking applies to how you use gadgets you own, how you shop for new ones, and how you dispose of those that you no longer want or need. The sections in this chapter briefly describe the philosophy behind each R and present a quick list of practices for each one.

Understanding your energy usage also plays an important role in helping you make more informed choices when you acquire new, ecofriendly gadgets. If you're like me, you want to spread the word about greener gadget living, so I wrap up this chapter by giving you some tips on sharing your gadget greenness.

Evaluating Your Energy Waste, er, Usage

When it comes to your gadgets, the single most important issue to consider isn't how much or how little energy *they* use or waste, but rather how much *you* do. A gadget, whether it's the latest and most energy efficient or it's many years old and inefficient, uses energy only when you use it — and, as I say in Chapter 1, even when you don't use it. Most gadgets, new and old alike, continue to draw power when they're turned off but remain in *Standby mode*. Turning off your TV, for instance, cuts most, but not all, of the power it draws as it stands by, ready to display the picture when you turn it on more quickly than if you had unplugged the power cord to completely cut its power draw. I refer to TVs and gadgets in Standby mode as *energy vampires*. Even a fully recharged mobile phone that you power off but leave plugged in the wall charger is an energy vampire. That's because most portable gadget chargers continue to draw power even after the gadgets they're charging have done their jobs.

Mobile phone and other gadget manufacturers are working on or have begun offering green phones and chargers that draw nearly zero power after they sense that the phone is charged. For instance, certain new Nokia phone models alert you when the phone is charged and then remind you to unplug the charger from the wall. And, a new line of high-definition TVs (HDTVs) from Sony draws only a tiny amount of power when they're turned off.

Although these undeniably positive moves promise that the new gadgets you purchase will be more ecofriendly than the ones you're replacing, remembering to apply greener decisions to the ones you're still using is a matter of appreciating how much energy you're using to power them.

Taking stock of how much energy you use, or waste, to power your gadgets can shed a powerfully motivating new light on actions you can take to start practicing a greener gadget lifestyle.

To practice what I preach in this section, I evaluated my own energy consumption by taking stock of the gadgets I typically use every day:

- At least one notebook computer, and sometimes as many as three when I'm writing about multiple operating systems (Macintosh, Linux, and Windows 7, Vista, or XP)
- A wireless mouse (or two)
- A mobile phone and Bluetooth headset
- A printer that's typically in energy-saving Standby mode because I print so infrequently
- An iPod nano on the days I go for a run
- A wireless network router and a broadband modem

✔ A TiVo digital video recorder (DVR) to record a few hours of news, which I watch while cooking supper and catching up on e-mail at the end of the workday

✔ An HDTV to watch the news and then to play a video game or watch a movie using one of my three movie download or streaming devices

✔ A universal remote control that controls the HDTV and devices plugged into it, like the TiVo, and my Apple TV music and movie player

✔ A rechargeable battery charger on days I need to recharge batteries for my electric beard trimmer or booklight — which count as three devices

✔ Assorted devices (and chargers that recharge many of the gadgets and gizmos in this list and others that I use only now and then), such as my AppleTV, Nintendo DS, Nintendo Wii, PlayStation 3, PlayStation Portable, and even more, which are piled in boxes

To find out how much energy all my devices and gadgets were consuming — and contributing to the carbon footprint I'm creating by using them — I decided to do some investigating. What I discovered was unsurprising yet so eye-opening that it motivated me to take additional actions beyond those I was already taking to live an even greener gadget lifestyle.

I investigated my energy use by using The Energy Detective (TED) power monitor. I can use it to instantly monitor exactly how many kilowatts I'm burning — and what they're costing me today and by the month. You can read about The Energy Detective, shown in Figure 2-1, and how I installed it in my house in Chapter 13.

Figure 2-1:
The Energy
Detective.

As I write this chapter, the devices in my household are drawing .850 kilowatts, about the equivalent of burning eleven 75-watt light bulbs at the same time. When the refrigerator turns itself on to adjust its interior temperature, the number on the monitor shoots up to 1,000 watts. According to The Energy Detective, my total energy cost for the day (just after noon) is $1.91.

Drawing the biggest gulp of electricity is the 1,500-watt stand-up radiator that's parked next to my writing table and set to its minimum setting. When I turn off the heater, the energy level in my house instantly drops to .100 kilowatts — the equivalent of a 100-watt light bulb. By turning off the radiator and bundling up on tolerably cold days, I can cut my electricity bill by a quarter or a third.

Reducing your household energy consumption by regulating the radiator is considerably easier when you have a monitor like The Energy Detective to visibly remind you exactly how much electricity you're using and paying for.

Alternatively, plugging a radiator, TV, computer, or other device into a power monitor like the Kill A Watt, shown in Figure 2-2, can instantly tell you how many kilowatts a device uses when it's turned on — and when it's turned off. Unlike The Energy Detective, which uses sensors you install in your circuit breaker to monitor your entire home's energy usage, the portable Kill A Watt has a single outlet. Plug in your TV or computer to measure how much energy each consumes. You can also plug in a power strip with several gadgets plugged into it, to find out how much energy they're consuming when they're all turned on, or when some are powered on and others turned off.

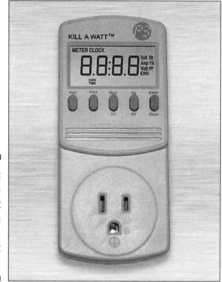

Figure 2-2:
The portable Kill A Watt monitors consumption gadget by gadget.

Another energy-saving step I took was the purchase of a Belkin Conserve power strip, which comes with a remote control that lets me instantly power off devices plugged into up to eight of its switchable outlets. Two additional outlets are for always-on devices that stay on even when the others are switched off with the remote. I also added a power timer switch and a 3-socket miniature power strip, which I use with the Belkin Conserve as I} follows:

- **Eight switchable outlets:** I plug in my notebook charger, HDTV, Xbox 360, PlayStation 3, VUDU movie downloading device, mobile phone charger, printer, and backup hard drive. The included remote control lets me instantly power off all these energy vampires at once while leaving two of the strip's always-on outlets turned on and receiving power.

✔ **Two always-on outlets and a 3-socket miniature power strip:** I plug my Wi-Fi router into one always-on outlet, and plug my broadband cable modem and TiVo into the 3-socket power strip, which is plugged into the second always-on outlet. That way, I can continue recording some later news programs and connect to the Internet with my notebook when I'm sitting on the sofa or in bed before turning in for the night.

✔ **Power timer switch:** I plug the Belkin Conserve power strip into a power timer switch that I set to turn off at 1 p.m., and turn back on at 6 a.m. All devices that are plugged into the Conserve, including the devices in the always-on sockets that I mention in the preceding bullet, are powered off. This action, according to The Energy Detective, cuts my energy vampire consumption to nearly zero.

Reducing Your Gadgets' Carbon Footprints and E-Waste

The first of the green living Rs — reduce — can be summed up in three words: Less is more. Using less energy by turning off gadgets and devices when you aren't using them, and adjusting their power settings to run more efficiently when they're turned on, can provide more savings in both kilowatts and the amount of money you pay for them. Reducing the carbon footprint of your mobile phone or notebook computer might sound like a small feat, so to speak — until you consider that they're only two of the many electronic devices most of us use every day.

Here's a case in point: According to the International Energy Agency (IEA), an estimated 5 to 15 percent of the world's domestic electricity is wasted by electronic devices idling their time in Standby mode.

If you take even the smallest energy-reducing actions against energy vampires and other power-wasting features, you can reduce the bigger-picture carbon footprint created by the sum of your gadgets' many parts. In many chapters, I tell you that plugging your mobile phone charger, TV, PC, and other "standby devices" into a power strip can help you easily pull the plug on all of them at one time when you shut off the switch. If you don't want to bend down or reach behind your gear to hit the switch, you can invest in a smart power strip, like the Belkin Conserve. Thanks to the included remote control, cutting the power to most of the Conserve sockets is just a tap away. Another option is the Smart Strip LCG3, which senses when you turn off a device and cuts power to the outlet accordingly.

Here are some actions you can take to reduce your gadgets' carbon footprint and keep them from contributing to the planet's already huge e-waste pile:

✔ Replace single-use disposable batteries in your gadgets with rechargeable ones.

✔ Unplug your mobile phone, MP3 player, and other gadget chargers when the devices are fully charged or not in use.

✔ Plug your home computer and its peripheral devices into a power strip that turns everything off at one time.

✔ Disable your computer's screen saver and change its power-saving settings to turn off the display when you aren't using it for more than five minutes.

✔ Adjust your computer's power-saving settings to switch the computer to either Standby or Sleep mode whenever you aren't using it for more than 15 minutes. Then switch to Hibernate mode after 30 minutes (if that feature is available).

✔ Read and review documents onscreen rather than print them on paper.

✔ Reduce the brightness of a display to its lowest comfortable setting — including mobile phones, MP3 players, digital cameras and camcorders, TVs, and notebook and desktop computers.

✔ Save trees and the carbon impact cost of buying printed books by downloading and reading e-books on your mobile phone or a dedicated e-book reader.

✔ Reduce fuel consumption and automobile emissions by shopping and banking online and by renting or buying downloadable and streaming movies and TV shows.

Reusing Your Gadgets and Electronics Gear

In certain instances, *reuse* and *recycle* (the second and third elements in the three Rs of green gadgets) are interchangeable. Reusing gadgets, computers, and other electronic devices rather than throwing them away or sending them to a recycler can help reduce your impact on the planet (and on your wallet). When you pass on to others who can use them your still-usable computers or other gadgets you've outgrown, you're practicing the ecofriendly act of reusing. Doing so extends the lives of usable products — and postpones their eventual entry into the waste stream.

The following list shows a few examples of the interchangeability of reusing and recycling. You can

✔ **Refill spent inkjet or toner cartridges.** This option is preferable to throwing them in the trash and buying new ones every time they're empty.

✔ **Add more memory to your computer and install a bigger hard drive.**
Help it run faster and give it more storage space.

✔ **Upgrade your Windows PC to Windows 7.** Your computer consumes
less power, thanks to new energy-saving features in Windows 7.

Repairing your broken computer, mobile phone, or other gadget can sometimes cost more than replacing it with a new one.

Even if it's the end of the line for your unwanted, damaged, or hopelessly useless gadget or device, salvaging still usable or saleable parts from them can
help reduce your overall impact on the environment when it's time to say "so
long."

Other *reuse* actions you can take to live a green gadget lifestyle include the
ones in this list:

✔ Replace single-use disposable batteries in your gadgets with rechargeable ones that you can reuse again and again.

✔ Choose rewriteable (CD-RW/DVD-RW) CD and DVD discs rather than
ones you can burn to only once (CD-R/DVD-R) for moving, sharing, and
backing up music, video, documents, and other computer files.

✔ Consider upgrading your current computer rather than buying a new
one. Adding internal memory, a bigger hard disk, a flat-screen display, or
the latest version of the operating system can make an aging desktop or
notebook feel new, or nearly new, again.

✔ Donate, sell, or give away gadgets, computers, and other electronics that
you no longer want or use but that someone else can use.

Recycling Gadgets the Green Way

Although the third R of green gadgets is *recycle,* it doesn't necessarily mean
that the items you want to dispose of will be broken down into parts and
ground up, melted, or otherwise destroyed. As I say in the preceding section,
the terms *recycle* and *reuse* are sometimes interchangeable. For example, if
you have someone repair or update a working gadget or computer that you
don't want or need and then put it back into someone else's hands, that process qualifies as both recycling and reusing. And yes, a bit of *rethinking* and
reducing take place in the mix.

Why do I talk more about trying to reuse or repurpose gadgets instead of
sending them off to a recycler? Here's where the rethinking comes into play.
Think about recycled paper. It comes from existing paper that is collected,
processed, and then repurposed as new paper. By selling a gadget or giving
it away, you're repurposing it, but you're also essentially recycling it. What's
cool here is that you're skipping the processing part of breaking down a

gadget the way a recycler would when the gadget has truly reached its end. What's more, reusing or repurposing a gadget means not having to purchase a new product to replace it, which in turn means you're *reducing* the resources and energy required to manufacture, package, ship, and use a new gadget.

Something you don't want to reuse is personal information that might be stored on a computer or gadget that you're giving away. Most repurposing programs promise to securely erase your personal information from your gadgets or computers before they send them to their eventual recipients. Regardless, I recommend checking out Chapter 15, where I show you how to prevent potentially unscrupulous recipients from snatching your personal information from unwanted gadgets and computers that you're saying good-bye to.

Here are some other places to look to incorporate recycling into your greener gadget lifestyle:

- **Computer manufacturer's Web site:** Check to find out more about the manufacturer's take-back, trade-in, and recycling programs.

- **Electronics trade-in Web sites:** Visit these sites to see whether your still-working but unwanted gadgets, computers, and other electronics can earn you cash or credit toward a new purchase.

- **Your local newspaper's classified ads or an Internet auction:** Sell your unwanted gadgets, computers, and other working but unwanted electronic products in your local newspaper's classified ads, or sell or auction them on the Web.

- **Any major wireless provider's retail store:** Drop off your working but unwanted mobile phone so that it can be repurposed or properly recycled. (Don't forget the charger and any accessories you no longer want.)

- **Your local video game store, such as GameStop or EB Games:** Trade in your unwanted but working video game consoles, games, and accessories for store credit.

- **A nearby or nationwide reputable recycler of e-waste** *(e-cycler):* Properly disposing of broken or otherwise hopelessly useless electronics rather than throwing them in the trash reduces potential hazards to the environment, and may also reduce waste if parts and materials can be extracted and reused or manufactured into new products.

Rethinking Your Gadget Purchases

After you deal with the standard three Rs of green gadgets, you have to consider the "bonus R" and *rethink* any new gadget purchases and whether you truly need them. For example, if the gadget you're thinking about replacing is still working, or if it can be repaired (if it isn't working) or upgraded (so that it can continue to serve you in a more useful way), maybe you don't even need the new gadget. If, however, your old gadget can no longer serve you — or if you simply want the newest model to replace it— consider whether you can donate or sell the old one or give it away to a friend.

Rethinking also means considering new products with expressly green features and benefits that have a smaller negative impact on the environment. For instance, a notebook computer is a greener choice than a desktop computer because notebooks require fewer resources and energy to build, require less packaging and therefore can be shipped in greater quantities, and are less expensive to operate. Do you really need a power-and-resource hungry desktop, or can a notebook serve your computing needs?

Replacing a cellphone that's smashed beyond repair presents another opportunity to put on your rethinking cap. Step 1 is to drop the broken phone at a retail cellphone store to make sure it's properly recycled (most do). Step 2 is to choose a new model with, for instance, a built-in solar recharger or housing case made from recycled water bottles. (See Chapter 11 to read about two cellphones with those exact attributes.)

Whatever you decide, the process of buying green gadgets and consumer electronics grows easier all the time. It seems that every company under the sun wants to be seen as green. As a consequence, major gadget manufacturers have "gotten hip" to behaving in an ecofriendly way and offering ecofriendly products.

Even so, sorting through what's real and what's greenwash hype can be dizzying. (See Chapter 9 for pointers on making your way through greenwash hype.) According to the Consumer Electronics Association (CEA) at myGreenElectronics.org, the good news is that more and more consumer electronics are now being produced that

✔ Contain fewer or no harmful chemicals or toxins

✔ Offer greater energy efficiency

✔ Are easier to upgrade, repair, and recycle

Here are some other actions you can take to rethink before you buy new gadgets:

✔ Visit Web sites, such as the ones in the following list, that evaluate, rate, and list greener electronics by category, brand, or another criteria:

- **myGreenElectronics.org:** http://mygreenelectronics.org

- **Greener Choices:** http://greenerchoices.org

- **Energy Star:** www.energystar.gov

- **Electronic Product Environmental Assessment Tool (EPEAT):** www.epeat.net

✔ Stay up-to-date on how the top electronics companies rank against each other by visiting the Greenpeace Guide to Greener Electronics at `www.greenpeace.org/electronics`.

✔ Visit the environmental sections on Web sites of companies that manufacture the products you're considering buying to find out about their greener products, programs, services, and policies.

✔ Read news, features, and reviews of the latest ecofriendly products by visiting green gadget blogs and consumer electronics Web sites, such as the following:

- **EcoGeek:** `www.ecogeek.org`

- *PC* **magazine's Green Tech section:** `www.pcmag.com/category2/0,2806,2256470,00.asp`

- **CNET News Green Tech page:** `www.cnet.com/greentech`

- **Good Clean Tech:** `www.goodcleantech.com`

Sharing Your Gadget Greenness with Others

Practice green gadget living by applying the three Rs (reduce, reuse, recycle) and the bonus R (rethink) to all the electronic and energy-consuming devices in your life. Doing so can help you reduce your carbon footprint for the good of the planet — and for the good of others. But some folks might not be living the greener gadget life that they could be living. What do you do about it? You share what you do, and spread the information so that others know what to do. Sharing with others how to practice the four Rs can be as simple as making suggestions in these venues:

✔ **At a gathering of friends, such as at a dinner party:** Ask everyone around the table if they're familiar with cellphone battery-zapping features, such as Bluetooth, that they can turn off if they aren't using them; if they're not familiar with the features, show them how to use them how and to turn them off when they aren't.

✔ **At work:** Help coworkers run screen savers and adjust their PC's power settings to shut off their screens whenever they're away from their desks for more than a few minutes.

✔ **At the homes of family members and friends:** Point out plugged-in gadgets and appliances that waste energy when they aren't in use, and suggest power strips that make it easy to turn off several gadgets at a time when they aren't being used.

Going a little further to turn other people on to the practices of living a greener gadget lifestyle can have a greater impact on reducing their carbon footprints. Consider taking these actions:

- ✔ **Encourage family, friends, and coworkers to steer their Web browsers to carpooling and ride-sharing Web sites.** Have them check sites such as Zimride (`http://zimride.com`), Rideshare Optimizer (`http://rideshareoptimizer.com`), or the community classifieds Web site Craigslist (`www.craigslist.org`).

- ✔ **Organize an e-cycling potluck party at work or among friends.** You can gather unwanted but potentially useful and hopelessly useless gadgets and other electronics to arrange for donation or proper disposal and recycling.

- ✔ **Visit the Stepcase Lifehack site to read the article "Arguing in Favor of Telecommuting: 5 Tips to Convince the Boss.** It's at `tinyurl.com/telecommuteyourboss`. The article tells you how to encourage your boss to allow you and coworkers to telecommute one day a week or more; if you're the boss, visit `tinyurl.com/telecommuteyourworkers` to read the article "9 Advantages to Companies Who Let Their Employees Telecommute."

The bottom line to sharing your gadget greenness with others is to lead by example. In other words: Practice what you preach.

Part II
Getting Green with Gadgets You Own

The 5th Wave   By Rich Tennant

"Okay, a patient is admitted with a comatose BlackBerry, a beeping pager, and a failing iPod–what do you do?! Think! Think!"

In this part . . .

The chapters in this part have one major goal in common: to save energy and money. Say goodbye to disposable batteries because rechargeable ones are the only choice for any ecoconscious person. And that's just one way you can "get green" with the gadgets you own. Another way is to adjust energy-saving settings, which can reduce how much energy a gadget uses — and how much you pay on your monthly utility bill. Still another way is to plug your home entertainment system into a smart power strip so that you can shut off everything at once when it's time to say goodnight.

Chapter 3

Saving Money (and the Planet) with Rechargeable Batteries

. . . .

In This Chapter

▶ Discovering the pros and cons of battery usage

▶ Becoming familiar with your battery-operated gadgets

▶ Getting the scoop on rechargeable batteries and chargers

▶ Replacing rechargeable battery packs in your gadgets

▶ Disposing of dead batteries the right way

. . . .

*R*eady to get all charged up?

Taking the smallest steps, such as replacing disposable batteries with rechargeable ones, can help you achieve long-lasting results when you "go green" with many of the gadgets you already own.

If saying goodbye to wasting money and energy on throwaway batteries makes good sense but you're not sure where to begin, you've come to the right place. In this chapter, I give you the lowdown on the pluses and minuses of typical rechargeable and disposable batteries, help you determine which of your battery-operated gadgets and devices can benefit the most from making the switch, and point you to rechargeable battery pack replacements that last longer than the ones supplied on your cellphone and other gadgets. Then I wrap it all up with advice on how to properly dispose of dead batteries after they lose their spark.

Recharge!

Understanding Basic Battery Pluses and Minuses

When you embrace the use of rechargeable batteries, you respect the three Rs: Reduce, reuse, recycle. When you replace disposable batteries with rechargeable batteries — which are also referred to as *cells* — you can

- ✔ **Reduce** the amount of money you pay from your pocket and reduce the amount of earth's resources required to produce each "one-hit-wonder" battery

- ✔ **Reuse** the same rechargeable cell or pack repeatedly, for many months or years

- ✔ **Recycle** energy with each reuse, until it's time to retire to a proper recycler the long-life-of-service rechargeable battery

Considering that a single rechargeable battery can be recharged and reused hundreds of times, buying and throwing out ordinary batteries is just plain wasteful — and potentially hazardous if they're improperly disposed of, because of the mercury and other toxins used to produce them.

An estimated 15 billion disposable alkaline batteries are produced and discarded each year.

Find out how to properly dispose of both kinds of batteries at the end of this chapter, in the section "Properly Disposing of Dead Batteries." To find out more about disposing of other gadgets and electronic e-waste, check out Chapter 16.

Hunting and Gathering Battery-Powered Gadgets in Your House

Making a game of searching for remote controls that might be lost in your sofa cushions is a helpful way to start saying *adios* to disposable batteries. I can think of a few other products and places (see Figure 3-1) that chew up and spit out disposable batteries like there's no tomorrow.

Here's a quick list of areas around the home to check for battery-operated gadgets, such as remote controls:

- ✔ **Living room:** This room of your house is likely to be Device Central, where remote controls live that drive your television or DVD player or that operate movie and music gadgets, such as Apple TV.

Figure 3-1:
Search
high and
low to find
all battery-
operated
gadgets in
your house.

✔ **Play room:** Wii controllers make you whirl your arms while bowling or whacking at a baseball, and the more you use them, the more you burn not only calories but also battery juice. While you're at it, grab any other nearby video game controllers, such as the ones for the Xbox 360 or PlayStation 3. Don't forget all those "old school" battery-powered games, such as Operation, Battleship, and Lite Brite (the precursor to the pixel).

✔ **Kitchen drawer:** You know where this drawer is — the one where you keep such items as your flashlight, electronic tape measure (when did *that* happen?), cordless hand mixer, digital egg timer, and other helpful cooking gizmos. While you're in the kitchen, don't forget the wall clock if it runs on a battery.

✔ **Bathroom:** Brushing up on battery-operated gizmos in the bathroom turns up reasonably cheapo devices, such as electric toothbrushes, beard and other body-hair trimmers, sing-in-the-shower radios, and digital scales.

✔ **Bedroom:** Although sleep is the first order of business in the bedroom, its mishmash of battery-powered devices can include TV and video player remote controls, a travel alarm clock, a book reading light, a cellphone, a notebook computer, or any other gadget you store at the bedside.

Rechargeables in my house: Part 1

Taking stock of battery-operated gadgets and gear in my house turned up the following inventory of computer-related items, listed with the types of batteries they use:

✔ **Notebook computer (four):** Replaceable rechargeable batteries

✔ **Notebook mouse (two), from Microsoft:** One AA battery and two AAA batteries

✔ **A pair of 3D virtual reality goggles, from Vuzix:** Built-in battery

✔ **A portable Bluetooth thermal printer, from PLANon Printstick:** Built-in battery

---

✔ **Home office:** Less officially speaking, this room is wherever you park your computer. The usual battery-operated suspects include wireless mice and keyboards, and also digital recorders and cameras that use ordinary batteries and other gadgets that connect to your computer, such as iPods and media players. These devices' built-in rechargeable batteries eventually wear out and need to be replaced and properly recycled.

✔ **Outdoors:** This smorgasbord of portable gadgets includes your cellphone, digital camera, camcorder, and personal digital assistant (PDA) as well as automobile GPS navigators and outdoor recreation companions, such as camping lamps and pedometers. And, those ubiquitous entertainers — the AM/FM radio, boom box, and DVD player — can suck down a six-pack of disposable cells before sundown.

You most likely recall the last time you groaned because a gadget's battery died and you didn't have a spare on hand. Think of all the times you shelled out greenbacks for single-use batteries. When you use rechargeable batteries, you don't have to waste money and energy on these duds.

Before you spend another dime on single-use batteries, step away from the store register, return to the battery rack, and pick up a rechargeable-battery kit. It typically has two or four AA or AAA cells (or a combination) and a charger. You'll thank yourself for making the investment — and you'll be relieved not to have to return to the store the next time you need a battery.

Sorting Out and Choosing Rechargeable Batteries and Chargers

Getting up to speed on the use of rechargeable batteries (and the chargers that juice them) to replace familiar disposable batteries is the topic I discuss in this section. In the "Finding Rechargeable Battery Packs" section, near the end of this chapter, I go over your options for replacing the rechargeable battery packs supplied with your cordless or mobile phone, electric tooth-brush, portable handheld vacuum cleaner, and notebook computer.

I also cover out-of-the-ordinary rechargeable solutions, such as flashlights and radios, that recharge with good ol' elbow grease (or, technically speaking, *kinetically* powered gadgets and gizmos), which I describe in various chapters in Part IV.

Before I get into the details of rechargeable batteries (and chargers), here is a list of general tips:

- ✔ Use rechargeable batteries in any gadget that takes alkaline batteries.
- ✔ Recharge rechargeable batteries hundreds of times (typically) — to save lots of money over the long haul.
- ✔ Avoid mixing new rechargeable batteries with old ones because a weaker battery (or more) prevents the combination from offering maximum capacity and performance.

The phenomenon of *memory effect,* which causes older rechargeable batteries to retain less of their total charge capacity over time, doesn't plague modern nickel-metal hydride (NiMH) rechargeable batteries.

Gauging matters of size, type, power, and price

The ability to replace single-use batteries with rechargeable ones is a matter of cell size and power capacity — which in turn determine price. Cheaper rechargeable batteries hold less power and drain faster than costlier, longer-lasting batteries.

Finding rechargeable batteries sized to fit your gadgets is a cinch because they're generally available in the most commonly recognized sizes, as shown in Figure 3-2.

Figure 3-2: Popular battery sizes.

AAA   AA   C   D   9-volt

Schooling yourself in battery matters

If you're looking for a depository of technical information about battery-related information, see BatteryUniversity.com, which offers practical battery knowledge for engineers, educators, students, and ordinary battery users alike.

The site's easy-to-read articles — a maximum of 1,000 words — cover battery chemistries, the best battery choices, and tips to make batteries last longer.

Battery energy capacity is measured in milliampere hours (mAh). Longer-lasting batteries have higher mAh numbers than their short-lived counterparts.

Battery maker Rayovac defines the three types of everyday rechargeable battery choices this way:

- ✔ **Everyday use**: Offers the best value in rechargeable power for high-drain devices and is generally available in all standard battery sizes.

- ✔ **High energy:** Adds power and is available in all standard battery sizes.

- ✔ **Precharged (which Rayovac dubs Hybrid):** Provides the most power and maintains its charge longer than ordinary rechargeable batteries — and is ready to use right out of the package. Unfortunately, this type is generally available in only two sizes: small (AA) and smaller (AAA).

The phenomenon of *self discharge* causes fully charged rechargeable batteries to run down even when they're lying around unused.

Duracell estimates that an ordinary rechargeable battery loses about 1 percent of its charge per day. Put another way, after 100 days, a charged rechargeable battery of this type dies whether or not it's inside a gadget.

Slow-discharge precharged batteries (such as the Rayovac Hybrid, the Duracell precharged, and the Sanyo eneloop line of rechargeable batteries) give up their power ghost v-e-r-y slowly — so slowly that a year after charging them, they're good-to-go into your gadget with nearly a full charge.

Sanyo says that its eneloop line of rechargeable batteries retains an 85 percent charge after one year of storage, as shown in Figure 3-3. For a technical explanation of how the company pulls it off, have a look at the nearby sidebar, "Sanyo's take on self-discharge."

A NiMH rechargeable battery is always the greener choice because it doesn't contain the hazardous toxins found in the older nickel-cadmium (NiCd) cell that the NiMH version has all but replaced. And, if that's not reason enough, I urge you to check out the nearby sidebar, "Memory effect, R.I.P." Don't say I didn't warn you.

Sanyo's take on self-discharge

The self-discharge of Ni-MH batteries is caused by three main factors::

✔ Chemical decomposition of the cathode

✔ Natural disaggregation of the anode

✔ Impurities of the anode

To reduce the self-discharge in its eneloop batteries, Sanyo uses a new hydrogen-absorbing superlattice alloy, which also increases the electrical capacity of the battery. By reducing internal resistance, the batteries have higher discharge currents than conventional rechargeables. Strengthening the anode by improving the electrolyte composition reduces the natural decomposition process, which also contributes to the eneloop's longer-lasting charge. Sanyo estimates that its eneloop batteries offer up to four times more power when used in a digital camera. The battery maker says the eneloop maintains its charge even in freezing temperatures down to 23 degrees Fahrenheit, and because they're ready to use right out of the box, you don't have to recharge them before you use them, as with ordinary NiMH rechargeables. Sanyo estimates that you can recharge an eneloop battery up to 1,000 times without experiencing a "memory effect" that plagues older.

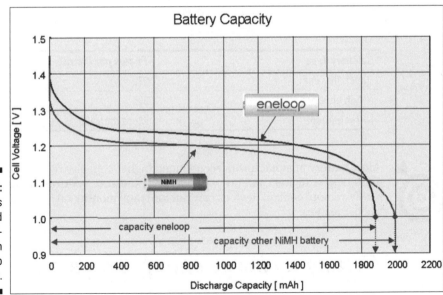

Figure 3-3:
Sanyo has reduced the self-discharge in its eneloop batteries.

Memory effect, R.I.P.

Once upon a time, longtime users of recharge-able batteries (like me) coped with a type of reusable-battery dementia known as *memory effect*. Memory effect describes how older types of rechargeable batteries that aren't allowed to fully discharge before being recharged "remember" the shortened cycle, thereby offering reduced capacity the next time they are charged. Trust me: I'm happy to forget all about it, which is why I mention it in a side-bar, where you're perfectly welcome to forget that you ever heard the term.

You can find a fuller explanation of memory effect at www.Zbattery.com.

Picturing how long battery types last

Because a digital camera requires lots of power to pull off its digital magic, especially when its flash feature is used, battery makers often point to this device as a real-world measuring stick that most people can relate to. The following minitable provides a snapshot of rechargeable-battery capacity and longevity based on the number of pictures per charge that Rayovac estimates can typically be snapped per battery type.

Battery Type	Photos per Charge
Everyday use	275
High energy	375
Precharged	More than 400

Most battery manufacturers recommend higher-capacity rechargeable batteries for digital cameras, whereas low-powered, low-drain gadgets such as TV remote control devices can run for many months on less pricey rechargeables.

Getting a charge out of chargers

Rechargeable battery chargers are available in many shapes and sizes. The most commonly sold chargers hold two to four AA or AAA batteries, or a combination of both types of batteries. Figure 3-4 shows a typical charger.

Figure 3-4:
Typical
charger
made by
Rayovac.

Although many rechargeable battery chargers look much the same, and you might think that they work the same way, the following charger characteristics can help you determine which charger type best suits your needs:

- ✔ **Charging speed:** Charging a rechargeable battery in a pricier fast charger can juice the cells to usable capacity in as little as 15 minutes, whereas a less costly "value" charger can spend several hours charging a battery to its full capacity.

- ✔ **Brand mixing:** You can charge one brand of rechargeable battery in another brand's charger as long as the other charger is designed to charge the same type of battery (NiMH or NiCD, for example).

- ✔ **Charging sensors:** A "smart" battery charger has built-in sensors to shut off the charger after the batteries are fully charged. Chargers without charging sensors continuously drain power even when they're not hungry for it. (These are known as *energy vampires*, and I discuss them further in Chapter 1.)

- ✔ **Mobile battery chargers:** A mobile battery charger, such as the one shown in Figure 3-5, looks and works like an ordinary battery charger — with a twist. Unplugged from the wall, a mobile battery charger can act as a portable charger for one or more gadgets, such as cellphones, iPods, and other MP3 players, digital cameras, and Bluetooth headsets.

If you're looking for rechargeable-battery reviews, check out the ConsumerSearch reviews, ratings, and top picks at www.consumersearch. com/batteries.

Figure 3-5:
Mobile
battery
chargers
function on
the go.

Rechargeable batteries that are too hot to handle in the charger are a sign of possible trouble with your home's power level. If the batteries in a charger feel hot when you touch them, unplug the charger, insert another set of rechargeable batteries, and then plug the charger back into the wall outlet. If the batteries still feel too hot, plug the charger into a different outlet in another room of your house, if possible.

Research the Web sites of the battery brands that most people know by name to find out what to look for when you shop for a rechargeable battery charger. The following minitable lists the Web sites of the most popular battery makers.

Battery Brand	URL
Duracell	www.duracell.com
Energizer	www.energizer.com
Eveready	www.eveready.com
Rayovac	www.rayovac.com

Rechargeables in my house: Part 2

An additional search of my house turned up the following batch of gadgets, listed with the types of batteries they use:

✔ **Beard trimmer, from Conair:** Two AA batteries

✔ **Electronic toothbrush, from Braun Oral-B:** Built-in battery

✔ **Nintendo DS and Sony PlayStation Portable game consoles:** Replaceable rechargeable battery packs

✔ **Game controllers (three) from Sony, Nintendo, and Microsoft:** Add-on rechargeable battery packs

✔ **iPhone, from Apple:** Built-in non-user-replaceable battery

✔ **iPod nano, from Apple:** Built-in non-user-replaceable battery

✔ **LED bike light, from Petzl:** Three AAA batteries (repurposed as a book light for bedside reading)

✔ **Power strip remote control, from Belkin Conserve:** An A23 12V battery

✔ **Smartphones (two) from Nokia and Palm:** Replaceable rechargeable battery packs

✔ **Smoke detector, from Black and Decker:** A 9-volt battery

Charging the batteries for my beard trimmer, reading light, and wireless notebook mice is a single Eveready eight-cell charger, which charges four AA and four AAA rechargeable batteries at the same time.

The only devices at my house that use single-use batteries are the smoke detector and the Belkin Conserve power strip remote control — oh, the irony!

Choosing rechargeable batteries and chargers

The process of buying rechargeable batteries to replace the single-use versions that power your numerous gadgets generally begins with a starter kit that includes a charger and a minimum of two batteries. Shapes, sizes, capacities, and prices vary, as you see in the following sections.

Basic AA and AAA rechargeable-battery kits

The types of rechargeable-battery kits that I often spot at drugstore chains and larger grocery stores are typically made by Duracell, Energizer, Eveready, and Rayovac. The kits charge as many as four AA or AAA batteries or a combination of the two types. The approximate price of each type of kit is included in this list:

✔ **Value:** This slow-to-charge type of kit, which comes with lower-capacity starter batteries, costs about $10.

✔ **Fast and smart:** This type of kit typically comes with higher-capacity starter batteries and a faster charger with features such as Energy Star sensors and On-Off buttons, costs about $25. An example is shown in Figure 3-6.

✔ **Mobile:** A mobile recharger kit, which costs about $30, has features similar to the type in the preceding bullet, and it can act as a portable charger for multiple USB-chargeable gadgets, such as smartphones, MP3 players, and Bluetooth headsets.

Figure 3-6:
Faster-charging battery kits cost about $25.

Recycling dead rechargeable batteries completes the recycle portion of "the three Rs" (reduce, reuse, recycle). Turn to the section "Properly Disposing of Dead Batteries," at the end of this chapter, to find out how to recycle yours.

Less common and wider-reaching chargers

Finding rechargeable batteries and chargers for sizes less common than AA and AAA — such as 9-volt, C, D, and hearing-aid and other flat, button cell batteries (see Figure 3-7) — may mean making a trip to your nearest superstore or Radio Shack. In these stores, you're most likely to find the larger-capacity chargers that hold and charge many batteries — and many sizes — at one time.

Visiting an electronics superstore or buying online offers the highest number of rechargeable-battery and -charger options, from solo 9-volt batteries and 4-cell kits to smart auto-shutoff and multicell decks that can charge a dozen or more rechargeables of different sizes and types at the same time (see Figure 3-8).

Figure 3-7:
Button-cell
batteries.

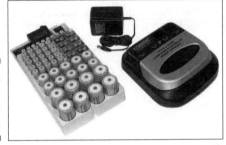

Figure 3-8:
A monster-
size
recharger.

One of these sellers is sure to have what you're looking for:

- ✔ www.amazon.com
- ✔ www.batteriesandbutter.com
- ✔ www.bestbuy.com
- ✔ www.buy.com
- ✔ www.greenbatteries.com
- ✔ www.longlast-battery.com
- ✔ www.megabatteries.com
- ✔ www.microbattery.com
- ✔ www.batteryspace.com
- ✔ www.radioshack.com
- ✔ www.staples.com

Finding Rechargeable Battery Packs

Buying higher-capacity rechargeable battery packs to replace dead or dying ones that are supplied with your gadgets can give them a longer-lasting boost that exceeds the original battery's running time.

Buying rechargeable batteries for less

Several specialty battery seller Web sites (see the earlier section "Less common and wider-reaching chargers") stock replacement-battery packs for your cellphone or smartphone, PDA, GPS tracker, cordless landline, digital camera and camcorder, answering machine, and lots of other gadgets.

Checking your gadget manufacturer's Web site for replacement rechargeable batteries is one option; however, you can often find a compatible fit for less money at reseller sites. These additional sellers specialize in replaceable rechargeable batteries for notebook computers and mobile phones:

- ✔ **1800Mobiles.com**
- ✔ **Batteries.com**
- ✔ **LaptopBatteries.com**
- ✔ **LaptopBattery.org**
- ✔ **YourWirelessSource.com**
- ✔ **All-Battery.com**
- ✔ **OnlyBatteries.com**

Replacing rechargeable batteries in iPods, iPhones, and other sealed gadgets

Replacing the rechargeable battery inside an iPod or MacBook Air or another sealed device isn't as easy as simply swapping the old one for a new one. Contacting Apple or the maker of another sealed gadget to make arrangements to send in your gadget for a rechargeable battery swap generally ensures an installation of the highest possible quality — and the highest price.

Saving money by replacing sealed device batteries with a do-it-yourself kit is another option for technically adept or adventurous types. LaptopsForLess. com sells a kit for less than $15 — battery, surgical tool, and instructions included.

Opening an iPod or most any other sealed gadget instantly voids its warranty.

To find out more about iPod and iPhone built-in battery issues, visit www. ipodbatteryfaq.com.

To help you prepare for your own gadget's battery-replacement microsurgery, search the Web for videos that show you how to open iPods and other sealed devices. Searching for the term **replace ipod battery** at YouTube turned up nearly 200 videos offering step-by-step replacement instructions.

These two online sellers offer do-it-yourself kits for the technically adept (and adventurous):

✔ www.ipodjuice.com

✔ www.ipodbattery.com

Properly Disposing of Dead Batteries

You don't have to just sit and stare at a pile of dead single-use batteries after swapping them out for rechargeable ones. By getting rid of batteries the green way (*and* those depleted rechargeable battery cells and battery packs), you can complete the cycle of the three Rs: Reduce, reuse, recycle.

Determining how to dispose of batteries depends on whether they're single-use or rechargeable cells.

Disposable batteries

Single-use, nonrechargeable batteries are categorized by the federal government as nonhazardous waste, which means that most states don't consider it unlawful to toss them in the trash.

Only two U.S. locales take exception to haphazard battery disposal:

✔ **California:** Requires nonhouseholds to dispose of batteries in accordance with the California universal waste rule.

✔ **Hennepin County (Minnesota):** Requires consumers and nonconsumers alike to treat batteries as hazardous waste.

Sending batteries to landfills or incinerators can cause the batteries' contents to potentially wind up in the soil, air, ground or surface water, and, ultimately, the food chain and drinking water supply.

Follow these guidelines to avoid this problem:

✔ Take the dead batteries to a local hazardous waste drop-off facility in your area, if one exists.

✔ Call your local municipality's public works department to find out whether it collects dead batteries or offers drop-off locations where you can dispose of them yourself.

✔ Check your local library, grocery, hardware, camera, electronics, drug, or other retail or superstore to see whether it offers collection bins for single-use, nonrechargeable batteries (see Figure 3-9).

✔ Call your local EPA office or check your state's environmental agency Web site (www.epa.gov/epahome/state.htm) to see whether it can point you to a nearby household battery drop-off location.

✔ Search your zip code on the Web site Earth911.org to find a battery recycling drop box in your area.

Figure 3-9: Look for recycle bins like these.

Searching Earth911.com for drop-off locations in rural areas (such as my own) turned up plenty that accept rechargeable batteries, but none for single-use batteries. Entering my old Manhattan zip code, however, revealed lots of drop-off locations, including the Whole Foods store not far from my last residence in the city.

If tossing your dead single-use batteries in the trash is your only option until better disposal ways are discovered, keeping these tips in mind can help lessen their potential negative impact on the environment:

✔ Remove and dispose of dead batteries immediately.

✔ Dispose of batteries in small quantities if you're throwing out more than a few.

✔ Make sure not to allow your batteries to be burned. They can explode and cause injury to you and to the environment.

Rechargeables in my house: Part 3

Hats off to the Logitech Harmony One remote (which comes with its own charging cradle), for its ability to replace eight remotes that would otherwise require lots of batteries. This list specifies which batteries I no longer need to buy for these devices because I control these with the Harmony remote control:

- **Apple TV:** One flat, nonrechargeable CR2032 battery

- **Five-port High-Definition Multimedia Interface (HDMI) switch:** Two AAA batteries

- **High-definition Digital Video Recorder (DVR) TiVo HD from TiVo:** Two AA batteries

- **High-Definition TV (HDTV), from Westinghouse:** Two AAA batteries

- **High-definition movie player, from Vudu:** Two AA batteries (and is also known as a "video store in a box")

- **Netflix player, from Roku:** Two AAA batteries

- **PlayStation 3 (PS3) Blu-ray DVD remote:** Two AAA batteries

- **Xbox 360 DVD remote:** Two AA batteries

Rechargeable batteries

Disposing of rechargeable batteries is a heck of a lot easier than disposing of single-use batteries, thank goodness! Finding a location that collects dead rechargeable batteries to see that they're properly recycled can take less than a minute of your time, thanks to the nonprofit organization Rechargeable Battery Recycling Corporation (RBRC).

To find a rechargeable-battery recycling drop-off location near you, follow these steps:

1. **Point your browser to www.rbrc.org.**

2. **Type your zip code in the text box in the lower-left area of the page and click the Go button.**

3. **Choose a location near you.**

4. **(Optional) If you need help navigating to your selection, click the Yahoo! link in the rightmost column to see a map.**

Other places that accept rechargeable batteries include

   ✔ Cellphone retail outlets

   ✔ Cellphone and computer corporate take-back programs (more infor-
     mation available on their Web sites)

   ✔ Consumer electronics stores, such as Radio Shack and Best Buy

To find out more about recycling other hopelessly useless electronics and
electronic waste, check out Chapter 16.

Chapter 4

Maximizing Energy Savings for Your Portable Gadgets

. . . .

In This Chapter

▶ Looking into some gadget energy-saving settings

▶ Extending the battery life on mobile gadgets

▶ Running mobile applications to track and adjust energy use

. . . .

*W*hether you're turning to this chapter first or moseying over from another one, this is the place to find out how to adjust the energy settings on your portable gadgets to gain maximum battery life on the go while minimizing power consumption.

I begin with the battery-consumption boot camp basics and then walk you through the steps to adjust energy settings for extending your gadgets' waking hours between visits to the wall outlet. I also turn you on to some cool, downloadable applications for monitoring and minimizing your gadgets' (and your own) carbon footprint.

Welcome to your new and longer-lasting (battery) way of life!

Getting a Grip on a Gadget's Energy-Saving Settings

Getting green and doing the right thing with all the gadgets and electronic items in your life is most likely why you're reading this book, but if you turned to this chapter before reading any of the others, I probably know the reason:

Blame it on the battery.

Am I right?

Let's face it: We've both done it (and possibly everyone else who reads this book) — blaming, or perhaps cursing, our most essential gadget's battery for running out of juice at the worst possible time. It might have happened in the middle of an important phone call or halfway through the motivating song you rely on to help push you to finish your run or workout. In the worst-case scenario, the battery dies and not until you awaken later than usual and plug in your gadget again can you call your boss and apologize for being late because your alarm didn't go off.

Although it's my job to know the ins and outs of every gadget I own, review, or write about in books like this one, I'm always happy to show friends or family members — or readers — how to adjust or turn off any energy-zapping features they might not know about.

That's what I do for you, by helping you adjust or turn off the power-draining features (see Figure 4-1) on your gadgets to make them last longer between charges.

Figure 4-1:
To extend a gadget's battery life, turn off wireless features you don't use.

Battery-draining items

You can less frequently blame your gadget's battery for bringing your productivity or playtime to a standstill if you pay attention to a few elements that most gadgets expend a lot of energy on — often gratuitously — to keep you happy.

Powerfully pleasing — but power-hungry — factors that have the biggest impact on how long batteries last between charges include the ones in this list:

✔ **Screen:** The screen, when putting on its brightest face possible, is generally the biggest drain on your gadget's battery life. Adjusting the screen's brightness setting to the lowest comfortable level and making adjustments to automatically dim or turn off the screen display after certain actions or periods of inactivity help to reduce the screen's draining contribution to your gadget's overall battery life. An example of a screen brightness setting is shown in Figure 4-2.

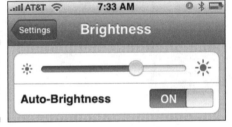

Figure 4-2: Dim the screen to save power.

✔ **Sound:** Pumping up the volume to get your attention or play a song takes lots of energy. Whether it's ultra-ear-awing polyphonic ringtones or a double-disc greatest hits collection, lowering the sound level lengthens battery life. Listening with headphones saves even more power. Shutting off sound completely if you aren't using it offers even longer stretches of time between charges. Turning on a mobile phone's vibrate feature is polite during meetings or movie moments, but that buzzing feeling comes at a price because it taxes the battery every time it gives you that quiet-loving feeling.

✔ **Wireless:** Turning on only features in use extends battery life. Using wireless technology for making and receiving phone calls, e-mails, and text messages; browsing the Web; pinpointing your current location in the world; beaming your business card to an associate or staying in sync with your computer; and listening to music or carrying on a conversation over an untethered headset makes your life easier — but not your gadget battery's life. The key culprits to look for are Bluetooth, WiFi, and GPS and speedier data service network boosters such as EDGE and 3G.

✔ **Hard drives:** A spinning hard disk inside a gadget, such as the older Apple iPod and its single hard-drive-based model, drains a battery faster than a solid-state memory device without a hard disk, such as the iPhone or the iPod nano. Some Windows netbook (miniature) computers have solid-state memory, while others have hard disks spinning inside them. Changing the Windows power options, shown in Figure 4-3, to stop the hard disk after a specified number of minutes extends battery life, as described in Chapter 7.

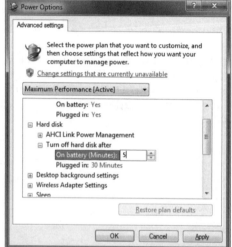

Figure 4-3: Turning off the hard disk to yield big energy gains.

✔ **Heat:** Batteries drain faster when they're hot rather than running warm and at room temperature. Keeping your gadgets cool by not letting them roast in car glove boxes or sit near winter-warming radiators extends battery life.

✔ **Dirt:** Dust, dirt, belly button fuzz, and other debris and impurities collect on your gadgets' battery contacts and can hamper proper contact and charging. First turn off the device and unplug it from its wall charger, and then gently clean exposed contacts with a cotton swab or dust-free cloth dipped in rubbing alcohol, as shown in Figure 4-4, to keep the battery's internal connection strong and unencumbered.

The more specific energy-saving settings described in the following sections can help you eke out the longest battery life possible from all your favorite gadgets.

The time for battery savings change is now!

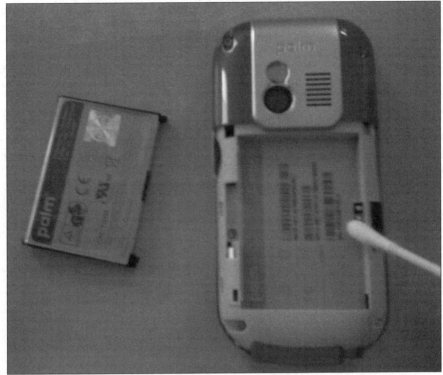

Figure 4-4:
Clean your gadget's battery connection to ensure better battery life.

Cellphones and smartphones

The heading of this section is sort of a catchall because the reality is that many gadgets nowadays are catchalls themselves. In the old days — which, in the world of technology, can mean last year, although I'm talking about ten years ago — gadgets did one or two tasks well. MP3 players played music. PDAs, such as the original PalmPilot, kept bits of information close at hand. Cellphones mainly made and received phone calls.

A little later, MP3 players began showing off photos. PDAs got connected and started running miniature applications that performed many of the tasks that computers could do, albeit on a Lilliputian scale. Cellphones became smarter too, and some, like the iPhone, even called themselves *smart*phones as they began doing the work of those other gadgets — while *still* letting you make and receive phone calls.

Bringing so many gadgets together into a single device that you can hold in one hand is by nature a greener way of getting along with the planet.

If the only setting you change on your cellphone is its ringtone, getting to know your device's other settings may reward you with longer talk times and less recharging.

Because settings vary widely depending on brand and model, you may need to poke around to find the individual energy-saving settings on your cellphone or smartphone.

To adjust the energy settings for my iPhone, for example, I access them from the same Settings menu. Although my Nokia also has a Settings menu, it isn't where I choose or change options such as the ringtone or vibration level. You find these options by opening the Profiles tab, shown in Figure 4-5, and then customize profiles to match different scenarios, such as Movie Time (shhh!) or Cityscape, where the ring volume is turned up full blast so that I can hear it over honking taxi horns.

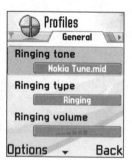

Figure 4-5:
Trying to
find a
setting.

Here are the top battery-busting energy settings you can adjust or turn off if you aren't using them:

- ✔ **On and off:** Powering off your phone when you know that you won't use it for a while is the basic way to save power.

- ✔ **Brightness:** Turning down the brightness level on a cellphone or smartphone to its dimmest level (while maintaining comfort) goes a long way toward lengthening your gadget's battery life. Activating a phone's automatic brightness feature adjusts the brightness to match your physical environment so that the screen dims at night or in a movie theater and increases to become visible on a sunny day or in a well-lit setting. Setting the screen to automatically dim after fifteen seconds or so is another option to activate if your phone has that setting.

- ✔ **Auto-shutoff, lock, and sleep:** Setting your phone to automatically lock itself or go to sleep prevents it from waking up in your pocket if you accidentally bump it. Some phones let you manually lock them by pressing a button, whereas you lock certain other phone models by pressing a combination of buttons.

✔ **Volume:** Turning down or shutting off your phone's ringtone helps save battery life. Adjusting sound effects and alerts for other actions — such as receiving a text or e-mail message or your phone's alarm clock — to the lowest level possible helps extend your phone's battery life.

✔ **Vibrate:** Turning on the vibrate feature can alert you to a call without making a sound, but keep in mind that vibrating uses battery juice. Setting your phone to vibrate only once or a few times is an energy-saving option on many phones.

✔ **Equalizer:** One other, often overlooked, power-gobbling option to turn off if your phone also plays music tracks is its equalizer, or EQ, as shown in Figure 4-6. Leaving this option on makes your phone work harder to produce the sound-quality effect you want. Turning off the option on your phone but keeping it activated on your computer's music-playing program, such as iTunes, is generally an option.

✔ **Network:** Sensing your wireless carrier's phone network signal is a task that your phone does continually to keep you connected. Turning off your phone's Network option when you're in rural areas where reception is spotty or unavailable can save power. Turning off the phone if you aren't using it for other tasks, such as listening to music, saves even more power. The Network option isn't the same as the one that connects to a WiFi network for accessing the Internet or files on your company's server, however. (That option is next on our list, in case your phone has it.)

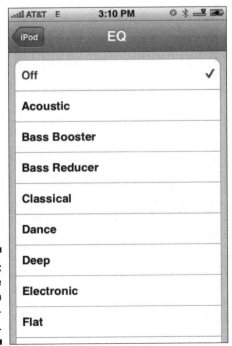

Figure 4-6:
Turn off the equalizer to extend battery life.

TIP

Leaving the Network option on but turning off data networking enhancements that give you faster Web access or clearer calls (if your phone has those options) can also help extend battery life. The most talked-about wireless carrier enhancement is 3G, which is an abbreviation for third generation.

✔ **Wi-Fi:** Turning off your phone's Wi-Fi connection if you aren't using it to connect to the Internet to browse Web pages, check e-mail, or download music can go a long way toward extending your phone's battery life. Keeping the Wi-Fi connection on if you're using it but turning it off to automatically search for and connect to new Wi-Fi networks your phone detects is a good compromise to keep the connection alive but minimize the power it uses, as shown in Figure 4-7.

Figure 4-7:
Sniffing for
Wi-Fi sucks
battery
juice.

✔ **Bluetooth:** Connecting your phone to a Bluetooth headset and turning it on saves you from having to hold the phone to your ear — and speeds up battery drain. Turning Bluetooth on only when you're using it and turning it off when you aren't can give your phone markedly longer battery life. Connecting to another Bluetooth-equipped phone or computer to send and receive pictures, files, business cards, or other types of information also drains a battery more quickly, and if you aren't using your phone for these tasks, by all means give Bluetooth the ax.

✔ **GPS:** Continually tracking your location by using your phone's global positioning system (GPS) feature makes a cinch of finding your way around on the road or locating a new restaurant in town (see Figure 4-8). Of course, this awesomely useful feature sucks more battery life when it's turned on than off, so if you aren't using it, turn it down.

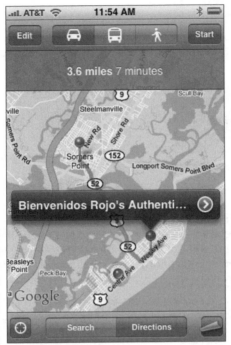

Figure 4-8:
Finding your
way with
GPS drains
the battery
faster.

✔ **Infrared:** Beaming business cards from your phone to a phone used by a work associate or friend or wirelessly sharing files between your phone and computer by way of infrared radiation, or IR (drum roll, please) shortens a gadget's battery life. Although IR isn't as common as it was before Bluetooth arrived on the scene, some new gadgets are supplied with the infrared option. Check the settings on your phone or other gadget to see whether it uses IR (like the Palm Centro does). If you aren't using it, you know what to do: Shut it off.

MP3 and media players

Adjusting or turning off some of the options and features described earlier in this chapter — such as brightness, Wi-Fi, and Bluetooth — applies here, and then some:

✔ **Brightness and Lock:** Watching a movie with your portable media player's screen brightness set to its maximum level makes sense, but keeping it that way when the gadget is in your pocket while you're listening to music wastes power. That power could keep your tunes playing longer if the brightness were turned down or off. Tucking your player into a pocket without turning on its lock feature, as shown in Figure 4-9, can cause it to start playing if you accidentally bump or brush it. Tend to these two options to ensure longer playing time.

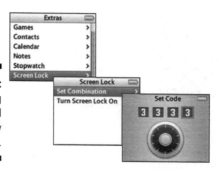

Figure 4-9:
Preventing
accidental
battery
rundown.

✔ **Battery capacity:** Opening your iPod or almost any other sealed gadget instantly voids its warranty, so be sure to contact the gadget's manu-facturer directly to arrange a swap for a longer-lasting battery if the warranty hasn't yet expired. Sending a sealed gadget to a seller that upgrades the battery for you is a smart choice if your device is out of warranty. A do-it-yourself kit is another option if you're technically adept or the adventurous type.

The Web site BatteryShip.com offers kits for players, such as the iPod and Zune, and replacement batteries for numerous other portable gadgets.

✔ **Hard drives and big audio files:** An MP3 player with a built-in hard drive, such as certain iPod and Zune models, copies as much of a music track as possible to a device's solid-state memory and then spins down the hard drive to save battery life. Playing huge files requires the hard drive to reactivate more frequently — which can cause the battery to run down more quickly.

To trim track sizes while retaining audio quality, you can adjust the way your computer's music player software converts CDs to digital music (which you then copy to your portable player). Changing either Windows Media Player's or iTune's default importing (that is, *ripping*) formats from their defaults to MP3 can double track sizes. Keeping the default importing formats — WMA for Windows Media Player, and AAC, as shown in Figure 4-10, for iTunes — can cut track sizes by as much as half.

If you changed your computer's music player's importing format to MP3 and want to change back to the more efficient (and default) formats, here's how:

> **For Windows Media Player:** From the Now Playing menu, choose More Options. On the Rip Music tab, choose Windows Media Audio from the Format drop-down menu (under Rip Settings).

> **For iTunes:** Click the menu iTunes (Mac) or Edit (Windows) and then choose Preferences. On the General tab, click the Import Settings button and then select AAC from the Import Using drop-down menu.

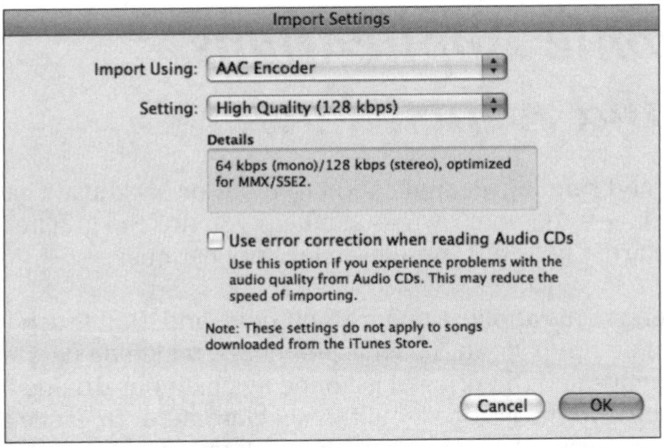

Figure 4-10:
Ripping a
CD with
battery-
friendlier
settings.

Import Settings

Import Using: AAC Encoder

Setting: High Quality (128 kbps)

Details

64 kbps (mono)/128 kbps (stereo), optimized
for MMX/SSE2.

☐ Use error correction when reading Audio CDs

Use this option if you experience problems with the
audio quality from Audio CDs. This may reduce the
speed of importing.

Note: These settings do not apply to songs
downloaded from the iTunes Store.

Cancel   OK

Digital cameras and camcorders

Just like with your other portable gadgets, making energy-saving adjustments to your digital camera or camcorder that extend battery life can increase the number of shots or hours of footage you can capture. And as with all portable gadgets that have backlit screens, turning down the brightness uses less battery juice.

For even longer camera and camcorder battery life:

- **Look through the viewfinder.** Turning off your camcorder's LCD viewfinder and looking through the lens instead (if your model has one) can help the battery last longer. Ditto for your digital camera's LCD viewfinder and preview feature. Shutting off the small screen and waiting until the gadget is plugged in again to preview snapshots or captured video also keeps the battery alive much longer.

- **Focus on focusing less.** Partly pressing the shutter release on your digital camera or camcorder to gauge or activate the autofocus feature makes the gadget's motor whir, which uses lots of power. Focus on testing the focus less often, until you're truly ready to take the shot.

- **Deactivate your digital camera's flash setting and your camcorder's spotlight.** Doing so prevents you from accidentally using either feature — and extends battery life. Turn them on when you need them, and turn them off when you don't.

- **Stay in charge.** Bringing along a second or third rechargeable battery can keep the action rolling throughout the day. Plugging in between shooting sessions to keep the battery topped off is another way to stay in charge of the battery on your camera or camcorder so that it lasts as long as possible.

Running Mobile Applications to Monitor and Adjust Power

Downloading and running an application to monitor or adjust a gadget's carbon footprint — and your own — can help you do "the greener thing" wherever you are. Check out these popular applications:

✔ **greenMeter:** This application for the iPhone and iPod touch helps lower your vehicle's impact on the environment by weighing parameters such as its tonnage and the price of gasoline against your driving behavior. By tapping into the iPhone's built-in accelerometer to gauge the vehicle's rate of forward acceleration, greenMeter, at `http://hunter.pairsite.com/greenmeter`, calculates vehicle readings such as fuel efficiency and carbon footprint (see Figure 4-11).

Figure 4-11: greenMeter keeps an eye on your carbon footprint.

✔ **Ecorio:** Running on a Google Android-based mobile phone near you, Ecorio (`www.ecorio.org`) taps into the phone's GPS feature to track movement to calculate your personal carbon footprint. Choosing your mode of travel — car, bus, train, or bicycle — determines how seriously green you are about getting around. Ecorio suggests carpool options by matching up drivers and passengers and lets fellow green-gadgeteers keep tabs on each other in the same town or across the country. The option to buy carbon offsets by way of Carbonfund.org is only a credit card number away.

✔ **Carbon-Meter:** Coming soon to Google Android and Blackberry smartphones, the iPhone version of Carbon-Meter (`www.viralmesh.com/carbon-meter`) rewards your green activities and efforts with coupons and specials sponsored by local advertisers, as shown in Figure 4-12. Run, walk, or bike your way to increase your ecosavings — and your savings account.

Figure 4-12:
Getting
there the
Go Greener
way.

✔ **UbiGreen:** Still only a research project and not yet a product you can hold in your hand (or install on a gadget), UbiGreen (http://dub. washington.edu/projects/ubigreen) gauges how you get around to calculate how much carbon dioxide you save during a week. Glancing at the UbiGreen background that runs on your cellphone can help you put your best foot forward when taking steps to reduce your carbon footprint.

Chapter 5

Energy Savings All Around the House

....

In This Chapter

▶ Applying basic energy savings at home

▶ Looking around your house for energy savings

▶ Intensifying your power savings on TVs and entertainment gear

....

Adjusting the options on the power-hungry electronic devices all around your house adds to your global contribution to helping save the planet. Just as importantly, the practice saves you money on your monthly electric bill.

I begin with a few reminders on green living practices, such as remembering to turn off the lights when you leave the room, and then describe the most common energy-saving opportunities on the consumer electronics in your house.

From there, I point out built-in energy-saving features that you might not know about, and then tell you which common settings to look for and how to adjust them.

This chapter focuses on energy savings for all gadgets and electronic devices in your house, except for your Mac and Windows computers — both of which receive full treatment in Part III.

Practicing Green Living in Your House

Use green living practices on the following items to gain greater savings benefits (which I describe in a few pages) from the energy settings on your electronic gadgets:

✔ **Off switch:** Turn off any device you aren't using.

✔ **Plug-in timers:** Turn lights and appliances on and off with automated timers set to match your schedule.

✔ **Thermostat:** Set your home's thermostat to 78 degrees in the summer and to 68 degrees in the winter.

If you have a programmable thermostat, set its standard Day, Night, Wake, and Sleep settings to maximize energy savings. See the following sidebar, "Use a programmable thermostat — and then walk away," for more information about this handy gizmo.

✔ **Your computer's screen saver:** Choose the None or Blank setting instead of an animated screen saver.

✔ **Your computer's monitor:** Use your computer's power-saving settings to turn off your monitor or notebook display after a few minutes of inactivity.

✔ **Your computer's sleep settings:** Put your computer in Sleep mode or Hibernate mode to power it down shortly after the display gets turned off as described in the preceding bullet. (See Part III for more information about reducing your computer's energy use.)

✔ **Devices that draw power even when they appear to be turned off:** Unplug these "standby power" devices — which are also known as *energy vampires* — including TVs, stereos, and cell phone or iPod chargers.

Plug energy vampires into a smart power strip, like the one shown in Figure 5-1, which senses the flow of electrical current through the strip's control outlet, and turns off selected outlets when devices plugged into them are not in use. Doing so minimizes the energy draw and makes it easier to automatically pull the proverbial plug on devices that aren't in use all at once.

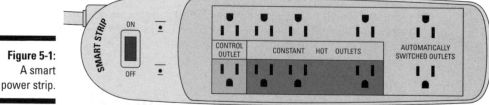

Figure 5-1:
A smart power strip.

To find out about all-around green living, read *Green Living For Dummies*, written by Yvonne Jeffery, Liz Barclay, and Michael Grosvenor (Wiley Publishing). Some of the basic energy-saving principles in that book apply also to the powered devices in your home.

Use a programmable thermostat — and then walk away

You can swap your manual thermostat with the Honeywell 5-2 Day Programmable Thermostat to set heating and cooling temperatures — and then forget them. Set this gadget to turn up the heating or air conditioning a few minutes before you wake up, adjust it downward when you head off to work, kick it up a few notches when you return home, and then adjust it again at bedtime for a night of sleep that's comfortable and energy efficient. If you're sleeping in on the weekend, setting the Honeywell device to keep you warm or cool beyond your usual wakeup time is par for the course.

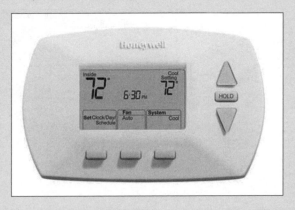

Reviewing Energy-Saving Opportunities in Your House

The biggest power-hungry, high-tech item in your house is probably the TV in your living room, followed by typically smaller sets in the bedroom, basement, or den. Several other pieces of home entertainment gear — including DVD players, audio systems, and game controllers — are vying for power, too.

In this section, I take you on a quick tour of your household gadgets and offer quick fixes for green living, such as using smart power strips, along the way. In the later section "Adjusting Power-Saving Options on TVs and Entertainment Gear," I detail which settings to look for and adjust to make your home gadgets more energy efficient.

Energy monitors

If you're wondering just how much power that room heater or printer, or any other electrically powered device, is drawing when it's turned on — and when it's turned off — plug it into the Kill A Watt, shown in the figure on the left. Then you can find out instantly how many watts it's drawing — and how much it's contributing to your monthly electric bill.

Skipping the plug-it-in approach is The Energy Detective, shown on the right, which taps directly into your home's circuit breaker to display in real-time the total amount of power you're using — and paying for. Turning appliances and gadgets on and off reveals how much each one is adding to your overall load.

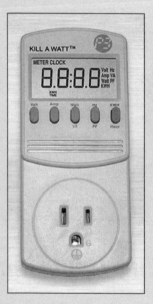

Televisions

Older sets are less efficient than newer ones, and all of them are energy vampires because they continue to draw power even when you switch them off. Some sip only a few watts when turned off — usually referred to as being in Standby mode — whereas others suck lots of juice in order to let you start watching almost immediately the next time you turn them on.

Replacing disposable, or *single use,* batteries with rechargeable ones in every remote control and other battery-operated gadget in your house is a supersmart, and supereasy, way to stop wasting energy, resources, and money. Read all about it in Chapter 3.

Plugging your TV into a power strip that you can turn off with the flick of a switch is an easy to way to cut down on not only its standby energy drain but also all the other gadgets typically plugged into your TV, including

- DVD and VHS players
- Video game consoles
- A/V receivers and surround-sound systems and the speakers connected to them
- Cable, satellite, and DVR devices, such as the TiVo

Choosing not to power off the trio of devices listed in the last bullet is understandable because they generally take a long time to start up again — and you run the chance of missing programs you want to record if they happen to air whenever your TiVo or DVR-enabled cable box is turned off.

Picking a smart power strip that combines several sockets that turn off at one time, or senses when a device isn't in use, yet leaves a couple of sockets powered on, provides a fair compromise to the all-or-nothing approach of turning everything off.

Computers and peripheral devices

Your computer and any devices connected to it are popular at-home, power-hungry culprits. If you use the same kind of smart power strip (refer to Figure 5-1) for your computer and its peripherals, you can leave it up to the power strip to sense when to turn off some sockets while leaving a few turned on. This type of flexibility lets you completely shut down such standby power drainers as monitors and printers when you turn off your PC, while allowing typically always-on gadgets (such as broadband cable or DSL modems and home networking WiFi routers) to keep perking along without pause.

This is helpful if you or someone else in your house is tapping into the Internet wirelessly with a notebook computer or video game console in another room. If not, turning off your broadband modem and router rewards you with even greater savings. Adjusting your computer's energy-saving settings is covered from head to toe in Part III.

Mobile phones, MP3 players, GPS trackers, and other personal gadgets

Leaving the charger for your mobile phone, GPS tracker, iPod, Nintendo DS, or other portable gadget plugged in to the wall socket after it's fully charged wastes energy.

Unplugging a charger after a gadget is fully charged saves energy because it stops the charger from wasting power by continually sipping juice even when it's no longer thirsty.

Taking advantage of individual energy-saving options for each of your personal gadgets is described in Chapter 4.

Adjusting Power-Saving Options on TVs and Entertainment Gear

In this section, I provide several power-saving tips for TVs and other common home electronics devices. These tips, which can help you save energy and money, are aimed toward making gadgets you already own more green. If you're interested in acquiring green home entertainment and other types of household gadgets, check out Chapter 13.

Taming TV power

Every TV in your house, whether it's old or brand-spanking new, can use less energy when you pay attention to the practices and settings mentioned in the next several sections.

You usually access your TV's settings by pressing one of the following buttons on your TV's remote control or on the TV set itself:

- Menu
- Settings
- Setup

Understanding that off means off

Plugging your TV into a smart power strip, which I describe earlier in this chapter — or just pulling the plug when you'll be away for more than a couple of days — cuts down on the power drain that a TV consumes when it's left plugged in and in Standby mode.

Saying not-so-fast to Fast Start

If your newer hi-definition TV (HDTV) has either a Fast Start or Quick Start option, turning it off means waiting a little longer after turning the set on before you can start watching. When you avoid using this feature, the TV uses up to 50 percent less energy than it normally consumes in Standby mode.

Playing to an audience of none

Leaving the TV turned on when no one is watching it is wasteful. Sure, you can reasonably leave the room to grab a beverage or use the (ahem) facilities, but turning off the tube if you won't be back for more than a few minutes is the energy-saving thing to do.

Initiating sleepy-time savings

Falling to sleep with the TV on happens, of course, and using your TV remote control's Sleep feature can ensure that your set sleeps as peacefully (and efficiently) as you if you happen to nod off during a snoozer. The Sleep button generally offers shutoff timer choices that range from 15 minutes to an hour or more. Check to see whether your TV remote has a Sleep button, and if so, press it repeatedly to become familiar with your snooze-you-don't-lose-energy choices.

Dimming the lights

Reducing your TV's brightness — and the brightness of the room you're sitting in when you're watching — can go a long way toward increasing your energy savings.

To dim the lights, so to speak, make one of these four adjustments:

- ✔ **Room lighting:** The use of low-level backlighting or curtained but light-allowing windows is easier on the eyes when viewing TV — and easier on the environment because you can dim your TV's brightness, as described in the next bullet.

- ✔ **Brightness and picture:** Most TVs leave the factory with all their picture-related settings cranked to the maximum level in order to stand out among all the competitors vying to catch your eye on the showroom floor. Turning down your TV's brightness setting increases your energy savings.

    Checking your TV's settings to see whether it has picture presets — such as Movie, Sports, Natural, Action, or Game — is another option. Some models offer a Power Saver setting that's generally the greenest choice you can make.

- ✔ **LCD backlight:** LCD flat-panel TVs typically offer a backlighting setting. The lower you set it, the less energy your set draws.

- ✔ **Professional calibration:** Consider hiring a professional TV technician to *calibrate* your higher-end HDTVs to provide picture-perfect performance for the room you're watching in. Your reward can be better savings — and greater viewing pleasure.

Benefitting from all-in-one remote controls

Replacing half a dozen (or more) remote controls with a rechargeable all-in-one model, such as the Harmony One, shown in Figure 5-2, eliminates the need to buy lots of batteries — and reduces multiple carbon footprint contributors in one fell swoop. I write more about the Harmony One remote in Chapter 3.

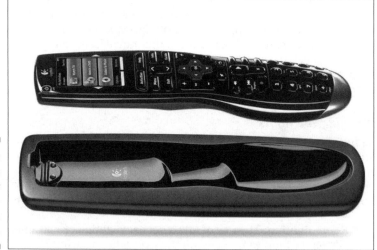

Figure 5-2:
Replace many remote controls with an all-in-one.

Reducing power consumption in DVD, video game, and other types of players

Adjusting your DVD or Blu-ray player's power-saving settings can help you save energy long after the curtains have closed. You can also keep the savings in play after you play games or movies on your video game console, thanks to the auto-off options built into the Xbox 360 and PlayStation 3.

DVD players

If you turn on your DVD or other player's auto-off option after the movie or other program ends and displays the main menu, you can save energy in case you forget to turn off the player yourself — or if you fall asleep before the end of the show.

Display your DVD or other player's settings by pressing a remote control button named Menu, Settings, or Setup.

VHS players

Activate the auto-off option on your VHS player, if it has one, so that the player cuts the power a set length of time after it senses that the tape has reached the end of the show.

Audio/video receivers and speaker systems

Booming bass surround-sound speaker systems are big-time energy drainers, and shutting them off or plugging them into a power strip can help increase your home entertainment system energy savings.

Plugging all the items connected to your audio/video (AV) receiver into its built-in switchable outlets can make it easier to turn everything on and off at one time — if your receiver is similar to the Yamaha RX-V2700, shown in Figure 5-3. It has two switchable power sockets for easier power-saving shut-offs, located in the lower right corner of the device.

Figure 5-3:
One AV receiver; two switchable power outlets.

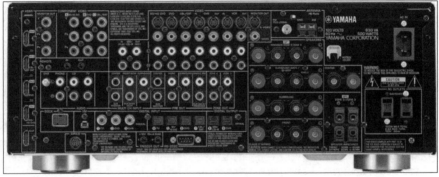

Xbox 360 and PlayStation 3

Activating the automatic power-off feature on your Xbox 360 or PlayStation 3 can help reduce your console's energy consumption whenever you leave the game — and leave the game box on.

Neither the Xbox 360 or the PlayStation 3 (PS3) ships from the factory with the option turned on, which is why it's up to you to make the change. Although Nintendo forgot to give its video game console, the Wii, any type of energy-saving settings, that doesn't mean it can't appear in a future downloadable update. (That's the approach Sony took to give the PS3 an auto-off option, similar to the one on the Xbox 360.)

Plugging any video game console into a smart power strip and shutting off the power strip with everything else all at one time can help save energy that's otherwise wasted by off-but-not-completely-off standby power drainers, such as the chunky power supply on the Xbox 360.

The great video-game-energy robbery

A study by the Natural Resources Defense Council, at `www.nrdc.org/energy/consoles/contents.asp`, found that video game machines eat up "an estimated 16 billion kilowatt hours per year," which is "roughly equal to the annual electricity use of the city of San Diego."

Gamers often leave consoles on when they're not playing in order to return to the middle of a level that can't be saved and reloaded in the same place if the power is turned off. Microsoft and Sony both offer options to automatically turn off the consoles after a set amount of time, but the study found that gamers often skip the option because they'll lose their place if the game doesn't have an auto-save or "save-any-where" feature.

Games like the futuristic role-playing game BioShock offer the capability to save your progress in a game anywhere, anytime, to reload right where you left off after turning off the game machine and returning to it later.

Mr. Horowitz believes a Hibernate mode similar to what Windows and Mac computers have would save energy and save the player's progress at the same time. When it came to locking in on how many gamers leave their machines on, Mr. Horowitz's team could not offer an answer as to what percent. As such, the study group's best guess is that about half of gamers leave their consoles running when they're not playing.

The study found that the Wii draws 16 watts of power when it's in use, while the Xbox 360 sits in the middle with a rating of 119 watts when it's on and doing its gaming thing. Sucking up 150 watts, the PS3 was the biggest energy consumer of the group.

Citing the PS3's main role as game machine, Mr. Horowitz said the console uses full power when it doesn't need to, such as while playing a Blu-ray DVD movie. Watching the movie Spider-Man 3, Mr. Horowitz found that the game console used more than 120 watts of power. Comparing the PS3 to one of Sony's standard Blu-ray players, Mr. Horowitz said the player uses five times less power than the PS3.

Hoping the study's findings prompt the console makers to make their boxes more energy efficient, Mr. Horowitz said the hibernation-like feature he described is doable, and if the manufacturers tried a little harder, they could fix it.

Granted, the Wii draws less than half the power of the Xbox 360 or PS3, but that doesn't mean you should leave it on morning, noon, and night whether you're playing or not.

Maybe you're wondering just how much energy is wasted every year because of video game consoles. Researchers estimate that the total drain is about 16 billion kilowatt hours per year or, put another way, "roughly equal to the annual electricity use of the city of San Diego." To read more about this study, check out the nearby sidebar, "The great video-game-energy robbery."

Turning off your Xbox 360 controller isn't a big deal because it does it itself after sensing that you're no longer using it. Not so with the PS3 controller — until you turn on its auto-off option.

To turn on the auto-off feature on your PlayStation 3 console and controller, follow these steps:

1. **From the main menu, choose System Settings⇨Power Save Settings and then press Select.**

2. **Select System Auto-Off and choose the number of hours your PS3 will wait when you're not playing it before it shuts itself off. Then press Select.**

   Your choices are 1, 2, 3, or 5 hours or Off. Choosing 1 hour is the greenest choice for maximum energy savings.

3. **Select the Turn Off System Automatically Even Under Special Conditions option and then select OK.**

   The console turns itself off after the selected length of time even if a game or Blu-ray disc is inserted in the console and the main menu is displayed.

   Leaving this option deselected prevents the console from turning itself off when you're watching a movie, playing a game, or just letting the console sit idle on the main menu.

4. **Return to the Power Save Settings screen and select Controller Auto-Off.**

   This step governs the controller's ability to toggle its power on or off whenever it detects that you're no longer playing with it.

To turn on your Xbox 360 auto-off feature:

1. **Press the Xbox controller's center X button, then navigate to Settings⇨System Settings⇨Console Settings⇨Shutdown.**

2. **Choose Auto-Off⇨Enable.**

   Your Xbox 360 turns itself off after six hours of inactivity, as shown in Figure 5-4.

3. **(Optional) Select Background Downloads.**

   After you turn off the console, the system completes any downloads that it put on hold while you were playing a game or watching a movie.

Auto-Off

Enable

Disable

Current Setting
Auto-Off Disabled

Enable auto-off to automatically turn
off your console after 6 hours of
inactivity.

Back
Select

Figure 5-4:
Bedtime for
the Xbox
360.

Part III
Minimizing Your Computer's Carbon Footprint

The 5th Wave   By Rich Tennant

"This model comes with a particularly useful function — a simulated static button for breaking out of long-winded conversations."

In this part . . .

Minimizing your computer's carbon footprint might sound daunting, but it's easier than most people realize. You have to roll up your sleeves and venture into parts of your system that you might have never seen. I provide step-by-step directions to help you do it, and before you know it, you'll tweak energy settings that leave you with a system that draws the least amount of power necessary when you're using it and draws little or no power when you're not using it.

Chapter 6

Your Computer's Energy Use

*P*Cs use a lot of energy, yet most people admit that they use their computers only half the time it's turned on (or even less). Adjusting your computer's power-saving settings to minimize energy consumption is an easy — and easily overlooked — way to reduce your personal carbon footprint.

Reducing your computer's power consumption increases your personal savings, knocking an average of $25 to $75 off your annual electric bill.

In this chapter, I discuss the general ins and outs of computer power consumption. I also briefly touch on how to adjust energy settings for your printer, monitor, and other peripherals. The results are beneficial to the planet — and your bank account. In the next two chapters, I discuss how to set specific adjustments for Windows computers (see Chapter 7) and Macs (see Chapter 8).

Quashing Computer Power Myths

Adjusting your computer's power settings for the largest possible energy savings is easier when you understand how much energy a PC consumes to start up, shut down, "nap" in Standby mode or Sleep mode, or power off completely with the deeper-sleep power-saving option known as *Hibernate*.

Plugging your computer and peripherals into a "smart" power strip such as the Belkin Conserve, shown in Figure 6-1, can take a bite out of energy vampires by reducing or completely cutting power consumption and costs. (See Chapter 1 for more about energy vampires.) If you have to bend over to reach a power strip that's on the floor or tucked behind your desk, you might not bother turning power strips off. Enter the Conserve's handy remote control — press it to instantly turn on or off all of the devices plugged into eight of the strip's ten outlets. The remaining pair of outlets stays on all of the time so that you can keep certain devices (such as your cable or DSL modem and Wi-Fi router) on around the clock.

Figure 6-1: Stop sucking power from your devices by using a smart power strip.

Playing a quick round of True or False can help you understand the ins and outs of PC power use while dispelling a couple of longstanding myths:

- ✔ **Shutting down your PC and turning it on again the next time you use it consumes more power than leaving the computer on most of the time.**

  False. A computer uses less energy to boot up and operate as needed than it does to leave it on all the time.

- ✔ **Screen savers save energy.**

  False. Setting your computer's energy-saving setting to turn off your monitor or notebook display rather than run a screen saver saves energy. Running a pretty 3D screen saver, such as Bubbles, shown in Figure 6-2, not only keeps the juice flowing to the screen but also might require the computer's graphics card to use more power because it's working harder to render the 3D animated scene.

- ✔ **Screen savers prevent screen burn-in.**

  True and false. It's true that older TV-like cathode ray tube (CRT) monitors suffered from image burn-in. *Burn-in* (also referred to as *screen fade* or *phosphor burn*) describes what happens when a screen is left on for hours at a stretch: Menu bars or the logo of a news channel, for example, leave a permanent shadow on the screen.

Figure 6-2:
The Bubbles
screen
saver in
Windows
Vista is
pretty but
also power-
hungry.

Running a screen saver on older CRTs can prevent burn-in — as does changing the energy settings to shut off the monitor after a certain amount of time. It's false, though, to suggest that a screen saver prevents burn-in on a notebook or computer with a liquid crystal display (LCD), because the technology that's used is impervious to the burn-in bummers of yore.

✓ **Computers use less energy when they're idling.**

True and false. Like cars, computers generally use less energy when they're just sitting there, not distracted by your fingertips or mouse clicks. But the same idling computer may be using more energy if it's running a graphically intensive program or downloading a huge file in the background. Many manufacturers now strive to cut idling energy consumption by half or more. For instance, at the time this book was written, the "greenest MacBook ever" from Apple used one-quarter of the power of an ordinary 60-watt light bulb when idling.

Picture this: In a perfectly energy-conscious world, your computer is fully powered on and running at a level of performance that suits your needs; when your computer isn't in use, it's dozing but ready to awaken instantly or in mere seconds when you return to it. Better yet, your computer awakens a minute or so before you sit down with your preferred beverage at the start of every workday; naps while you're at lunch and awakens just before you return; and thoughtfully remembers to shut itself off a few minutes after your typical quitting time, in case you forget to "pull the plug" yourself. In fact, your perfectly energy-conscious computer is so energy-savings-savvy that it even knows not to wake itself until noon on weekends because that's when you typically check your weekend e-mail and it's smart enough to put itself to sleep or completely shut down if you don't even check in, which saves the largest possible amount of energy.

My description sounds like a science fiction dream, doesn't it? It's not, because it can all be done right now, thanks to automated power schedulers, such as the one built into the Mac's Energy Saver preferences, shown in Figure 6-3.

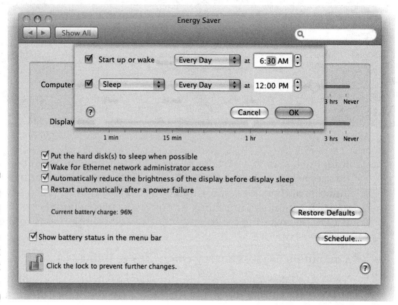

Figure 6-3: Scheduling your Mac to automatically start up and shut down.

Okay, in a more perfect world, perhaps your computer will be so smart that rather than rely on an energy settings schedule that you set up, built-in sensors will detect when you're out of bed and wake the computer at the same time, and other sensors will listen for such phrases as "I'm heading to lunch," giving the computer permission to take a nap until it senses your return.

In the meantime, setting your computer's energy settings to respond to your work and play needs on a strict day-to-day basis — or in a manner that's more relaxed and generally eco-aware — is a cinch after you have a better handle on your true computer usage and consumption habits and routines.

Evaluating Your Everyday Computer Needs

Getting a handle on how you use your computer on a daily, nightly, and weekend basis is the first step to creating a friendlier energy-saving relationship with your computer — and with the environment. You can calculate the estimated energy usage of your home computer (and other electronic devices) in dollars and cents — a task that's made easy when you use an energy calculator like the Web-based offering at `http://mygreenelectronics.org`. If number crunching is your preferred way of doing business, download the free energy calculator spreadsheet available at `www.energystar.gov`.

You must consider the kinds of tasks you use your computer for to help determine which settings to adjust to give back positive energy — and costs savings — without negatively affecting your workflow or your computer's performance (and by extension, your own).

This list highlights which tasks require the most power and speed and which ones are relatively easy on a computer's resources:

- ✔ **Video editing:** If you have a Mac and you're using a program such as Final Cut to edit video, you need all the power and speed the machine can provide. Turning down settings that affect performance isn't an option, however, because the computer's main central processing unit (CPU), graphics processing unit (GPU), and hard drive must work fast and furiously to capture the necessary number of video frames to make movies and broadcast-quality video look natural to viewers.

- ✔ **Photo editing, uploading, and so on:** To your computer, a picture is a data file made up of thousands to millions and millions of bits of data. Keeping a handle on all of those millions of dots (or pixels), and rendering each new view after you make changes, pushes your computer's processors and hard drive to the max. Uploading your pictures or illustrations to Facebook or e-mailing them to family and friends, on the other hand, isn't too taxing on your computer's electronic brain.

- ✔ **Any tasks that require specialized applications:** Using computers to perform complicated tasks such as editing feature films, playing ultrarealistic video games, or analyzing DNA chains in 3D (I made that one up, but you get the idea) are considered specialized applications and therefore require computers to run at their maximum performance level to process all the data that's involved.

- ✔ **Word processing and/or number crunching (in a spreadsheet program):** These everyday tasks are in the category of general computing, which are tasks that generally access the hard drive only when saving (or autosaving) a document or looking up a word in the thesaurus, for example.

> ✔ **Web browsing**: This is also mainly a light-duty task for your computer's processing brains, requiring the machine's brawnier browsing powers on an as-needed basis, such as when visiting sites loaded with tons of design gizmos and animated graphics or video.

No matter what you do with your computer — calculating rocket science or playing solitaire — it's always smart to turn it off when you're not using it.

Setting a reliable energy-saving schedule and scheme is generally easier if you adhere to a strict schedule. Even so, no law specifies that if you're keeping a strict schedule, you must set your computer's energy settings to turn on and off at the same time every day, or at different times on the weekend.

Setting even the most basic energy-saving settings reduces your personal carbon footprint. For example, you might make the display turn off automatically after you're away from the computer for several minutes, followed by switching to Sleep mode or Standby mode a little later, and then powering off if you're not back within an hour.

If you're like most people, you probably travel to an office or other out-of-the-house workplace. That means your computer doesn't belong to you, and maybe your company doesn't allow employees to fiddle with certain settings. If you work for this type of company, you might change your bosses' minds if you can help them understand that the settings you want to adjust to conserve energy also save the company's money. Whose boss wouldn't love that result?

Understanding Computer Energy-Saving Settings

Adjusting how much power your computer consumes depends on the brand, model, and platform.

Knowing the difference between Standby, Sleep, and Hibernate modes — and any other power-conservation variables you might hear your friends and neighbors bandying about — goes a long way toward increasing your energy savings and your savings account. So without further adieu, here's a quick-and-dirty primer on computer power-saving modes:

> ✔ **Sleep/Standby:** This mode is called Sleep on the Mac and Standby in Windows. Activating either turns off the screen and hard drive and most of the power to the processor and memory while continuing to sip just enough juice to wake the computer instantly at the touch of a key or click of the mouse.

✔ **Hibernation:** In Windows, Hibernate mode is a selectable option that saves to the hard disk the state of all running programs and open documents before completely powering off the computer. The Mac has no Hibernate option to do the same. Translation: You have no way to explicitly order your Mac to shut down completely and then power on and resume where you left off, as you can in Windows. Sorry, Mac fans!

✔ **Safe Sleep:** Putting a Mac to sleep *does* in fact copy all the contents of memory to the hard drive as a safety measure in case the desktop's power is cut off or the notebook's battery runs down or is removed before being plugged back into a power outlet. Apple calls this nicely integrated feature Safe Sleep.

If you're a Mac techie-type who's comfortable running system commands in the Terminal program, you can find out how to force the Mac to always hibernate and shut down when it's put to sleep by issuing the commands in the nearby sidebar, "Shut 'er down, Mac!"

✔ **Hybrid Sleep:** This Windows Vista setting works like Safe Sleep mode on the Mac, by copying the contents of open programs and documents to the hard drive before putting the computer to sleep, where they're safe and sound in the event of a power failure or drained battery.

So you can see how the two platforms (Windows and Mac) are similar in that both offer Standby/Sleep *and* Hibernate modes, yet how you invoke the completely powered off Hibernate mode demonstrates how they differ.

Considerations beyond platform and operating system version (Windows Vista and XP have their own standby and hibernation differences that also determine a computer's energy-saving features and adjustable settings) include whether your computer is equipped with any of these features:

✔ Energy Star or EPEAT ratings, or both, and if so, to what level of compliance (see Chapter 1)

✔ A preloaded, custom power-management program to enhance, extend, or simplify making adjustments to the operating system's standard energy option settings (Windows only)

✔ A CPU specifically engineered to consume less power

✔ Built-in ambient light sensors that monitor room lighting to automatically brighten or dim the display and, if equipped, the keyboard backlighting brightness

✔ Additional powered hardware such as WiFi, Bluetooth, or power-adjustable graphics processor or card

Shut 'er down, Mac!

Apple sets its Macs to Safe Sleep mode by default, which means that your Mac goes to sleep and awakens almost instantly. Also, if your notebook battery dies or you accidentally kick out the power cord on your desktop, the next time you power on your Mac, it reawakens exactly where you left it, with all your programs open to exactly where you left them.

In Safe Sleep mode, your Mac doesn't shut down completely — which explains why it reawakens so quickly — but maybe you want it to power off completely to use less energy and save more money on your electric bill. Keep in mind that a Mac, when awakened, takes longer (like a Windows computer) to return from Hibernate mode than when it's awakened from Standby mode (Windows) or typical Sleep mode (Mac).

To shut down your desktop or notebook Mac when you put it to sleep and it's plugged in or running on the battery, launch the Terminal application and enter the following line:

```
sudo pmset -a hibernatemode 1
```

To hibernate your notebook Mac only while it's running from the battery but not when it's plugged in, type the following command instead:

```
sudo pmset -b hibernatemode 1
```

To restore your Mac to the default Safe Sleep mode, type 3 rather than 1.

Basic energy-saving settings available on all Mac and Windows computers include the ability to adjust how long (and whether) the computer is allowed to sit doing nothing before it:

- Activates a screen saver or blanks the display.
- Dims or puts the display in Standby (also known as Sleep) mode, but doesn't put the computer in Standby or Sleep mode.
- Puts the display and computer in Sleep or Standby mode.
- Puts the hard disk to sleep.
- Senses whether, in the case of notebooks, the computer is plugged in or running on battery juice, and switches above settings accordingly, based on user's power source preferences.

Birth, death, taxes and basic energy-saving settings are all you can count on, and now that you're in tune with the main points, let's change the world one PC at a time by adjusting your own computer's power settings for greater energy efficiency. How you'll change your computer's energy settings depends on how much control you want to gain.

Changing your computer's energy settings the easy way

If applying energy-saving settings with an easy-to-use utility or widget sounds more appealing than getting down and dirty with all your computer's power settings, you've come to the right place. This section offers a quick tour of several easy-to-use power management utilities and widgets that take the guesswork out of adjusting your computer's energy settings. Downloading one or more of these helpers lets you "set it and forget it."

Tables 6-1, 6-2, and 6-3 show a few of my favorite add-ons for monitoring, managing, and minimizing your Mac or Windows computer's power tconsumption.

Table 6-1	Mac-Only Add-Ons to Save Energy			
Add-On	*Web Site*	*What It Does*	*Cost*	*Free Trial Period?*
Power Manager 3	www.dssw.co.uk/ powermanager/ index.html	Offers multiple schedules to turn your Mac on or off and to put it to sleep.	$28.95	Yes
Energy Schedule Widget	www.dssw.co.uk/ energyschedule/ index.html	Displays scheduled power events created by using either Power Manager 3 or your Mac's Energy Saver scheduling feature.	Free	N/A
Lights Out	www.northern softworks.com	Provides additional control over the Mac's Energy Saver program by offering customized savings settings for individual programs, the ability to toggle Safe Sleep on or off, and more.	$9.99	Yes
iBatt	raynersoftware. com/ibatt	Supplies an advanced MacBook and PowerBook battery-monitoring and diagnostics utility that displays geek-savvy information such as total capacity, voltage output, and rate of charge and discharge.	$19	Yes
Sleep Monitor	http://dssw.co. uk/sleepmonitor/ index.html	Keeps track of your Mac's energy use by recording power events, battery changes, and other factors that can help troubleshoot and solve power problems.	$28.95	Yes

Table 6-2   Energy-Saving Add-Ons for the Mac and Windows

Add-On	Web Site	What It Does	Cost	Free Trial Period?
Power Save	www.faronics.com/html/PowerSave.asp	Aimed at businesses; lets administrators deploy and manage power-saving configurations to one or more computers throughout an enterprise.	$14.40	Yes
Monitor Off	http://widgets.yahoo.com/widgets/monitor-off	Instantly switches the display to Standby mode.	Free	N/A

Table 6-3   Windows-Only Add-Ons That Save Energy

Add-On	Web Site	What It Does	Cost	Free Trial Period?
Easy Shutdown	www.easyshutdown.com/	Automates energy-saving actions such as Shut Down, Hibernate, and Wake Up plus hot keys for fast, on-the-fly power mode switching.	$5	Yes
Energy Saver	desktop.google.com	Eliminates the guesswork of adjusting your computer's energy-saving settings.	Free	N/A
Edison	www.verdiem.com/edison	Calculates your estimated savings based on the "green level" you choose.	Free	N/A

Figure 6-4 shows the Power Manager (the first entry in Table 6-1). The Energy Schedule Widget (the second entry in Table 6-1) is shown in Figure 6-5. To use Edison (the last entry in Table 6-3), drag the slider, shown in Figure 6-6, to choose a green level for your computer. Who says it ain't easy being green?

Taking greater control of your computer's energy settings

When you adjust Mac and Windows energy-saving settings, the goal is the same — to achieve a good balance of power savings without sacrificing performance. The steps you take vary from platform to platform and in Windows, from version to version. In this section, I discuss the myriad ways you can adjust your computer's energy-saving options.

Figure 6-4:
Adjusting
energy sav-
ings based
around the
clock —and
your
schedule.

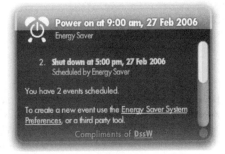

Figure 6-5:
Reminders
show you
which
events are
scheduled
and when.

The Environmental Protection Agency (EPA) suggests setting your computer to enter either Standby mode or Hibernate mode after 15 to 60 minutes of inactivity, and for monitors to enter Sleep mode after 5 to 20 minutes of inactivity.

Mac folks like to remind Windows users how much simpler it is to do things the Mac way over "that other way" of computing. Well-versed Windows types, on the other hand, like to point out the wider range of choices and options in Windows — even if all that flexibility can sometimes cause confusion.

My MacBook is my main machine, and I usually have one or more Windows PCs on hand for review or to serve a particular project — or simply because I'm always curious about other ways of doing things, including dabbling with Ubuntu Linux now and then.

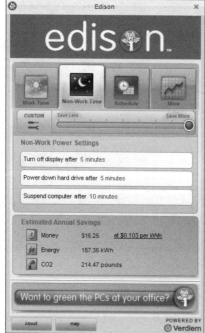

Figure 6-6:
Edison
makes being
green a
drag — in a
good way!

Because I'm familiar with both Mac and Windows PC energy-saving settings and options, it's fair to say that each side has its pluses and minuses. The Mac's settings are supereasy to figure out, though I wish that the Mac offered a way to easily force it into "deep sleep" Hibernate mode. As for Windows, I like its ability to create a custom power scheme (in Windows XP) or power plan (in Windows Vista) to best suit my energy needs, depending on what I'm working on — or not working on.

Although this chapter and the next two talk mainly about your computer's power-management settings, those settings aren't the only ones you should think about. Disconnecting, adjusting, or disabling other connected or built-in devices can further reduce consumption — and extend battery life between visits to the wall outlet if your computer is a notebook. Key power-drainers to shut off or disconnect when you're not using them include the ones in this list:

- ✔ Bluetooth
- ✔ External hard drives
- ✔ Sound
- ✔ Wireless networking (WiFi)

In Chapters 7 and 8, I show you how to disable these energy-zapping devices — and how to squelch a few not-so-obvious power-hogging features you might not know about.

Turning off your screen saver and setting your monitor to shut off after a few minutes — right now, before you do anything else — earns you instant kudos from Mother Nature. Think globally, act locally!

iPods, Printers, Hard Drives, and Other Connected Devices

In Chapter1, I explain how leaving cellphone chargers and other devices plugged in when you're not using them wastes energy. The same explanation holds true for your Mac or Windows computer: Leaving a fully charged iPod, iPhone, cellphone, digital camera, or most any other rechargeable device plugged in wastes energy. Although a few gadgets have smart charging sensors to turn themselves off, most don't — yet.

Make a habit of plugging rechargeable gadgets into your computer only when they need charging or when you intend to use them — such as when you want to sync your iPod with your MP3 music or movies using iTunes, or import pictures from your digital camera to Windows Photo Gallery — and then unplug them when you're done.

Here are four examples of potential energy-sucking "vampires" connected to my computer:

- ✔ **iPhone 3G:** I connect this device only when I'm charging it or syncing it with iTunes.

- ✔ **iPod nano:** Ditto.

- ✔ **LaCie portable USB hard drive:** I use this drive to shuttle large numbers of files between my computers. I don't need to do it all the time, so I unplug the drive when I'm not using it.

- ✔ **Microsoft Bluetooth Notebook Mouse 5000:** My beloved digital rodent is always on when I'm working. When I'm not working, it puts itself into energy-saving Sleep mode or I power it off completely by using the switch on its underbelly.

If unplugging certain devices — such as printers, network routers, and backup hard drives — isn't an option, inspect each one to see whether it offers power-reducing options.

Here are three examples of power-saving options built into my own computing gear:

- **A three-year-old Brother HL-2070N laser printer has a Sleep Time option that powers down the printer five minutes after I print.** The printer also offers toner cartridge savings options, such as the ability to print at a lower resolution, and Toner Saver mode, which uses half the normal amount of toner when the feature is turned on. You adjust the Toner Saver mode and Sleep Time settings by using the Printing Preferences control panel.

- **A Western Digital 150GB hard drive backs up my MacBook every hour, thanks to the Mac's awesomely useful Time Machine backup program.** Like my printer, the hard drive has a sleep function that spins down the drive and powers it off after a specified number of minutes. Accessing this option works only when the drive is connected to Windows computers, so I can't use it. Then again, Time Machine accesses the drive every hour anyway, and although the drive doesn't power off completely, it stops spinning after Time Machine finishes backing up any changes on my Mac that occurred since the previous backup, an hour earlier.

- **An Xbox 360 streams music and video from my computer to my HDTV, with the help of the cool program Connect360** (www.nullriver.com/products/connect360). Though I turn on my Xbox 360 only when I'm playing a game, watching movies, or streaming music and video from my Mac, I mention it here to point out the console's energy-saving auto-shutdown option. It's the same for my PlayStation 3. To find out how to adjust your video game console's energy-saving settings — and power-saving features for your TV, DVD player, cable or satellite TV box, and other home entertainment devices — check out Chapter 13.

Chapter 7

Reducing Energy Consumption in Windows

....

In This Chapter

▶ Saving money with energy conservation

▶ Minimizing Windows energy use on-the-fly

▶ Adjusting the Windows automatic Power Options settings

▶ Making additional adjustments to the Windows Power Options

....

*Y*ou aren't one of those people who uses your computer only one-quarter of the time it's turned on, are you? I didn't think so. You're one of those people who wants to reduce your computer's carbon footprint as much as possible, and you've come to the right chapter. Adjusting your Windows computer's power-saving options is fairly easy, and you can generally choose one of these four methods (all of which I explain further throughout this chapter):

✔ **On-the-fly:** Choosing on- the- fly options are those that you can change quickly and easily, such as pressing the power button on your desktop computer to shut it down, or closing the lid on your notebook computer to put it in *Standby* — also known as *Sleep* — mode).

✔ **Automatically:** Choosing one of the Windows preconfigured energy-saving settings — known as Windows Vista *power plans*, or Windows XP *power schemes* — tells the computer to make certain energy-saving changes and to take action based on general usage scenarios.

✔ **Customized:** Modifying an existing power plan or creating a new one tailored to your specific needs gives you greater control over when and how Windows activates individual energy-saving modes.

✔ **Specialized:** Running a power management utility preloaded on your computer by the manufacturer — or running one of several power utilities and widgets you can download — is the fourth way to minimize your computer's power consumption, as I describe in Chapter 6.

Making ¢ents of power-saving options

According to the government-backed program Energy Star, you can shave as much as $75 annually from your electric bill by choosing the right Windows energy-saving settings. This list gives you a quick rundown of the key Windows power options — it describes what they do and how much they can save you:

Hibernate

- ✔ Drops monitor and computer power use to 1 to 3 watts apiece

- ✔ Wakes after 20 seconds or more

- ✔ Saves work in the event of power loss

- ✔ Saves $25 to $75 per PC annually

Standby

- ✔ Drops monitor and computer power use to 1 to 3 watts apiece

- ✔ Wakes in seconds

- ✔ Saves $25 to $75 per PC annually

Turn Off Hard Disk

- ✔ Saves little energy

Turn Off Monitor

- ✔ Drops monitor power use to 1 to 3 watts

- ✔ Wakes in seconds or less

- ✔ Saves half as much as system Standby or Hibernate, or about $10 to $40 per PC annually

Preloaded energy-saving utilities generally aim to take the guesswork out of tweaking the Windows Power Options control panel settings. Some or all of the categories mentioned in the preceding list are called into play when running a specialized or add-on energy-saving program or widget. Not all computers come with specialized power-management programs, such as the Power Manager that Lenovo ships with the ThinkPad X200s notebook, shown in Figure 7-1.

Making other adjustments — such as disabling Bluetooth and wireless networking features if you're not using them — also helps reduce your computer's carbon footprint. I describe making these energy-saving adjustments and others in the section "Making Additional Windows Vista and XP Power Options Adjustments," later in this chapter.

Note: Although Windows 7 was not shipping when I wrote this, I did run the prerelease beta version of the operating system; Microsoft has been burning the midnight oil to improve its newest operating system's energy efficiency smarts beyond all versions that came before it. The improvements are mainly under-the-hood, and I'm happy to report that accessing and adjusting the Windows 7 power options are nearly identical to doing so in Windows Vista, which I describe in the following sections. To read more about how Windows 7 pulls off its better energy-saving abilities, check out the product design group's blog (Engineering Windows 7) at `http://blogs.msdn.com/e7`.

To follow the step-by-step instructions in this chapter, open Classic View in the Windows computer's Control Panel. With Classic View turned on, we're both on the same page, so to speak, which means you won't stumble when following how-to steps. To turn on Classic View, choose Start➪Control Panel, and then click Classic View, as shown in Figure 7-2.

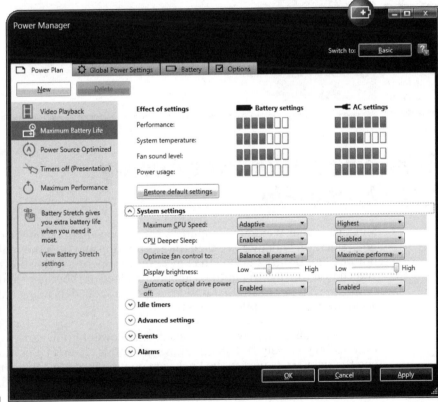

Figure 7-1:
The Lenovo ThinkPad comes with its own advanced, energy-saving program.

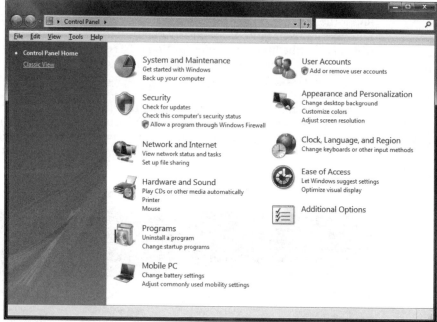

Figure 7-2:
Turn on
Classic view
so that you
can follow
my lead.

Minimizing Windows Energy Use On-the-Fly

Minimizing your Windows computer's energy consumption on-the-fly is a no-brainer: On Windows XP, click the Start button and then the red Power button (Shut Down). Clicking the Power button opens a dialog box to let you choose whether to put the computer in Sleep or Hibernate mode (hold down the shift key to see that option) or power it off, depending on how the Windows XP Power Options are set.

If you're running Windows Vista, clicking the Power button carries out whatever action you assign it (which I show you in this chapter). Clicking Start and the right arrow next to the Lock icon opens a fly-out menu with options to Switch User, Log Off, Lock the computer, Restart, Sleep, or Shut Down.

Here are some other ways to activate the Windows energy-saving features, which I describe in more detail in the next section:

✔ **Close the lid on your Windows notebook:** You can put it in Sleep, Hibernate, or Shut Down mode, based on which option you select in the Power Options control panel.

✔ **Press your computer's power button:** You're prompted to suspend, shut down, or hibernate — or the action automatically completes based on whether one is chosen in the Power Options control panel.

✔ **Press the Fn key and another, assigned key:** This combination puts the computer in Suspend mode or Hibernate mode.

✔ **Press a special button to instantly switch power-saving modes:** This button is available only on certain computers.

Pressing the power switch to turn off your Windows desktop computer's external monitor is another easy way to blank the screen and save energy when you leave your computer for more than a few minutes — unless, or course, your PC is an all-in-one model with a built-in display.

Adjusting the Windows Automatic Power Options Settings

Performing the smartest energy-saving actions need not rest on your shoulders alone. Letting your computer remember for you is easy — all it takes are a few simple adjustments to the Power Options control panel. You change the power options — such as how long your computer waits before it turns off the display, powers off the hard disk, or enters Standby or Hibernate mode — by using the Power Options control panel.

Note: Many of the following options are based on notebook settings. You can ignore those instances if you're using a desktop computer because they don't apply to you.

To open the Windows power options, click the Start button and then choose Control Panel⇨Power Options.

Choosing a preconfigured power plan in the center of the Power Options control panel is just a click away. As Figure 7-3 shows, Windows Vista comes with three preconfigured power plans.

Your computer may have additional power plan choices that may be ordered differently from the ones you see in Figure 7-3 and other figures in this chapter.

If you're running Vista, clicking the Change Plan Settings link beneath each of the power plans shows you what each one tells your computer to do after the computer is idle for specified stretches of time (see Figure 7-4.)

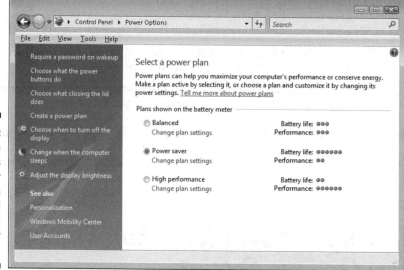

Figure 7-3:
The
Windows
Vista Power
Options
control
panel and
power
plans.

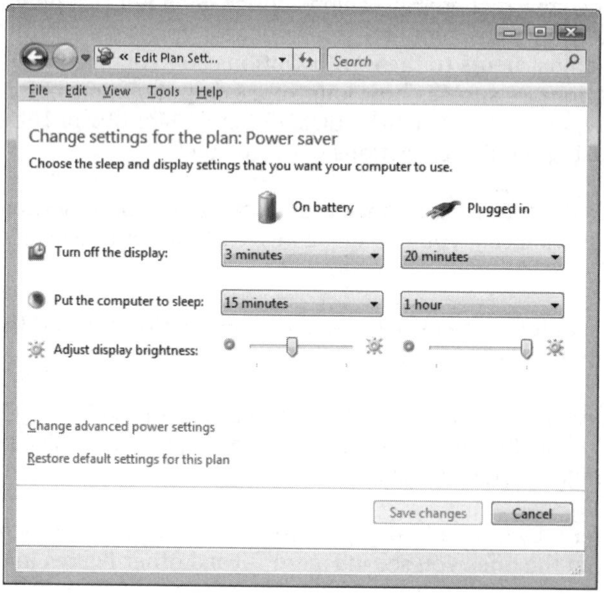

Figure 7-4:
Power plan
settings
tell your
computer
when and
how to save
energy.

If you're running Windows XP, clicking the individual drop-down menus in the settings section lets you adjust how much time passes before your computer turns off the monitor and hard disk, or switches it into Standby or Hibernate mode, if your computer supports hibernation.

To quickly change power plans and keep tabs on your Windows notebook's battery level, click the battery or power icon in the Task Bar (as shown in Figure 7-5). If you don't see the battery or power icon in your Task Bar, you can turn it on:

- ✓ **Windows Vista:** Choose Start⇨Control Panel⇨Taskbar and Start Menu, and then select the Power check box under the System Icons section.

- ✓ **Windows XP:** Click Start⇨Control Panel⇨Power Options, then click the Advanced tab and click the checkbox Always Show Icon on the Task Bar.

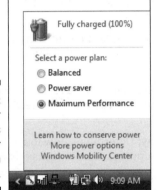

Figure 7-5:
Adjust your notebook's power usage with a few clicks.

Choosing and customizing Windows Vista's power plans

The Windows Vista power plan settings (refer to Figure 7-3) for running your notebook on battery power are

- ✓ **Balanced:** Turns off the display after 5 minutes, puts the computer in Sleep mode after 15 minutes, and automatically reduces the screen brightness. When your notebook is plugged in, its display is set to maximum brightness and goes dark after 20 minutes. After an hour, it enters Sleep mode.

- ✓ **Power Saver:** Turns off its display after 3 minutes, puts the computer in Sleep mode after 15 minutes, and automatically reduces the screen brightness even more than the Balanced setting does. When your notebook is plugged in, its display is set to maximum brightness and goes dark after 20 minutes. After an hour, the computer enters Sleep mode.

✔ **High Performance:** Turns up the brightness setting on the display, turns it off after 20 minutes, and puts the computer in Sleep mode after an hour. When the notebook is plugged in, it's also set to maximum brightness, goes dark after 20 minutes, and is set to never enter Sleep mode.

The power options listed on the left side of the control panel are the following (refer to Figure 7-3):

✔ **Require a Password on Wakeup:** Prompts you to type in your password when your computer wakes from Sleep or Hibernate mode.

✔ **Choose What the Power Button Does:** Prompts Windows to take an action after you press your computer's power button, such as to power it off or put it in Suspend or Hibernate mode.

✔ **Choose What Closing the Lid Does:** Prompts the same actions as for the preceding option, but occurs when you close the lid of your notebook computer.

✔ **Create a Power Plan:** Enables you to create and save a power plan that you can easily switch to without having to re-create the settings all over again.

✔ **Choose When to Turn Off the Display:** Determines how much time will elapse when you're not using the computer before it turns off the screen.

✔ **Change When the Computer Sleeps:** Determines how much time will elapse when you're not using the computer before it puts the system in Sleep mode.

✔ **Adjust the Display Brightness:** Adjusts your screen's level of brightness.

Choosing one of the first three options opens the Power Options System Settings control panel, shown in Figure 7-6.

Under Power and Sleep Buttons and Lid Settings (refer to Figure 7-6), choose which energy-saving action your computer will take while it's running on battery and while it's plugged in. Your choices are

✔ **Do Nothing:** Exactly what it says.

✔ **Sleep:** Puts your computer in energy-saving Sleep mode.

✔ **Hibernate:** Puts your computer into more efficient energy-saving mode.

✔ **Shut Down:** Powers off your computer.

Under Password Protection on Wakeup (refer to Figure 7-6), if the Require a Password (Recommended) option is grayed-out, click Change Settings That Are Currently Unavailable. When the permissions alert appears, as shown in Figure 7-7, click Continue. Now you can select the Require a Password option and click the Save Changes button. From now on, your computer prompts you for your password whenever it awakens from either Standby or Hibernate mode.

Figure 7-6:
Decide
what your
notebook
will do when
you press
the power
button.

The last three options in the left column of the main Power Options control panel open the Edit Plan Settings control panel (refer to Figure 7-4). Choosing to change any of these options keeps them in effect until you change plans. Clicking the Save Changes button saves your changes so that you can restore them after changing to another power plan.

Click the Restore Default Settings for This Plan option (refer to Figure 7-4) to reset the preconfigured plan to its original settings if you goofed up the settings and want to start over.

Creating a new power plan rather than changing one of the ready-to-go choices is another option. To do so, click the Create a Power Plan link (in the main Power Options control panel; refer to Figure 7-3), and then follow the prompts to choose the power options that best match your needs.

Figure 7-7:
Granting
permission
to request
your
password.

Customizing Windows Vista's advanced power settings

Tweaking a power plan with the Vista advanced power settings can yield energy-saving benefits.

To get under your computer's proverbial hood to access and adjust a number of additional energy-saving settings, follow these steps:

1. **Choose Start⇨Control Panel⇨Power Options.**

2. **Select the Change Plan Settings option beneath the power plan you want to customize.**

3. **Click the Change Advanced Power Settings link.**

4. **Click the plus (+) icon beside a setting to expand it, and then click the setting's drop-down menu to choose different options.**

Figure 7-8 shows the options, which are largely self-explanatory. Click the Question Mark button (in the upper-right corner) to open Windows Vista help for more information about Advanced Power Settings.

Figure 7-8:
The Windows Vista advanced power settings unlock energy savings.

5. **To reveal even more advanced power option settings, click the Change Settings That Are Currently Unavailable link and then click Continue to close the permission alert box.**

6. **When you finish making changes, click OK.**

You can always revert to the original settings by clicking the Restore Plan Defaults button.

Choosing and Customizing Windows XP Power Schemes

Running Windows XP on a notebook? If so, you'll see two columns of options in the middle of the Power Options Properties control panel — Plugged in and Running on batteries — as shown in Figure 7-9. Windows XP desktop users will see only one set of options.

Starting with the first tab — Power Schemes — and working to the right, here's a rundown of Windows XP's Power Options settings.

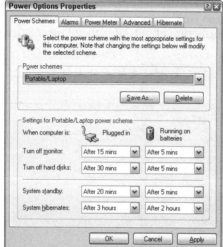

Figure 7-9:
The
Windows
XP Power
Options
control
panel Power
Schemes
and
settings.

Power Schemes

Choosing a preset energy setting Power Scheme to match your Windows XP computer's usage is easy: Simply click the drop-down menu to the right of the Power Schemes list and pick the one that closely matches your kind of computer usage.

Notice how each one changes the settings time limits listed in the lower half of the Power Options Properties control panel. Choices include:

- **Home/Office Desk:** Shuts off the display after 20 minutes when plugged in, and after 5 minutes when running on batteries. Doesn't turn off the hard disk or go into Standby or Hibernate mode when plugged in, but does all three when running on a notebook's battery.

- **Portable/Laptop:** Greener than Home/Office for both desktops or notebooks because it turns off the display and hard disks after several minutes, and also puts the computer in Standby mode and then Hibernate mode.

- **Presentation:** Choose this if your notebook is plugged in and you're giving a presentation but don't want the screen to go blank while you're pausing to expound on a particular slide. When running on batteries, the screen will stay on for up to 15 minutes before the system goes into Standby mode.

- **Always On:** Not green, but definitely the one to choose if you're playing an action game or running a complicated graphics or video-editing program. Just remember to switch to one of the greener schemes when you're done playing!

✓ **Minimal Power Management:** Greener than Always On, with reasonably accommodating stretches of time before the monitor and hard disk shut off; the computer goes into Standby mode after one hour.

✓ **Max Battery:** A good choice for on-the-go notebook users because it blanks the screen after 1 minute, spins down the hard disk after 3 minutes, and (inexplicably) goes into Standby mode after 2 minutes, which means that the hard disk will enter Sleep mode then as well, rather than wait 3 minutes to do so.

Changing the individual time limits and actions for each scheme allows you to tailor a Power Scheme to suit your unique computer usage style. Choices include

✓ **Turn Off Monitor**

✓ **Turn Off Hard Disks**

✓ **System Standby**

✓ **System Hibernates**

After making changes to a Power Scheme, click Save As to save your custom settings so you can select them again if you change schemes. Name it whatever you like — Joe's Ultimate Power Scheme has a nice ring to it, don't you think?

Alarms

Adjusting the options on the Alarms tab tells your notebook to shout out when its battery is running (almost) on empty (see Figure 7-10).

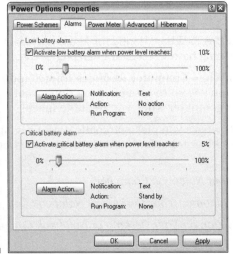

Figure 7-10:
Alarming options to warn you when your notebook's battery is running down.

Drag the sliders left and right to determine just how low the battery is allowed to go before warning you the party's almost over and you need to plug into a power outlet soon before your notebook shuts itself off.

Click the Alarm Actions buttons to choose what kind of wake up call you prefer. Choices include:

- ✔ **Sound Alarm**
- ✔ **Display Message**
- ✔ **When the alarm goes off, the computer will:**
  - *Stand By*
  - *Hibernate*
  - *Shut Down*
- ✔ **Force Stand By or Shutdown Even If a Program Stops Responding**
- ✔ **When the Alarm Occurs, Run This Program**

Power Meter

Select the Show Details for Each Battery option if your notebook has more than one battery; otherwise, leave it deselected to see how much juice is available when you're not plugged into a power outlet — and how much more juice the battery needs when you're plugged in and recharging.

Advanced

Clicking or changing the Advanced options tells your Windows XP notebook computer to

- ✔ **Always Show Icon on the Taskbar:** Handy for keeping visual tabs on your notebook's remaining battery level or changing power schemes.
- ✔ **Prompt for Password When Computer Resumes from Standby:** Definitely something you'll want to turn on if you don't want coworkers snooping around your computer while you're out to lunch!
- ✔ **Power Buttons:** Here's where you pick automatic power-saving options that tell your Windows XP notebook what to do when you choose one of these options:
  - *Close the Lid of Your Notebook Computer*
  - *Press the Power Button on Your Desktop or Notebook Computer*
  - *Press the Sleep Button on Your Desktop or Notebook Computer*

Choices for the Power Button options include:

- ✔ **Do Nothing:** Dangerous if you're putting your notebook into your back-pack or messenger bag because it will keep running — and possibly burn itself out without proper ventilation.

- ✔ **Stand By:** A good choice for desktops but not wise for notebooks because sometimes Stand By mode allows the computer to wake. See Do Nothing, above, for the 411 on why this isn't a smart choice.

- ✔ **Hibernate:** Smart for desktops and notebooks alike because it completely powers off your computer so it isn't wasting any energy at all. Note that this mode does return you to your running programs when you turn it back on.

- ✔ **Shut Down:** Does exactly what it says, and powers off your computer.

Hibernate

Click Enable Hibernation if it appears; if not, your Windows XP does not have what it takes — technologically speaking — to use the Hibernation power-saving mode. Rest assured when you're ready to upgrade to a new Windows computer you can bet it will hibernate if that's your preference.

UPS

Though you don't see a tab labeled UPS in Figure 7-9, a *UPS (Uninterruptible Power Supply)* tab will appear on your Power Options Properties panel if Windows XP detects your computer is attached to a battery backup power supply. Here's where you can check on the status of your UPS. Click Configure to set notifications to alert you when the UPS's battery is running low, as well as instruct your computer to shut down when the UPS is almost out of juice.

Making Additional Windows Vista and XP Power Options Adjustments

You can tweak the Windows Vista and XP power options as described in the previous section to automatically move a few seats closer to the front of the class for minimizing energy consumption when you're using — and not using — your PC. Well done, old chap. But why settle for anything but the best energy-saving setup possible? Making a few additional adjustments can move you to the head of the computer conservation class, earning you the right to stick a green star on your forehead, if that's your idea of fun. Why not? You certainly will deserve it after tending to these extra-savings extra credits.

Take a stroll through the following smorgasbord of power-related settings, features, and other options, and follow the appropriate steps or actions to turn off or tweak those that can help make your increasingly green PC even greener. Unless otherwise noted, these settings and options apply to both Windows Vista and Windows XP.

Windows Mobility Center (Vista only)

This handy control panel is an all-in-one dashboard of modules for gauging and controlling a number of Windows Vista settings of the energy-saving variety. To open it, choose Start⇨Control Panel⇨Windows Mobility Center. Settings you can monitor and change on any Vista notebook include those shown in the upper two rows in Figure 7-11:

- Battery gauge and power plan chooser
- Display brightness
- External display
- Presentation settings
- Sound volume and mute
- Sync Center
- Wireless network

Certain manufacturers may also include additional Windows Mobility Center modules, such as the ones included with the Lenovo ThinkPad X200s, shown in the bottom two rows of Figure 7-11.

Throughout this section, I give you details about other ways of adjusting these settings to garner energy savings.

Brightness

This setting is easy to understand — and change — for better energy savings. Simply put, lowering your display's brightness uses less energy. Personally, I've never been able to dim the screen even one notch without feeling as if it's too dim. Other people I know have no problem working on their computers with the screen brightness knocked down a few notches.

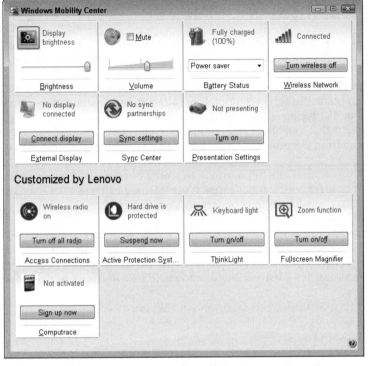

Figure 7-11:
The
Windows
Mobility
Center
makes
changing
energy-
saving
settings a
cinch.

You can adjust your Windows computer's display by doing one of the following:

✔ On notebook computers, press the Brightness Down key until the screen is black, and then press Brightness Up one keypress at a time until you reach a level that's easy on the eyes — and, hopefully, on your energy use.

✔ On Windows Vista computers, choose Start⇨Control Panel⇨Power Options⇨Adjust the Display Brightness, and then drag the slider to the left to dim the screen or to the right to make it brighter.

✔ On stand-alone monitors and LCD displays connected to desktop computers, or all-in-one desktop computers follow the instructions in the first bullet if your computer has dedicated brightness keys. If it doesn't, use your Vista computer display's brightness control to decrease, and then increase, the brightness until it's just right for your eyes, as described in the preceding bullet.

Screen saver

Yes, screen savers are pretty to look at. And, once upon a time, they were darned helpful when it came to preventing permanent damage to your monitor.

But nowadays screen savers are mostly useless because the green choice is to blank the screen completely rather than consume power by keeping it on to display an animated sequence or other eye-catching, energy-wasting delight that's probably going unnoticed anyway because you are, after all, away from the computer in the first place, right? Phew, that was a mouthful!

Okay, I admit I'm a hypocrite in this area because I *do* run my screen saver — but only for a minute, because it's a learning experience. I have the Word of the Day scroll past to broaden my vocabulary!

Instead of running a screen saver, set your Windows computer to turn off the monitor when you aren't using it. I describe how to do so earlier in the chapter. See the "Choosing and customizing Windows Vista's Power Plans" and "Choosing and Customizing Windows XP's Power Schemes" sections.

To turn off the screen saver on your Windows computer:

Windows Vista:

1. Choose Start⇨Control Panel⇨Personalization⇨Screen Saver.

The Screen Saver Settings dialog box appears, as shown in Figure 7-12.

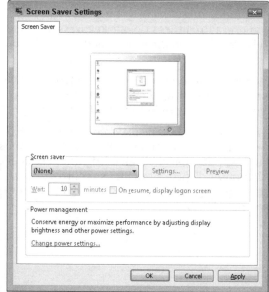

Figure 7-12: Turn off your screen saver for greater energy efficiency.

2. **Click the arrow on the drop-down menu and choose (None), and then click OK.**

Windows XP:

1. **Choose Start⇨Control Panel⇨Display, and then click the Screen Saver tab.**

2. **Click the drop-down menu and choose (None), and then click OK.**

Keyboard brightness

Got a slick new notebook or desktop computer with a backlit keyboard? Sweet! The keyboard is definitely eye-opening when playing a game in the dark or working in low-light situations, but it's also a sucker for power when you aren't using it.

You typically dim your Windows desktop or notebook's keyboard backlighting by pressing the keyboard buttons dedicated to doing just that. Check your computer's or keyboard's documentation for specific instructions on how to adjust or deactivate keyboard backlighting.

Wireless networking

Think about how your computer connects to the Internet. It might be connected with an Ethernet cable running from your cable or DSL modem, or network router, to your computer's Ethernet port. Or, your computer might be connected wirelessly to your Wi-Fi router or the one at the café you're sitting in that lets you connect free — or almost free, when you factor in the cost of a cup of joe or tea.

If your computer is plugged in with an Ethernet cable, there's no reason to have your Windows computer's built-in wireless networking adapter turned on. The reason is that it's wasting energy — and draining your notebook's battery more quickly when you're away from a wall adapter but not connected to a Wi-Fi network, if yours is a notebook PC.

To turn off your Windows computer's wireless networking option when you aren't using it:

Windows Vista:

1. **Click Start⇨Control Panel⇨Network and Sharing Center, and then Disconnect.**

2. **Click the Close button to close the Network and Sharing Center control panel.**

Windows XP:

1. **Choose Start⇨Control Panel⇨Network Connections⇨Wireless Network Connection, and then click the Disable button.**

2. **Click the Close button.**

To monitor Wi-Fi status, or to quickly connect and disconnect (as shown in Figure 7-13 for Windows XP), click the Network icon on the taskbar. If you don't see the Network icon in your Windows XP or Vista taskbar, here's how you can turn it on:

✔ Windows Vista: Choose Start⇨Control Panel⇨Taskbar and Start Menu, and then click the Notification Area tab and check the box next to Network under System Icons.

✔ Windows XP: Choose Start⇨Control Panel⇨Network Connections⇨Wireless Network Connections, and then click the Properties button and select the Show Icon in Notification Area When Connected check box.

Figure 7-13:
Turning off
the wireless
connection.

Most notebook computers have a function key (Fn) combo to turn Wi-Fi networking (and Bluetooth) on or off.

Many notebooks also have dedicated on-off switches or buttons along their front or side edges, or above the keyboard, often near the computer's power button.

Bluetooth

Turning on your Windows computer's built-in Bluetooth feature (if it has it) lets you connect to other devices, such as

✔ **A wireless mouse:** For clutter-free mousing around

✔ **A hands-free headset:** For clearer Skype webcam voice and video chats

> ✔ **Another Mac or Windows PC:** To send files back and forth
>
> ✔ **A Palm, BlackBerry, or other brand of smartphone:** To keep your device and your address book and calendar in sync.

If you have no idea what I'm talking about, you probably aren't using Bluetooth, which means that it's wasting energy — and draining your notebook's battery more quickly when you're away from a wall adapter.

To turn off your computer's Bluetooth feature when you're not using it, choose one of these options:

> ✔ Press the Fn key and then, on the upper row of the keyboard, the key bearing the Bluetooth symbol.
>
> ✔ Switch off your notebook's dedicated Bluetooth power button if it has one (usually located on the front or side of the keyboard or above it).

Turning off the Bluetooth devices you connect to your computer, such as a headset and mouse, helps extend their battery life so that you don't need to recharge them as often.

A wireless mouse may come with its own charging base, which should be unplugged from the wall outlet or USB port unless the mouse needs a recharge.

Sound

Lowering your computer's sound volume or turning it off uses less energy than when you have it cranked up full blast. Of course, then you can't hear music or the alert sound whenever a new e-mail message lands in your inbox. Press the Volume Up, Volume Down, and Mute keys to adjust your computer's sound level accordingly.

If your keyboard has no sound control keys, don't worry. Adjusting your computer's volume or muting it altogether is easy — just turn on the Sound icon on the taskbar by following these steps:

> ✔ **Windows Vista:** Choose Start⇨Control Panel⇨Taskbar and Start Menu, click the Notification Area tab and select the Volume check box under System Icons.
>
> ✔ **Windows XP:** Click Start⇨Control Panel⇨Sound and Audio Devices, and then click the Place Volume in the Taskbar check box.

To adjust the volume, click the Speaker icon on the taskbar and drag the slider up or down to adjust the volume. Or, click the Mute button (Vista) or check box (XP) to silence your computer.

The following list highlights other measures you can take to reduce the amount of energy used by your computer's sound system:

✔ **Use headphones.** Plugging in headphones is another way to save energy because they draw less power than speakers — and they're helpful for blocking out the chatterbugs and other distracting sources of noise when you're working on your notebook at a café or another public place.

✔ **Turn off surround sound subwoofer and speakers.** This is the biggest sound setting step you can take to reduce your computer's power consumption in a meaningful way — if your sound setup includes a subwoofer and three or more surround-sound speakers.

Indexing options (Vista only)

The speedy Windows Vista search option gets its fast-finding action kick by frequently performing indexing, which means that it's regularly scanning your computer's hard disk to keep track of all the files on it — and files no longer on it.

If you're running your Windows Vista notebook on battery power more often than not, deactivating Windows Indexing Options can lengthen how long you can keep working before having to plug in again to recharge your battery.

To stop Windows Vista from sucking down power by regularly indexing your computer's hard disk, follow these steps:

1. **Click Start⇨Computer.**

2. **Right-click the Hard Disk (C:) icon, then choose Properties.**

3. **Deselect the Index This Drive for Faster Searching option and then click OK.**

4. **Click OK to accept the default option, Apply Changes to Drive C:\, Subfolders and Files, as shown in Figure 7-14.**

5. **Click Continue if prompted for permission, and then click Continue again.**

6. **When you're finished, click OK to close the Hard Disk Properties dialog box.**

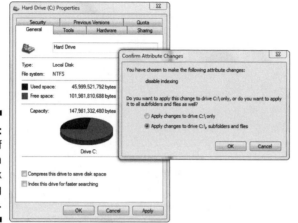

Figure 7-14:
Turning off
the Vista
hard disk
indexing
option.

Deselecting the Vista indexing option as I describe stops any indexing of your hard disk — but not the underlying indexing process that Windows constantly runs in the background, whether you're using it or not. To disable the indexing service, follow these steps:

1. **Click the Start button and choose Run.**

2. **Type services.msc and press Enter.**

3. **In the right column, scroll down to and double-click Windows Search.**

4. **Click Stop if the button is not grayed, and then choose Disabled from the drop-down menu.**

5. **Click OK and then click the Close button.**

Chapter 8

Conserving Power with Your Mac's Energy-Saver Settings

● ●

In This Chapter

▶ Instantly minimizing your Mac's energy use

▶ Automatically adjusting your Mac's Energy-Saver settings

▶ Fine-tuning energy-saving settings on the Mac

● ●

*I*n this chapter, I tell you how to adjust your Mac's energy settings to save greenbacks while doing a little something for the environment. You manage your Mac's energy usage and settings in three general ways:

✔ **On-the-fly:** By on-the-fly, I mean those options that you can change quickly and easily. Examples include moving the mouse pointer to a hot corner to instantly shut off the display or closing the lid on your Mac to instantly put it in Sleep mode. I cover the gambit of on-the-fly options in the chapter's first section.

✔ **Automatically:** Adjust your Mac's Energy Saver preferences to specify how long to wait before the display or the computer enters Sleep mode. Activate the Energy Saver Schedule option to tell your Mac when to turn itself on or off or enter Sleep mode, based on day and time choices that you set to suit your individual workday, nighttime, and weekend routine.

✔ **Specialized:** Run a power management utility or Dashboard widget that you can download for free or for a fee, as I describe in Chapter 6. These utilities and widgets generally aim to let you simplify or enhance the Mac's Energy Saver Preferences panel.

Making other adjustments, such as disabling your Mac's Bluetooth and AirPort wireless features if you aren't using them, also helps reduce your Mac's carbon footprint. Applying these energy-saving adjustments, and others, is described in the section "Making Additional Mac Energy-Saving Adjustments," later in this chapter.

Minimizing Your Mac's Energy Use On-the-Fly

Minimizing your Mac's energy consumption on-the-fly is a no-brainer: Press your Mac's power button and then click either the Sleep or Shut Down button in the dialog that opens (see Figure 8-1). Or, skip the mouse click and press the S key to choose sleep, or press Return to tell your Mac to shut down.

Figure 8-1:
Instant
energy
savings!

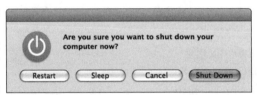

Are you sure you want to shut down your computer now?

Restart   Sleep   Cancel   Shut Down

Close the lid on your MacBook to instantly put it to sleep. Waking it is just as easy: Open the lid, and your Mac snaps instantly awake, ready to serve. That's what I call instant green gratification. Unfortunately, this method of closing the lid to induce sleep doesn't work on desktop Macs, so don't bother tipping your heavy monitor or LCD display face down onto the keyboard or desktop. (I speak from experience).

You can also move the mouse to one of the Desktop hot corners to instantly put the display in Sleep mode. (A *hot corner* is a corner on your Mac's display which, when you move your mouse pointer to it, causes your Mac to take one of a number of actions you've assigned it.) You can also activate other events with hot corners — start the screen saver or display your Mac's Dashboard Widgets, for example.

To put your Mac's display in Sleep mode when you move the pointer to a hot corner, follow these steps:

1. **Click the Apple menu and then choose System Preferences.**

2. **Click the Desktop & Screen Saver icon.**

3. **Click the Hot Corners button.**

4. **Click the button corresponding to the corner of your choice, and then choose Sleep Display, as shown in Figure 8-2.**

   If you want, choose Sleep Display for a second or third corner — or even all four.

5. **Click OK and then click the Close button to close System Preferences.**

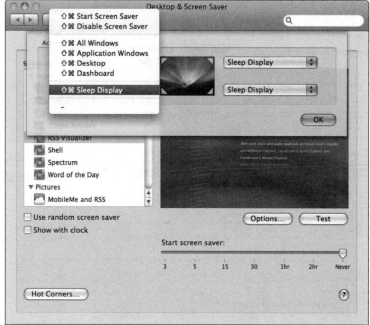

Figure 8-2:
Instantly
turn off
your Mac's
screen by
assigning a
hot corner
to Sleep
Display.

 Cutting the power to your desktop Mac's external monitor (if you're using one) is another easy way to blank the screen and save energy when you leave your Mac for more than a few minutes.

Being responsible and remembering to perform the smartest energy-saving actions need not rest on your shoulders alone, however. Let your Mac remember for you, by setting it up to take care of its energy-saving options for itself. All it takes are a few simple adjustments to your Mac's Energy Saver Preferences panel, as described in the following section.

Adjusting Your Mac's Automatic Energy-Saver Settings

To change your Mac's energy-saving options — such as whether it powers off the hard disk when possible, or how long it waits before turning off the display, or entering Sleep mode — you use the Energy Saver Preferences panel.

To open the Energy Saver Preferences panel, follow these steps:

1. **Click the Apple menu and choose System Preferences.**

2. **Click the Energy Saver icon.**

If you use a MacBook, you see two clickable tabs, Battery and Power Adapter, at the top of the Energy Saver preferences panel (see Figure 8-3). Desktop Mac users see two options: Sleep and Options.

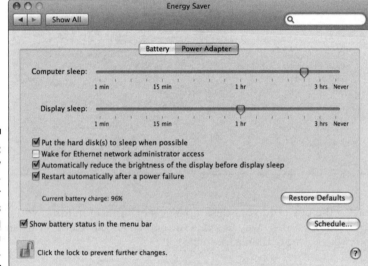

Figure 8-3: The Energy Saver no-brainer controls make saving energy a cinch.

If you can't move the sliders or select and deselect the check boxes, the likely reason is that the settings are locked. To unlock the settings so that you can change them, do what it says alongside the tiny lock icon in the lower-left corner: Click the lock to make changes.

Starting from the top, here's a description of the Energy Saver options:

✔ **Computer Sleep:** Moving this slider to the left is the greener way to go. Moving to the right is less efficient because it allows a smart device to do nothing other than burn energy for no good reason.

✔ **Display Sleep:** Maybe you take a break and then return to your computer at regular intervals and you don't want to wake your Mac from lots of catnaps several times a day. Fair enough. Set the Computer Sleep slider (see the preceding bullet) a little farther to the right and then drag the Display Sleep slider to the left to snap your Mac to attention in a flash, with only the slightest pause before the screen comes back to life.

✔ **Put the Hard Disks(s) to Sleep When Possible:** Select this option to "snooze" the hard disk whenever it determines that the programs you're running don't need to keep the drive (or drives) spinning. If you regularly perform hard disk intensive tasks, such as edit videos or play 3D games, deselect this option.

✔ **Wake for Ethernet Network Administration Access:** If you don't know what this option means, deselect it. If you're told not to, you probably work in a company or an organization that reserves the right to oversee, maintain, start up, shut down, manage, or regulate computer usage in ways beyond your control. In that case, it's beyond my control to advise you do anything other than leave this option selected. If you routinely access your Mac remotely when you're away from it, however, leave this option selected to keep the connection alive.

✔ **Automatically Reduce the Brightness of the Display Before Display Sleep:** When you select this option, the brightness level on the display drops a few notches before blanking out the screen after the length of time you select in the Display Sleep setting (see preceding bullet).

✔ **Restart Automatically After a Power Failure:** Whether it's brownouts, blackouts, or black cats knocking out power cords, power failures happen. Use this option to specify how your Mac should react when the lights come on again after a power failure. Select the check box if you want your Mac to restart, and deselect it if you prefer to turn it back on yourself after the power is running again.

For a greener choice, deselect this option unless your Mac is pulling duty as a server or performing some other service that absolutely requires it to be on 24/7 — no ifs, ands, or buts.

✔ **Show Battery Status in the Menu Bar:** Selecting this option on your MacBook lets you keep visual tabs on how much battery juice remains when your machine is unplugged from the wall outlet — and how long you need to wait until its battery is fully charged after you plug into a power outlet. To change the information you see, click the Battery Status icon and then Show, and then choose Icon Only, Time, or Percentage to see your battery's status the way you like it.

✔ **Schedule:** Click the Schedule button to open these scheduling options:

- *Start Up or Wake:* Choose when you want your Mac to greet you on weekdays or weekends, every day, or one day in particular. (The scheduler has no option for folks whose "Friday night" begins on a weekday.) Click the up and down arrows to adjust the time, as shown in Figure 8-4 — or just click the time slots and enter your preference directly.

- *Sleep/Restart/Shutdown:* Choose one of these pop-up options if you want your Mac to do as instructed and adjust the time, as described in the preceding bullet, to suit your schedule.

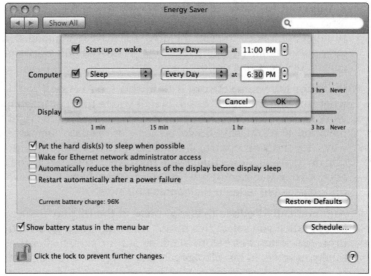

Figure 8-4:
Awaken
your Mac on
a schedule.

Taking advantage of your Mac's Energy Settings undoubtedly helps minimize its carbon footprint, but wait — there's more! You have more ways to
minimize your Mac's power usage by switching off certain features or other
devices. You have more ways to save running downloadable miniprograms or
widgets that simplify the process of making the smartest energy-saving settings possible.

Making Additional Mac Energy-Saving Adjustments

Tweaking your Mac's Energy Saver options as described earlier in this chapter automatically moves you a few seats closer to front of the class for minimizing energy consumption when you're using — and not using — your Mac.

Well done, 'ol chap. But why settle for anything other than the best energy-
saving setup possible? Making a few additional adjustments can earn you the
right to stick a green star on your forehead, if that's your idea of fun. Why
not? You'll certainly have deserved it after tending to these extra-savings
extra credits.

Have a stroll through a smorgasbord of power-related settings, features,
and other options by following the appropriate steps or actions to turn off
or tweak those that can help make your increasingly ecofriendly Mac even
friendlier.

Brightness

The brightness level is easy to understand — and change, for better energy savings. Simply put, lowering your display's brightness level uses less energy. I've never been able to dim the screen even one notch without feeling like it's too dim. Other people I know have no problem working on their Macs with the brightness level knocked down a few notches.

Adjust your Mac's display brightness by using one of these methods:

✔ **The Brightness Down key:** Press this key until the screen is black, and then press Brightness Up one keystroke at a time until you reach a level that's easy on the eye — and, hopefully, on the energy use.

Note: Older Mac models may not have Brightness keys on their keyboards.

✔ **The Displays Preference Panel:** Click the Apple menu, choose System Preferences, and then click the Displays icon. Slide it to the left to dim the display, and slide it to the right to brighten the scene.

You can set a newer MacBook to automatically adjust the brightness, depending on how light or dark it is where you're working, if you select the Automatically Adjust Brightness As Ambient Light Changes check box, shown in Figure 8-5.

On stand-alone monitors and LCD displays, follow the guidelines in the preceding list, using your display's brightness control to decrease, and then increase, the brightness level until it's just right for your eyes.

Figure 8-5:
Adjust
your Mac's
brightness
level — or
have it
adjusted for
you.

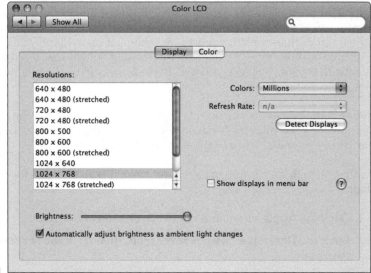

Word of the Day: Deadhead

Repeat after me: "I shall not let my Mac's screen saver run for more than a few minutes (the minimum amount of time allowed) before blanking the screen." I set mine to three minutes because that's all the idle time my MacBook needs in order to pop up my screen saver of choice: Word of the Day. It appears after I haven't touched my MacBook after three minutes, a length of time that easily passes while I'm fixing a sandwich or setting up another round of tea in the autodrip. Because my workspace is stationed next to my kitchen (in a one-room house, which room *isn't* next to it?), my MacBook's switch to Screen Saver mode always catches my eye, and rarely do I fail to move closer to learn a new word I didn't know — or relearn the meaning of one I *thought* I knew so well. Today's word that appeared as I was waiting for the Word of the Day Screen Saver to kick in? *Deadhead.* My favorite Grateful Dead song of late? "Touch of Gray." Learning new words every day? Priceless.

If your Mac's Brightness Up and Brightness Down keys aren't responding, hold down the Fn key and press the Brightness keys again. To change your Mac's keyboard so that the Brightness key and others work without holding down Fn, click the Apple menu and choose System Preferences, then click the Keyboard & Mouse icon➪Keyboard, and then deselect the Use All F1, F2, Etc. Keys As Standard Function Keys check box.

Screen saver

Yes, screen savers are pretty to look at. And once upon a time they were helpful for preventing permanent damage to your monitor. But nowadays screen savers are mostly useless because the green choice is to blank the screen rather than consume power by keeping it on to display an animated sequence or other eye-catching, energy-wasting delight that's probably going unnoticed anyway because you are, after all, away from the computer in the first place, right? Phew!

I admit that I'm a hypocrite on this topic because I run my screen saver — but only for a few minutes because it's a learning experience, as I explain in the nearby sidebar, "Word of the day: Deadhead."

To shut off your Mac's screen saver and make it fade to black, follow these steps:

1. **Click the Apple menu and choose System Preferences.**

2. **Click the Desktop & Screen Saver icon, then click the Screen Saver tab.**

3. **Drag the Start Screen Saver slider to Never.**

4. **Click the Show All button at the top of the System Preferences window.**

5. **Click the Energy Saver Preference icon.**

6. **Drag the Display Sleep slider to choose the number of minutes** (3 or 5, for example) that you want the display to wait before turning off when your Mac is idle.

7. **Click the Close button to close System Preferences.**

Keyboard brightness

Dimming, turning off, or automatically adjusting the keyboard backlighting on a newer MacBook can help save energy — and extend battery life when your machine isn't plugged into a wall outlet.

To adjust your MacBook's keyboard backlighting, follow these steps:

1. **Click the Apple menu, choose System Preferences⇨Keyboard & Mouse, and click the Keyboard tab, if it isn't selected.**

2. **Select or deselect the Illuminate Keyboard in Low Light Conditions check box.**

3. **If you choose to select the option, click and drag the Turn Off When Computer is Not Used For slider to adjust how long your Mac should wait before it does just that.**

   This step specifies how long your MacBook waits before turning off keyboard backlighting when you aren't using it.

Require password to wake computer from sleep

Read this handy tip if you work in an office or another environment where you don't want someone snooping on your computer when you're away from your desk. (If it's only you and your dog, cat, or goldfish in the house, this feature can be annoying, especially if your Mac goes to sleep after only a few minutes.)

To make your Mac ask for your password whenever it awakens from Sleep mode or when it's running the screen saver:

1. **Click the Apple menu and then choose System Preferences.**

2. **Click the Security icon.**

3. **Select the Require Password to Wake This Computer from Sleep or Screensaver check box.**

4. **Click the Close button to close System Preferences.**

If you can't deselect the check box in Step 3, it's because the settings are locked. To unlock them so that you can change them, click the little lock icon in the lower-left corner, and then enter your password and press Return.

AirPort

Your machine might be plugged in to the Internet by way of an Ethernet cable running from your cable or DSL modem or your network router and into your Mac or MacBook's Ethernet port. Or, it might be connected wirelessly to a WiFi router either at home or, if you're out with your MacBook, at the local café that lets you connect for free.

If your machine is plugged in using an Ethernet cable, you have no reason to leave your Mac's built-in AirPort wireless networking feature turned on, because it's wasting energy.

To turn off your Mac's AirPort wireless networking feature when you aren't using it, click the AirPort icon on the menu bar, as shown in Figure 8-6, and then choose Turn AirPort Off.

Figure 8-6:
Turn off AirPort when you aren't using it.

If you don't see the Airport Icon in the menu bar, follow these steps:

1. **Click the Apple menu and choose System Preferences.**

2. **Click the Network icon to open the Network Preference panel.**

3. **Select the Show AirPort Status in Menu Bar check box and then click the Close button to close the Preference panel.**

Bluetooth

Turning on your Mac or MacBook's built-in Bluetooth feature lets you connect other devices, such as the ones in this list:

- **Wireless mouse:** For clutter-free mousing around

- **Hands-free headset:** For clearer iChat Webcam video chats

✔ **Another Mac or Windows PC:** To send files back and forth

✔ **A Palm, BlackBerry, or other brand of smartphone:** To keep the phone and your address book and iCal calendar in sync.

If you have no idea what I'm talking about, you probably aren't using Bluetooth, which means that your Mac is wasting energy — and if you're using a MacBook, draining its battery more quickly when you're away from a wall adapter.

To turn off your Mac's Bluetooth feature when you aren't using it, simply click the Bluetooth icon in the menu bar and choose Turn Bluetooth Off, as shown in Figure 8-7.

Figure 8-7:
Turn off
Bluetooth
when you
aren't
using it.

If you don't see the Bluetooth icon in the menu bar, follow these steps:

1. **Click the Apple menu and choose System Preferences.**

2. **Click the Bluetooth icon to open the Bluetooth Preferences panel.**

3. **Select the Show Bluetooth Status in the Menu Bar check box and then click the Close button to close the Preference panel.**

Turning off the Bluetooth devices that you connect to your Mac, such as a headset and mouse, helps extend their battery life so that you don't need to recharge them so often.

A wireless mouse may come with its own charging base, which should be unplugged from the wall outlet or USB port unless the mouse needs a recharge.

The "powerful" tale of one tailless mouse

My favorite Mac mouse is the Microsoft Bluetooth Notebook Mouse 5000, which runs on two AAA batteries (I use rechargeable ones, of course) and automatically enters Sleep mode after a few minutes of inactivity.

Reawakening the mouse can take a few seconds after moving it. You gain smarter energy savings when you flip over the little creature and turn off the tiny power switch to cut the juice.

Thanks to the shareware program SteerMouse (`plentycom.jp/en/steermouse`), the mouse's programmable buttons work fine with my Mac — but not with my Windows notebooks because Microsoft never created a driver specifically for this particular mouse model.

Sound

Turning your Mac's sound output down or off uses a little less energy than turning it up full blast. Of course, you can't hear music or the alert sound whenever a new e-mail message lands in your inbox. Press the Volume Up, Volume Down, and Mute keys to adjust your Mac's sound level accordingly.

The following list highlights other measures you can take to reduce the amount of energy used by your Mac's sound output:

- ✔ **Plug in headphones:** They draw less power than speakers do — and they're helpful for blocking out the chatterbugs and other distracting noisemakers when you're working on your MacBook at a café or another public place.

- ✔ **Turn off surround sound subwoofer and speakers:** This method can reduce your Mac's overall power consumption in a meaningful way — if your sound setup includes a subwoofer and three or more surround-sound speakers.

Spotlight

Pressing ⌘+spacebar opens the most helpful time-saving feature: Spotlight search. Type the first letters of a name or word and Spotlight instantly turns up such potential matches as Address Book contact cards, e-mail messages, music tracks, and documents.

But pulling off the fast-acting finding magic comes at a price if you're running your MacBook on battery juice. To find things darn fast, Spotlight performs *indexing*, which means that it regularly scans the hard disk to keep track of all the information on it — and no longer on it.

If you run your MacBook on battery power more often than not, deactivating Spotlight can lengthen the time between recharges.

To prevent Spotlight from indexing your Mac's hard disk, follow these steps:

1. **Click the Apple menu and then choose System Preferences⇨Spotlight.**

2. **On the Privacy tab, shown in Figure 8-8, click the plus (+) button near the lower-left corner.**

3. **Click Macintosh HD (or whatever you renamed your hard disk) and click Choose.**

4. **Click the Close button to close the window.**

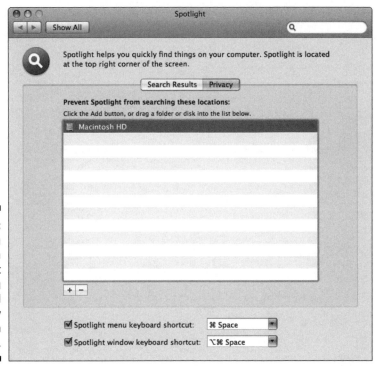

Figure 8-8:
Shutting
down
Spotlight
searching
can extend
your battery
life on
the go.

Part IV
Acquiring Green Gadgets and Gear

The 5th Wave   By Rich Tennant

"It's a fully furnished, 3-bedroom house that's designed to fit perfectly over your iPod."

In this part . . .

*I*t's time for a virtual shopping trip to Planet Green Mall. The ecofriendliest energy-efficiency technologies now available are found in the latest greener gadgets. So, when you choose the most ecofriendly gadgets that money can buy, your rewards double: You have a greater sense of having made the smartest choice for the planet, and you have a greater sense of having made the smartest choice for your wallet.

I help you figure out whether a company's supposed green products are truly ecofriendly or just greenwash. I also show you what makes the tiniest wind-up flashlight or the largest energy-efficient high-definition TV green.

Chapter 9

Knowing the Difference Between Truly Green and Greenwash Hype

. . . .

In This Chapter

▶ The "It" thing of our time: Paying to be (seen as) green

▶ The Greenpeace Guide to Greener Electronics

▶ The Greenpeace Electronics Survey

▶ Another take on green gadgets, from the Consumer Electronics Association

▶ Company information straight from the source

. . . .

*Y*ou can't turn on the TV, open a magazine, or listen to the radio without hearing about this product's green benefits or that company's efforts in improving the planet by being green. That's because every company under the sun wants to be seen as green. It's the "It" thing of our era. Sorting through what's real and what's hype isn't so glamorous and can be dizzying.

In this chapter, I explain the difference between being truly green and just *greenwashing,* or making misleading or false claims about a company's eco-friendly practices and the products it produces. Understanding this difference can help you make the greenest choices possible before buying new gadgets and other consumer electronic goods.

I also point you to regularly updated resources for staying on top of how high-tech manufacturers rank on the list of the greenest (and not so green) giants in the industry.

Paying to Be (Seen As) Green Is Big Business

It pays to be green, and most major corporations are spending lots of green in ad dollars to ensure that you know how hard they're working on their ecofriendly marketing. So figuring out on your own which claims companies make are true, false, or somewhere in the middle can be next to impossible. Fortunately, many companies are pulling back the veil and making public their environmental impact on many or all levels, including internal practices and policies for reducing consumption. In addition, many companies are detailing the resources and processes involved in producing, packaging, and distributing the digital stuff they sell.

As you navigate companies' ecoclaims, check out a study by TerraChoice (http://terrachoice.com), an agency that offers its environmental marketing services to companies. It made news in 2007 for its "Six Sins of Greenwashing" study. In it, TerraChoice reported that of the slightly more than 1,000 consumer products making environmental claims the company surveyed, all but one product committed at least one of the six sins. As the chart shown in Figure 9-1 points out, the Sin of Hidden Trade-Offs takes the cake — er, pie — as the most commonly committed greenwashing "sin."

Sins Committed by Category

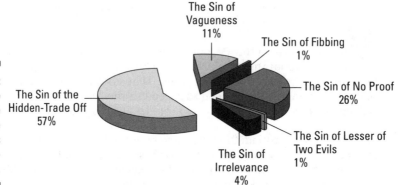

Figure 9-1: Slicing up the pie among the six sins of green-washing.

Here's a rundown of the six greenwashing sins — they're also listed on a TerraChoice downloadable wallet card for easy reference when making purchases:

- ✔ **Sin of the Hidden Trade-Off:** The product focuses only on one or two environmental issues while ignoring others of equal importance.

- ✔ **Sin of No Proof:** Neither the company nor the product can give evidence of its claim.

- ✔ **Sin of Vagueness:** The manufacturer provides little detail, if any, for issues such as amount of packaging, manufacturing process, and product disposal.

✔ **Sin of Irrelevance:** The company makes claims that are true of all products in a particular category.

✔ **Sin of Fibbing:** The manufacturer cannot back up certified claims or prove certification.

✔ **Sin of the Lesser of Two Evils:** The claim tries to make you feel "green" about a product category that's basically "ungreen." Is organic tobacco, for example, truly a green product?

Many, if not most, companies are making changes and improving their production, packaging, distribution, and recycling policies and practices to truly become green and produce greener products and services. As far as wanting you to take a company at its every ecofriendly word, the makers of computers, mobile phones, video game consoles, digital cameras, GPS locators, and other high-tech, chip-based products are no different from companies that produce paper towels or potato chips. They all want to be seen as green.

Reviewing the Greenpeace Guide to Greener Electronics

Taking companies' green claims to task are organizations such as Greenpeace, which analyzes and publicly details which (and where) companies meet, exceed, and fall short of promises — and how they stack up against their competitors.

Every quarter, Greenpeace releases its *Guide to Greener Electronics* (www. greenpeace.org/electronics). It focuses on overall corporate policies and practices for the 18 high-tech companies it reviews and features on its easy-to-read summary widget, shown in Figure 9-2.

Figure 9-2:
The
Greenpeace
Guide to
Greener
Electronics.

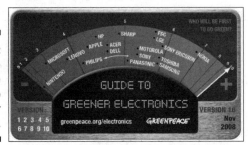

Checking the guide online can keep you up-to-date on which companies have gone up or down or stayed the same in the ranking.

Table 9-1 shows the February 2009 rankings from the Greenpeace guide.

Table 9-1	Company Rankings from the Greenpeace Guide to Greener Electronics	
Rank	*Company*	*Scoring Rationale*
6.9	Nokia	Maintains a comprehensive, voluntary take-back program
5.9	Sony Ericsson	Implemented new environmental warranty that guarantees take-back and recycling for individual products regardless of location
5.9	Toshiba	Increased its score based on energy efficiency and use of renewable energy
5.9	Samsung	Scores well on energy efficiency and toxic-chemical handling but poorly on recycling
5.7	Fujitsu Siemens	Scores well on energy efficiency but poorly on electronic-waste management
5.7	LGE	Improved its score in recycling and energy efficiency
5.3	Motorola	Improved its energy, waste, and recycling scores
5.3	Sony	Leaves room for improvement on energy efficiency
5.1	Panasonic	Achieves maximum points on energy efficiency but scores poorly on establishing e-waste criteria
4.9	Sharp	Improved its energy policy but maintains weak reporting of product energy efficiency
4.7	Acer	Needs improvement in the areas of reducing toxic chemicals and recycling
4.7	Dell	Withdrew from its commitment to eliminate all PVC plastic and brominated flame retardants (BFRs) by the end of 2009
4.5	HP	Needs to improve its e-waste handling.
4.3	Apple	Reports its carbon footprint status; newer iPods are free of polyvinyl (PVC) and brominated flame retardants (BFRs)

Rank	Company	Scoring Rationale
4.1	Philips	Scores well on toxic-chemical handling and energy use but scores zero on most other e-waste criteria
3.7	Lenovo	Handles toxic chemicals well but not recycling or energy
2.9	Microsoft	Registers low scores on recycling and energy Efficiency
0.8	Nintendo	Scores a zero on most criteria except chemical management and energy efficiency

Tapping In to the Greenpeace Electronics Survey

The second annual Green Electronics Survey evaluated in 2008 a total of 50 products manufactured and submitted by 15 companies. The survey evaluated such factors as whether products contain hazardous chemicals, level of energy efficiency, lifecycle based on ability to recycle and upgrade, design innovation, and the promotion of environmental friendliness.

The types of products submitted for the survey included

- Desktop and notebook computers
- Mobile phones, smartphones, and personal digital assistants (PDAs)
- LCD and plasma TVs and LCD monitors

And, here's a list of participating companies:

- Acer
- Dell
- Fujitsu Siemens
- Hewlett Packard
- Lenovo
- LG Electronics
- Motorola
- Nokia
- Panasonic
- Research in Motion (RIM)
- Sharp
- Samsung
- Sony
- Sony Ericsson
- Toshiba

Companies that were invited by Greenpeace to submit products but opted out of the survey include Apple, Asus, Microsoft, Nintendo, Palm, and Philips.

Although Sony submitted its PlayStation 3 for review, the report couldn't include a category for video game consoles because of the absence of Microsoft and Nintendo. In a Chapter 5 sidebar, I describe a study in which video game machines were found to gobble an estimated 16 billion kilowatt hours per year, or the approximate amount used annually, as the report states, by the city of San Diego. The PlayStation 3, shown in Figure 9-3, draws more power than the second-place Microsoft Xbox 360, and the Nintendo Wii, which requires the least amount of power to keep you in the game.

Figure 9-3:
High-
powered
gaming —
and energy
consump-
tion.

Greenpeace found that although none of the products included in the survey could claim the title of Truly Green, many companies scored higher and more competitively than they did in the previous year.

The good news is that fewer products now contain PVC plastic or hazardous chemicals. Greenpeace also found that most companies adhere to the latest Energy Star requirements while also rolling out better voluntary take-back and recycling programs.

The highest-scoring products in each category on a scale from 1 to 10 — such as the Lenovo L2440x, shown in Figure 9-4 — are listed in Table 9-2.

Table 9-2	The Greenpeace Electronics Survey Top-Scoring Products by Category	
Score	*Category*	*Company and Product*
6.9	Computer monitor	Lenovo L2440x
5.92	Television	Sharp LC-52GX5
5.88	Desktop computer	Lenovo ThinkCentre M58

Score	Category	Company and Product
5.57	Notebook computer	Toshiba Portégé R600
5.45	Mobile phone	Samsung F268
5.2	Smartphone	Nokia 6210

Figure 9-4:
The
ecofriendly
Lenovo
L2440x
monitor.

The not-so-good news, as Greenpeace points out in its survey, is that the greenest new gadgets and other electronic devices are generally green in one or more areas but not in others.

Although the gadget-and-electronics industry is moving in the right direction from the Greenpeace perspective, the organization believes that companies need to "up the ante" by applying the innovations of their most ecofriendly products across all product lines.

Considering Another Take on Green Gadgets: The Consumer Electronics Association

The Consumer Electronics Association is a trade association that promotes growth in the $171 billion U.S. consumer technology industry (2009 forecast) through events like the annual Consumer Electronics Show (CES), research, promotion, policy, and the fostering of business and strategic relationships. A study by the CEA found that nearly 90 percent of consumers consider energy efficiency to be an important factor in picking out a television to buy. The name of the study is "Environmental Sustainability and Innovation in the Consumer Electronics Industry" and you can find it here:

```
www.ce.org/GovernmentAffairs/2267.asp
```

A few choice nuggets from the study are in the nearby sidebar, "I want my greener MTV!"

At the same time, less than half of the nearly 1,000 study participants felt comfortable with understanding the ins and outs of green gadgets and electronics and the companies that manufacture them. To put it bluntly, many people aren't sure what being green means when they choose gadgets and other high-tech devices to buy. Here's a case in point: Although nearly three-quarters of people surveyed said that they expect companies to do everything in their power to protect the planet, fewer than 20 percent were confident about the practices, policies, procedures, and promises of the companies building the items they buy — or intend to buy.

I want my greener MTV!

Here are some highlights from the Consumer Electronics Association (CEA) report "Environmental Sustainability and Innovation in the Consumer Electronics Industry:"

✔ The top 20 companies included in the study build roughly half of the consumer electronics units in the world.

✔ In 2007, Best Buy sold seven million products with the Energy Star label on them. According to Environmental Protection Agency (EPA) accounting, these purchases saved those people $100 million in utility bills while preventing an estimated 1.4 billion pounds of carbon emissions from flaking out into the atmosphere. *That's similar to plucking nearly 130,000 cars off the street.*

These companies stood out in the recycling category:

✔ **Crutchfield:** The gadget and electronics retailer and e-tailer replaced polystyrene peanuts with biodegradable starch pellets in nearly 1 million outbound shipments — an estimated 600,000 pounds of waste that might have otherwise wound up in local landfills.

✔ **Hewlett-Packard:** HP recycled more than 400 million pounds of computer hardware since it began its recycling program in 1987.

✔ **Kodak:** The company collected 120 million single-use cameras of all manufacturer types for recycling in 2007. Single-use cameras might seem at first to be a drag on the planet, but the CEA survey cites that Kodak has recaptured an estimated 1.2 billion cameras since the company began the program in 1990. Why all the fuss? Nearly all Kodak single-use cameras now in production use recycled parts.

Fifty percent of people interviewed felt that companies will do whatever it takes to sell their products — even if it means exaggerating ecofriendly corporate policies and product features. And, slightly more than half of the study participants questioned the validity of the information they read about green gadgets and gear.

The CEA Web site for finding out about green gadgets, computers, and other consumer electronics is www.myGreenElectronics.org. The Web site also offers an energy calculator to figure out how much your electronics are costing you to use them, and a recycling location finder.

Taking Companies at Their Own Green Word, Sort Of

When you visit the Web sites of companies that build the products you're thinking about purchasing, or that you already own, you can find out about their environmentally friendlier products, initiatives, attitudes, actions, reactions, and satisfaction-guaranteed promises. You might also discover that the maker of that to-die-for gadget you're itching to purchase has a take-back recycling option to relieve you of the gadget several years down the road.

Browsing gadget-makers' ecocentric Web sites

Visiting the Web site of a company that builds gadgets, computers, and other high-tech gear that you're interested in buying can help you gauge how serious it is about creating ecofriendly products.

This list presents a sampling of eye-catching company Web pages that aim to educate you about their green leanings:

> ✔ **Apple:** The new Apple notebook model is pitched as "the greenest MacBook ever." At its Web site, Apple reports on its recent green achievements, as shown in Figure 9-5. Although Apple is often portrayed in the media as an underdog and the darling of the public's eye, its less-than-green history belies its image (www.apple.com/environment).

Figure 9-5:
An environmental update from Apple.

✔ **Dell:** Dell publicly states that it's aiming to become the "greenest technology company on the planet." Go to `http://dell.com/environment` to find out how the company hopes to achieve its goal, including compliance and waste and pollution prevention and suggestions for steps you can take to help protect the planet. You can also find information about Dell's recycling policies, including its global efforts, as shown in Figure 9-6.

Figure 9-6:
Ecofriendly Dell info is online.

✔ **Hewlett Packard:** At `www.hp.com/environment`, you can read up on HP corporate commitments and find tips for trimming your computer's energy use, recycling those empty inkjet and laser toner cartridges, and trading in used or hopelessly useless gadgets, computers, and other unwanted electronics.

✔ **Nokia:** Go to `www.nokia.com/environment` to find out how you can recycle your old mobile phone at a nearby recycling location, read about the company's efforts to minimize its global environmental impact while helping you make sustainable choices, and grab a handful of tips to help you minimize your mobile phone's carbon footprint, as shown in Figure 9-7.

✔ **Samsung:** "All good things come to an end. Let's make sure it's a green end." That's the Samsung opening on its green-minded Web site (at `http://samsung.com/green`), where you can determine how to upgrade and recycle your electronics, find a nearby drop-off location for unwanted gadgets and gear, and tap into a toner recycling or mobile phone take-back program.

✔ **Sony Ericsson:** At `www.sonyericsson.com/sustainability`, you can read the Sony Ericsson sustainability policy and find out more about the company's efforts to safeguard profitability while making an effort to improve its influence on the living and working conditions of the people who build its products. You can also check out its latest take-back programs and see how the company reduces energy consumption.

✔ **Toshiba:** Check up on the latest Toshiba corporate social responsibility (CSR) efforts at `www.toshiba.com/csrpub/jsp/home/SResponsibility.jsp`, including its corporate policies and ecofriendly vision for the future.

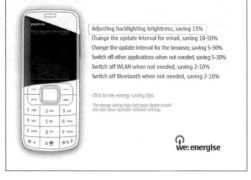

Figure 9-7: Grab an energy-saving tip from Nokia.

Adjusting backlighting brightness, saving 15%
Change the update interval for email, saving 10-50%
Change the update interval for the browser, saving 5-30%
Switch off other applications when not needed, saving 5-30%
Switch off WLAN when not needed, saving 2-10%
Switch off Bluetooth when not needed, saving 2-10%

Click to see energy saving tips

The energy saving may vary upon device model and also upon operator network settings.

we: energise

Seeking a second, third, or tenth opinion

To make the greenest possible buying choices, you have to consider a company's claims of what it does, or promises to do, about being green and then weigh those claims against other resources, such as the Greenpeace *Guide to Greener Electronics* and the CEA's current and future surveys, both described earlier in this chapter.

Check out Web sites that are focused on green gadgets, like the *PC* magazine Green Tech section at `www.pcmag.com/category2/0,2806,2256470,00.asp`, shown in Figure 9-8. There you can review electronics products and stay on top of manufacturer trends and developments in the high-tech world of gizmos and digital gear.

Figure 9-8:
The *PC* magazine Green Tech section.

Chapter 10

Choosing Green Mac and Windows Computers

*I*n this chapter, I show you the ins and outs of buying computers the green way before you even enter the store.

Before you whip out your credit card, I tell you about upgrades that can make your computer feel like new again — or nearly new — and save you from having to buy a whole new computer. Upgrading the PC you already own also helps save the environment because it reduces your consumption — and the use of resources necessary to build and ship a new computer.

If you can't upgrade, I help you get a handle on the latest computer energy standards and ratings, such as Energy Star and EPEAT (Electronic Product Environmental Assessment Tool), and point out ways to evaluate how computer manufacturers stack up against one another when it comes to being green.

With a number of new desktop and notebook choices to illustrate green computing trends, I take you on a tour of standout Windows and Mac models.

Considering Upgrades to Make Your Computer Feel New Again

When you upgrade your existing desktop or notebook computer rather than buy a new one, you honor the *three Rs* — reduce, reuse, recycle — all at once by

- ✔ **Reducing** the need to use raw elements and resources to build, ship, and power a new computer.

- ✔ **Reusing** a computer you already own by making it more useful with hardware upgrades to increase performance, or upgrading the operating system (OS) to give you new features and functions absent from the old OS

- ✔ **Recycling** the computer's power to serve you better by adding upgrades while compelling you to properly recycle parts you swap out but can't use

Upgrading hardware

You can make your computer feel new again by upgrading its internal hardware parts and components, or adding new ones. To enhance your existing computer's hardware, you generally

- ✔ Exchange or add more *random access memory (RAM)* so that you can run more applications at one time and more quickly.

- ✔ Replace the internal hard drive with a faster, larger capacity, more energy-efficient model (or add an external model) so that you can store and access more programs and files more quickly — while using less power

- ✔ Add an external monitor, keyboard, and mouse to your notebook computer, as shown in Figure 10-1, so that you can work more comfortably with it without having to buy a new desktop to achieve the same result

- ✔ Add a network router that lets you print to a connected printer or share files on a connected hard drive rather than having separate printers and external hard drives all around the house

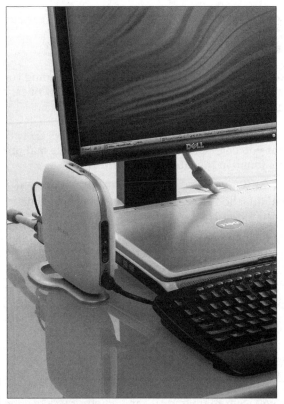

Figure 10-1:
Turn your
notebook
into a desk-
top with
add-ons
like this one
from Belkin.

Upgrading operating systems and applications

You can also make your computer feel new again by upgrading your computer's operating system (OS) and applications, or adding new ones. To enhance your existing computer software, you generally

✔ Upgrade or replace your computer's Mac or Windows OS with a newer version so that you can benefit from the performance and productivity enhancements found in the latest versions.

✔ Give your Mac or Windows PC a totally new look and feel by replacing (or adding and dual-booting) its OS with a free Linux OS distribution, such as Ubuntu (www.ubuntu.com).

✔ Run Windows on your Mac in a separate partition with Apple's Boot Camp (or a with *virtualization* program, such as Parallels or Fusion) so that you can run Windows applications without having to buy a second Windows computer.

✔ Add new applications or upgrade ones you already have to the latest version so that you can benefit from more features and functions.

Choosing and installing upgrades

Figuring out what you want to upgrade — and whether you can install it yourself — depends on which options from the previous two sections can make your old computer feel new again. Consider these tips when upgrading your computer:

✔ Install more memory in your desktop or notebook computer, which is typically easy, whereas replacing or adding a new internal hard drive is generally not so simple.

✔ Check your computer's manual or visit the support section of your computer manufacturer's Web site to find out what upgrade options are available for your particular model.

✔ Buy from online discount computer and gadget retailers rather than directly from the computer manufacturer, which can save you money. The following three, which I use, offer savings:

• **Amazon.com:** Memory upgrades, peripherals, and software

• **Crucial:** Memory upgrades at http://crucial.com

• **TigerDirect.com:** Memory upgrades, peripherals, and software

✔ Check prices before buying by searching the product price comparison sites, such as MySimon.com or Froogle.com, which can turn up even larger savings. Pay attention to Star ratings and user comments, which can often spell the difference between spending a few bucks more and getting what you want on time versus paying the absolute lowest price and then winding up waiting a week for your goods to show up.

✔ Reuse or repurpose components or programs you've upgraded or replaced by selling, giving away, or recycling them.

Getting Up-to-Speed on Computer Energy Standards and Ratings

In Chapter 1, I talk about the basic charters of the two key players in the electronics energy efficiency standards game — Energy Star and EPEAT. Becoming acquainted with them can help you choose the greenest gadgets, computers, and other electronics.

I recap briefly here as each pertains to buying a new computer:

✔ **Energy Star:** Launched in 1992 by the U.S. Environmental Protection Agency (EPA), this program is designed to help consumers identify energy-efficient products. Initially, computers and monitors were the first products to wear the Energy Star logo, and since partnering with the Department of Energy in 1996 for additional product categories, the label can now be found on everything from major appliances and office equipment to DVD players and set-top cable TV boxes. (Not to mention notebook and desktop PCs, printers, and other computer-related products.) Check out www.energystar.gov.

✔ **Electronic Product Environmental Assessment Tool, or EPEAT:** This procurement system helps buyers consider, compare, and choose computer products based on environmental attributes. Earning one of the three EPEAT ratings is sort of like winning an Olympic medal — which is exactly how the three levels of accomplishment are named:

- **Bronze:** Products meet all required criteria

- **Silver:** Products meet all required criteria plus 50 percent of optional criteria

- **Gold:** Products meet all required criteria plus 75 percent of optional criteria

All EPEAT-registered products are automatically Energy Star qualified. The EPEAT and Energy Star Web sites have information about whether a specific computer, printer, or other peripheral makes the Energy Star (www.energy star.gov) or EPEAT (www.epeat.net) grade — and if so, at which level.

Evaluating Computer Manufacturers' Levels of Greenness

In Chapter 9, I discuss how you can make your way through the muck of greenwash hype to find out what products are truly green and who's making those products. Computer companies, such as Apple, Dell, HP, Lenovo, Toshiba, and others, have all spoken publicly about their own green efforts, and they all have sections on their Web sites to back up their claims.

The Greenpeace Guide to Greener Electronics, which I discuss at length in Chapter 9, helpfully ranks the top 18 consumer electronics manufacturers of TVs, computers, video game consoles, and cellphones based on their policies on toxic chemicals, recycling, and climate change.

The Electronics section of Consumer Reports Greener Choices Web site (www.greenerchoices.org; look under the Products and Green Ratings heading) also can help you narrow down potential computer picks organized by three categories:

- ✔ **Budget:** Suffices for basic tasks; has a DVD burner and two-piece speakers.

- ✔ **Workhorse:** Faster and more powerful for multimedia needs; has a DVD burner and three-piece speakers.

- ✔ **High end:** Optimal for graphic design and gaming; has a Blu-ray drive, TV tuner, and three-piece speakers.

At the time of this writing, Lenovo, Gateway, and HP, respectively, took top honors in those three categories.

Consider whether a computer company offers a program to take back, repurpose, or properly recycle your old computer to help you choose which company gets the green from your wallet. Visit their Web site and navigate to the green or environment section to find out.

Some companies take back only their own products, whereas others, such as Dell, will come to your doorstep to pick up old computers and peripherals made by other manufacturers.

Getting a Handle on Green Computers

Windows or Mac? That is the question. And it's typically the first decision you make when choosing a new desktop or notebook computer. Of course, you might also consider a Linux-based computer, especially if you're thinking about buying a new and inexpensive, ultralightweight *netbook,* such as the ASUS Eee PC model (see Figure 10-2), which is useful for light duty tasks such as e-mail and browsing the Web.

Figure 10-2:
Netbook:
No energy-
saving
lightweight.

Although I don't dedicate a whole section to Linux-based computers, I do give a nod to the ability to run Linux on some of the choices described later, in the section "Looking at Green Windows Computers."

The next question you'll want to ask is "Desktop or notebook?"

Whatever way you go — Mac or Windows, desktop or notebook (or netbook) — keep the following general computer energy usage points in mind to help you make the greenest choice possible:

- ✓ **Notebooks use less power than desktops.** Except for honker-sized ultra-whiz-bang (and heavy) notebooks such as the ones Alienware builds for playing high-end games with the panache of a full-blown desktop PC, notebooks use less power than desktops.

- ✓ **LCD displays are more efficient than monitors.** I can't remember the last time I've seen an old-fashioned cathode ray tube (CRT) monitor, and maybe you can't remember either. If someone tries to sell you one, say no thanks and go with an LCD screen. The newer LED type offers the best energy savings — and instantly powers on to full brightness rather taking a while to warm up to full brightness, the way non-LED type displays do.

- ✓ **Faster processors use more power.** Buying the fastest PC available rewards you with speedier performance, but not without paying a price in consuming more power and increasing your electric bill to boot.

✔ **Adjust energy saving settings to save more power.** Tweak your new computer's energy settings, which can cut its energy usage by half. I talk briefly about making adjustments a little later in this chapter, and for more on the subject, check out Part III.

✔ **Make a future-proofed purchase.** The ability to upgrade a computer means that you can keep using it longer than one that's not as adaptable to changing with the times. The Apple MacBook Air, for instance, excites techno-lust for its sleekness, but garners groans for its sealed case design, which makes it impossible to replace the rechargeable battery yourself if the battery stops holding a charge. For that, you have to send it to Apple or another company that specializes in opening and upgrading sealed products such as the MacBook Air.

✔ **Lots of connections are a good thing.** Paying a little more for features, such as built-in Bluetooth and Wi-Fi wireless networking, can ensure your new computer can connect to your other gadgets — such as digital cameras, headsets, wireless routers, keyboards, and mice — well into the future before some new standard comes along and renders those means obsolete.

Other features to look for include

- *The most current operating system (OS)* so that you don't have to spend more money just to catch up with the OS Jones's, so to speak.

- *Lots of Universal Serial Bus (USB) ports and, ideally, at least one FireWire port,* for connecting other devices, such as cellphones, PDAs, printers, digital cameras, externals hard drives, and memory keychains.

✔ **Smart power strips save even more power.** Plugging any type of computer or peripheral into a smart power strip such as the Belkin Conserve, as shown in Figure 10-3, can take a bite out of energy vampires by reducing or completely cutting power consumption and costs. Check out Chapter 1 to read how to stop sneaky energy vampires all around the house.

Figure 10-3:
Stop your
PC from
sipping
power when
it's off.

Positively green printers

All the major printer manufacturers — I'm talking about Canon, Epson, HP, Kodak, and the rest of the majors — are hip to building green printers. They're also working harder to make it as easy as possible to recycle used toner and ink cartridges. Visit the companies' same-name-dot-com Web sites to catch up on the latest green printing products and policies that can help you hang onto a little extra printed green of your own. In Chapter 17, I discuss a green printer from Canon and an ecofriendly ink system that's good for your wallet, too.

Picking Green Macs

Apple launched its new MacBook last year, which says a lot about where the company and its products are today when it comes to getting green. In his 2008 Environmental Update, Apple CEO Steve Jobs wrote, "We are constantly working to reduce the emissions associated with Apple's products. This means making them more efficient in size and energy consumption." A few months later Apple described its newly designed 13-inch MacBook as "the greenest MacBook ever."

Although green-gadget watchers gave the 13-inch MacBook mostly good reviews, Greenpeace noted that "not all toxic pieces have been eliminated yet." Those not-so-nice pieces are generally made of polyvinyl chlorides (PVCs) or brominated flame retardants (BFRs), which are poisonous when burned — which is par for the course in the polluted overseas recycling markets where much of Western e-waste winds up. In the MacBook's case, Greenpeace is referring not to the notebook unit itself, but rather to the PVCs contained in the external power adapter and cord included with the MacBook.

According to EcoGeek.org editor Hank Green, "the one revolutionary aspect of the MacBook — its solid aluminum brick construction — is not green at all." Apple's claim that "a single piece of solid, recyclable aluminum that replaces dozens of extraneous pieces once destined for landfill," may be accurate, but EcoGeek's Green wrote on his Web site that the design creates unnecessary energy expenditures, which he deems "a step backward."

What about the rest of the MacBook's green qualifications? With both Energy Star 4.0 compliance and EPEAT Gold status, the MacBook earns its place with more than 100 other notebooks green enough to wear the gold star, so to speak.

If you want to know more about your computer's general power issues and energy-saving options, I cover that in greater detail in Chapter 6 (along with information on how to run easy- to- use energy-saving utilities). Chapter 8 covers how to adjust your Mac's specific Power Saver preferences.

Breaking down the MacBook, piece by piece

The MacBook has both green and not-so-green parts, some of which come out as recyclables, including:

- ✓ **Aluminum all-around:** The single slab of recyclable aluminum, or the *unibody enclosure,* along with an aluminum lid and base equal three easily separable pieces of metal when the MacBook reaches the hopelessly useless stage at the end of its life. Still, reviewers such as EcoGeek's Hank Green believe creating the unibody enclosure uses more energy than it's worth.

- ✓ **Mercury- and arsenic-free glass screen:** All LCD screens are glass; however, most get covered with plastic shields. No shield gets in the way of the MacBook's LED backlit LCD recyclable glass display, which is free of the mercury or arsenic found in older displays. The display consumes 30 percent less power than conventional LCD displays, and as I mention earlier, it lights to full brightness when powered on, without needing time to warm up, like non-LED–type LCD displays.

- ✓ **BFR- and PVC-free (almost):** Although Apple eliminated brominated flame retardants — or BFRs — from the circuit boards and polyvinyl chlorides (PVCs) from the internal cables and connectors, at the time of this writing, Apple has yet to eliminate PVCs from the external power adapter and cord. Apple says it's working to achieve PVC-free status for its external parts — and it may get there by the time you read this.

- ✓ **Less packaging:** Made from a minimum of 25 percent post-recyclable material, the MacBook's completely recyclable packaging, as shown in Figure 10-4, is 41 percent smaller than the preceding model's packaging. This reduction is not only appreciable to the buyer but also to the environment because Apple says it can fit 25 percent more units into shipping containers, thereby reducing greenhouse gases by way of reduced shipping sizes and materials.

Figure 10-4:
Minimizing
packaging.

✔ **Sensors and energy savings:** A built-in light sensor gauges the room you're in and automatically dims or brightens the screen and keyboard, as shown in Figure 10-5. When powered on and sitting idle (but not entering Sleep mode, per se), the MacBook uses about as much power as a 15-watt light bulb.

MacBook Pro

Illuminated Keyboard
An ambient light sensor activates the illuminated keyboard in low-light conditions. It also controls the brightness of the display, the sleep indicator light, and the battery indicator lights.

Figure 10-5: The MacBook adjusts keyboard brightness automatically.

Considering other Macs and products

Many of Apple's green choices, which I describe in the preceding section, carry over to all its products as the company works to achieve greater green status. The Apple Mac mini desktop, as shown in Figure 10-6, is tiny, quiet, and uses very little energy — that's because many of its internal parts are based on notebook computer components, which means they sip less power to do their thing.

Figure 10-6: Apple Mac mini — quiet as a mouse.

Other Apple choices are the high-powered, high-performance Mac Pro tower desktop and the all-in-one iMac desktop. Unlike the Mac Pro, which requires the additional purchase of a display, the iMac binds the computer and the display into a single, thin ecofriendly package that has you doing a double-take because it looks like a monitor, minus the computer. For that reason, it's the greener choice of the two desktops.

If you're thinking about buying an Apple desktop, notebook, or peripheral, such as the LED Cinema Display, go to Apple's Web site at www.apple.com. There you can find the most up-to-date information about what green features the LED Cinema Display may have, as shown in Figure 10-7.

Environmental Status Report

The LED Cinema Display is designed with the following features to reduce its environmental impact:

- Arsenic-free glass
- Brominated flame retardant-free
- Mercury-free
- PVC-free internal cables
- Highly recyclable aluminum and glass enclosure

The greenest Apple display ever.

The LED Cinema Display is the most environmentally friendly display Apple has ever created.

Toxin free
One thing that makes the LED Cinema Display so remarkable is what it lacks. Namely, environmentally harmful mercury. And like the latest-generation iPod, iPhone, and Mac computers, the glass used in the display is arsenic-free. Even the internal cables and components are BFR- and PVC-free.

Highly recyclable
Because of its glass and aluminum construction, the LED Cinema Display is highly recyclable. So when you eventually part with it, rest assured it can be remade into something new.

ENERGY STAR
The LED Cinema Display is designed to meet the low power requirements set by the EPA and the U.S. Department of Energy, giving it the ENERGY STAR certification. The result is a display that reduces energy consumption and your carbon footprint.

EPEAT Gold
The Electronic Product Environmental Assessment Tool, or EPEAT, ranks the performance of a product throughout its lifecycle according to its environmental attributes. The LED Cinema Display earned the highest rating of EPEAT Gold.

Figure 10-7: Visit Apple online to research a product's green features.

Keep tabs on Apple's progress in achieving its green goals by visiting the company's green section of its Web site at www.apple.com/environment.

Looking at Green Windows Computers

Although Apple's high-stylin' products consistently make the company something of a media darling, lots of companies manufacturing computers that run Windows are just as ambitious when it comes to enacting — and being seen as a leader of — green policies, production processes, and recycling programs.

Go to the Energy Star (www.energystar.gov) and EPEAT (www.epeat.net) Web sites to find out whether a specific computer, printer, or peripheral is up to specifications when it comes to energy efficiency.

Note: At the time of this writing, the computers described in the following sections were not yet commercially available with Windows 7. Chances are good that updated models of these computers and a whole lot of others will ship with Windows 7.

To get the most thorough understanding of all things energy saving — especially with the PC you already own — check out Chapters 6 and 7. In those chapters, I tell you how to

✔ **Maximize your computer's energy-saving options:** Chapter 6 has the details.

✔ **Adjust specific Windows power options and tweak other settings for green personal computing:** I fully explain these options in Chapter 7.

✔ **Download and run easy-to-use energy-saving gadgets or applications:** One such gadget is Edison (it's free!), and I discuss it in Chapter 6.

Two green Windows desktops

The Dell Studio Hybrid PC isn't much bigger than a hardback book and can change its casing *skins* faster than a chameleon — and a bamboo one at that — while the HP TouchSmart IQ800t allows you to skip the keyboard and reach out and touch its screen to surf the Web. (In the nearby sidebar, "A teeny PC with its head in the clouds," I describe a third ecofriendly PC that deserves kudos even though it doesn't run Windows.)

Dell Studio Hybrid PC

The Dell Studio Hybrid PC earned EPEAT Gold status, which means it's among the greenest PCs you can buy. In my book, it also deserves the Best Dressed award as well, thanks to slip-on sleeves to change the computer's look and feel. Touchy-feely sleeve choices include a rainbow of colors, leather, and my favorite, bamboo.

Note: You need to add a keyboard, a mouse, and a monitor in order to interact with the Studio Hybrid. The following less superficial features make the Studio Hybrid an interesting green PC choice:

✔ **Smaller size:** Eighty percent smaller than standard desktops, which makes it easy to move from room to room.

✔ **Wireless options:** Wireless mouse and keyboard options follow along without tripping you up with cords; Wi-Fi networking keeps you tapped into the Internet no matter which room you wind up in.

✔ **Energy efficient processors:** Energy efficient Intel Core 2 Duo Mobile Processors sip as much — make that, as little — energy as a notebook rather than a hulking desktop PC.

✔ **TV tuners and Blu-ray:** An optional digital/analog TV tuner enables you to watch, pause, and record live TV — and reduce your carbon footprint by eliminating the need for a separate TV. An optional Blu-ray disc player turns it into a high-def movie theater in a box.

✔ **Efficient standards:** Uses about 70 percent less power than a typical desktop and meets Energy Star 4.0 standards with an 87 percent efficient power supply.

✔ **Recyclable packaging:** Packaging is made from 95 percent recyclable materials. In addition, the Hybrid comes with about 75 percent less printed documentation then typical tower desktops, so fewer materials are used in this regard, too.

✔ **System recycling kit:** Comes with a system recycling kit so that you can help preserve and protect the environment.

HP TouchSmart IQ800t series

Sandwiching the display screen and computer together makes the HP TouchSmart IQ800t, as shown in Figure 10-8, easy to move from room to room — or to the kitchen counter.

Figure 10-8: It *can* stand the heat in the kitchen.

Simply touch the screen to flip through recipes on the Web or change channels on the built-in TV. Earning EPEAT Silver status, the TouchSmart IQ800t balances energy efficiency with beefed up performance for playing high-end games or editing pictures with Photoshop.

Other features that make the HP TouchSmart IQ800t an interesting green PC choice include the ability to

- ✔ Hold video chats with the built-in Webcam and microphone

- ✔ Watch, pause, rewind, and record live high-def TV on the built-in wide-screen — which saves you (and the planet) from buying a new or second HDTV

- ✔ Expand as needed via the built-in pocket media drive bay and optional drive

- ✔ Reduce your PC energy use up to 45 percent

- ✔ Use 55 percent less metal and 35 percent less plastic than standard PCs and monitors

- ✔ Is packaged in a reduced amount of plastic foam cushioning

A pair of green Windows notebooks

Choosing one of these notebooks can be as easy as deciding which style suits you best: Are you a button-down business-type, or someone who likes to wear his oh-so-greenness on his sleeve where no one can miss it?

A teeny PC with its head in the clouds

By eliminating a built-in hard drive and skipping a cooling fan, the EPEAT Gold and Energy Star 4.0 rated Zonbu PC (www.zonbu.com), shown here, is a super energy-saving choice for light-weight duties, such as browsing the Web. The Zonbu PC is referred to as a *cloud* computer, which means you pay a monthly subscription to store your files on an Internet-based file service rather than on the computer itself. The Zonbu PC is less vulnerable to sneaky spyware or virus attacks because it runs on Linux rather than Windows, and, of course, you can't do anything with Zonbu PC until you plug in a monitor, a key-board, and a mouse, sold separately. Whether standalone, cloud-based, microsize PCs such as the Zonbu PC catch on (remember 3Com's Audrey or MSN TV — oh-oh, I think I'm dating myself), one thing seems certain: More and more smartphones and computers are tapping into cloud-based services, such as MobileMe, SugarSync, and others. Who says you can't be in two places at once?

In Chapter 1, I describe the Toshiba Portégé R600 which, at the time I was writing this book, had earned the title of "greenest notebook."

Lenovo ThinkPad X200s

Encased in protective Magnesium-alloy and armed with built-in airbag-like hard drive protection in case you drop it, the Lenovo ThinkPad X200s means serious business — and EPEAT Gold status means it's just as serious about saving energy as well.

You can carry around the 2.5 pound notebook without stressing your shoulder. You can also snap the notebook into an optional dock when you're home to ease eyestrain by turning it into a desktop with a keyboard, a mouse, and a monitor.

Standout aspects that make the ThinkPad X200s particularly ecofriendly include

- ✔ Custom power management features, low-voltage processors, a less power hungry display, and the latest battery technology to help you eek out up to 12 hours of all-day computing before it's time to plug in for a recharge.

- ✔ The solid-state drive option means no moving parts, faster performance, and less power consumption than a traditional hard drive.

- ✔ A spill-resistant keyboard, sealed and contained within a tray with special drain holes to channel spills to the bottom of the system to lessen opportunity for damage, means knocking your coffee on this notebook won't spell death.

- ✔ A fingerprint scanner embedded in the wrist rest ensures only your fingerprint can unlock the X200s and not a thief's.

- ✔ A built-in nightlight illuminates the keyboard in dark settings — drawing less energy than turning on a desk lamp or other room light.

ASUS U6V-V1-Bamboo Laptop

Enshrouded quite literally with nature, the ASUS U6V-V1 Bamboo notebook is, at its core, as ecofriendly on the inside as the outside.

Standout features that make this notebook the most eye-catching computer you've ever laid eyes on include

- ✔ EPEAT Gold status
- ✔ LED backlit LCD display that instantly turns on to full brightness and consumes less power than non-LED LCD displays

- ✔ Super Hybrid Engine extends battery life between 35–53 percent when compared to other notebooks

- ✔ A security fingerprint scanner to protect your identity and personal files in the event of loss or theft

- ✔ A built-in Webcam with face-scanning capabilities for even greater personal identity protection and security

- ✔ Instant movie-watching in ten seconds to save power without requiring the computer to fully boot up to Windows

Enjoying the beauty and bamboo touch isn't limited only to the ASUS notebook or the Dell Studio Hybrid PC, which I describe earlier in the "Two ecofriendly Windows desktops" section. Bamboo-accented peripherals and computer-related add-ons are just some of the choices I show you in Chapter 17.

Chapter 11

Buying Green Mobile Phones and Handheld Gadgets

*Y*ou've come to the right place if you're looking for the latest multiple-personality gadgets — including MP3 and video players, handheld video games, e-book readers, and supersmart phones that pull quadruple duty on all those products — because they *are* those products yet also happen to work as phones.

Other handheld or multifaceted green gadgets covered in this chapter include windup radios with built-in flashlights that convert your elbow grease into raw power and a solar-powered Bluetooth headset that gets its charge from daylight.

Getting Up to Speed on Green Gadget Matters

Choosing green mobile phones and other multiple-personality gadgets such as iPods or windup radios (see the Freeplay Companion in Figure 11-1) means keeping in mind a number of ecofriendly factors. A few examples of green gadget personality traits include gadgets which:

✔ **Are manufactured, distributed, and eventually taken back and recycled by companies that use fewer — or zero — toxins:** These companies also practice the highest level of ecofriendly compliance possible, as judged by organizations such as Greenpeace, the EPA's Energy Star program, and the Consumer Electronics Association.

✔ **Are highly energy-efficient:** A gadget uses the least amount of energy while offering the longest battery life possible, thereby decreasing how frequently you plug it in to the recharger.

✔ **Can be charged using energy sources other than a wall outlet:** Some examples include built-in cranks to recharge gadgets by winding the crank, or a built-in solar panel that can convert sunlight to energy — two features you'll find on the combination radio/flash light shown in Figure 11-1.

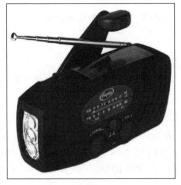

Figure 11-1: Turning elbow grease into energy.

Before forking over your hard-earned greenbacks for a new green gadget, check manufacturer Web sites, green-gadget blogs, and product-review Web sites to find the latest green gadget information. In Chapter 9, I explain how you can find out how companies and the products they build rate among each other in ecofriendliness. A good starting point is the Greenpeace *Guide to Greener Electronics,* which I discuss further in that chapter.

Taking my own advice (which I give in Chapter 9), I selected the assortment of green gadgets populating the following pages to illustrate ecofriendlier factors, features, and follow-through at the end of the products' lifecycles. Of course, keep in mind that this overview is subject to change. New gadgets are introduced every day; new models and updated versions are par for the course.

After buying your new phone, check out Chapter 4 to find the most energy-efficient ways to use your green gadgets.

Ready to shop?

Dialing in to Green Mobile Phones

Choosing the greenest mobile phone — or carrier, as described in the nearby sidebar, "CREDO's green mobile phone mission" — can be helped by researching the latest models on the Web. Opening your Web browser and searching for **greenest cellphone** or **greenest mobile phone** turns up a number of results that point to stories or product pages for mobile phones claiming the title.

Knowing whether the claims are still current (or, for that matter, accurate) can be tricky. Was the claim staked last week — or last year? Using the Google Advanced Search option can help you winnow your results to show recent ones rather than older ones that have become outdated.

To use the Google Advanced Search option to search for new or recent green mobile phones:

1. **Type** google.com/advanced_search **in your Web browser's address field and press Return or Enter.**

2. **In the Find Web Pages That Have All These Words field, type** greenest mobile phone.

3. **Scroll down to the middle of the page and click Date, Usage Rights, Numeric Range, and More, as shown in Figure 11-2.**

4. **Click the Date pop-up button and select Past Week or Past Month (refer to Figure 11-2), and then click Advanced Search in the lower-right corner.**

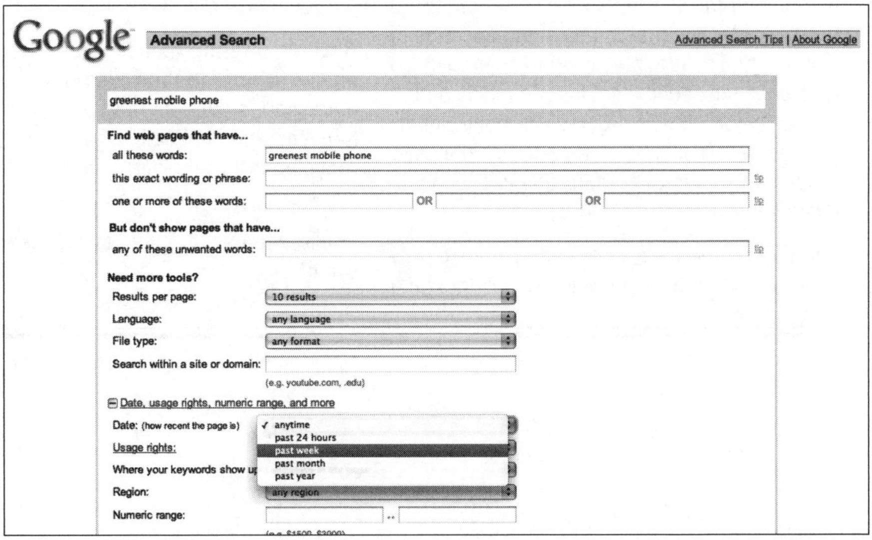

Figure 11-2:
Narrow
search
results by
date.

Google Advanced Search   Advanced Search Tips | About Google

greenest mobile phone

Find web pages that have...
all these words: greenest mobile phone
this exact wording or phrase: tip
one or more of these words: OR   OR   tip

But don't show pages that have...
any of these unwanted words: tip

Need more tools?
Results per page: 10 results
Language: any language
File type: any format
Search within a site or domain:
                          (e.g. youtube.com, .edu)

⊟ Date, usage rights, numeric range, and more
Date: (how recent the page is)   ✓ anytime
                                   past 24 hours
Usage rights: past week
                                   past month
Where your keywords show u   past year
Region: any region
Numeric range:
                          (e.g. $1500..$3000)

Using this search method, as well as contacting company sources and using the resources I talk about in Chapter 9, all helped me choose the following handful of mobile phones that epitomize the greenest gadgets money can buy.

You might notice that one visible product — the Apple iPhone — is absent from the roster of green mobile phones. At the time this book was written, the iPhone 3G still contained not-so-nice-for-the-environment toxins, as detailed by Greenpeace in the report *Missed call: the iPhone's hazardous chemicals* (www.greenpeace.org/usa/news/iphone-s-hazardous-chemicals). Apple got it right for the iPod nano, however, which I detail later in this chapter.

CREDO's green mobile phone mission

"It was the greed-is-good 1980s. Gordon Gekko, and all that," says CREDO Mobile CEO Laura Scher. "A lot of my friends got out of college and headed straight to Wall Street. But I wanted something different — or rather, I wanted to make a difference." And so began the story of CREDO (www.credomobile.com), a mobile-phone provider that is on a mission to be the greenest carrier in the world.

Originally founded as Working Assets in 1985, the company was formed by a small group of idealists aiming to further causes such as human rights, women's rights, peace, and environmentalism. The vision was simple: to turn everyday purchases into automatic acts of generosity. The group developed an innovative long-distance service that functioned as both a phone company and a progressive lobby, donating 1 percent of monthly phone-bill payments to progressive nonprofit organizations chosen by customers.

The Working Assets movement grew steadily over the next 23 years, providing steadily growing support for a wide range of progressive nonprofits, before making the leap to mobile phones, which prompted a new name to better reflect its charter: CREDO Mobile.

At the time this book was written, CREDO says that it and its members have donated more than $60 million to the groups that members themselves help select, including Doctors Without Borders, the American Civil Liberties Union, the Global Fund for Women, Greenpeace, and Planned Parenthood. Along the way, CREDO has generated 5,652,914 letters, 15,785,829 e-mails, and 932,992 calls to political and corporate decision-makers.

Besides offering mobile phones and service plans, CREDO Mobile also sells ecofriendly accessories such as the Iqua solar Bluetooth headset, and cool cellphone cases made from recycled tires salvaged from Colombian cargo trucks.

"Hello, Mother Nature? Can you hear me now? Good!"

Ranking the greenest mobile phones

At the time this book was written, the latest Greenpeace *Guide to Greener Electronics* report (www.greenpeace.org/electronics) gave top honors to Nokia 6210 Navigator smartphone, followed by the Sony Ericsson G900. Both devices are PVC-free, but the Nokia gadget earned extra credits for its better energy efficiency and lifecycle.

Judging cellphones, the Samsung SGH-F268 came in first, followed by the Motorola V9, the Nokia 3110 Evolve, the Sony Ericsson C905, and the LG Electronics KT520, taking fifth place. In the report, Greenpeace stated that the phone makers have taken major steps in reducing toxic chemicals, and "all but the LG phone claimed to be PVC-free, and Samsung's phone being free of BFRs, well below the commonly used so-called 'halogen-free' industry limit of 900ppm bromine."

Motorola MOTO W233 Renew

www.motorola.com

Motorola states that the MOTO W233 Renew, shown in Figure 11-3, is the world's first carbon-neutral cellphone, thanks in part to a plastic housing made entirely from recycled water bottles. The phone ships in a smaller package, and it and all the printed materials inside it are made from 100 percent post-consumer recycled paper.

As the first mobile phone to earn carbonfree certification, Motorola's alliance with Carbondfund.org means that the company offsets the amount of carbon dioxide it uses to manufacture, distribute, and use the phone.

Other green perks are described in this list:

- **Longer-lasting charge.** Motorola estimates that you can expect up to nine hours of talk time with the Renew — which means less tapping in to the recharger and more energy savings for you.

- **Trees are planted.** Furthering the phone's ecofriendly theme, mobile carrier T-Mobile will plant a tree in your name if you sign up for the company's paperless billing option. Partnering with the Arbor Day Foundation, T-Mobile reportedly planted more than a half-million trees in 2008.

- **Recycling is made easy.** To recycle the phone at the end of its life, you can just drop it off at the nearest T-Mobile phone store, or mail it in, using a pre-printed mailing label you create on the T-Mobile or Motorola Web sites.

✔ **Sustainability is ongoing.** Proceeds gained from T-Mobile's handset-recycling efforts contribute to the company's social investments, and to schools participating in Race to Recycle, which is part of T-Mobile's sustainability practice.

Although the MOTO W233 Renew was offered exclusively to T-Mobile customers for six months after it launched in early 2009, your carrier may be offering the green mobile phone by the time you read this. To find out, visit your carrier's Web site and browse the selection of mobile phones its supports and sells.

Figure 11-3:
Your phone's housing brought to you by recycled water bottles.

Samsung SGH-W510, SGH-F268, and E200 Eco

www.samsung.com

Even though you couldn't buy either product at the time I wrote this chapter, the Samsung SGH-F268 earned top honors in the 2008 Greenpeace *Guide to Greener Electronics,* and the SGH-W510 made news as the first mobile phone to use parts made from *bioplastics,* which are extracted from natural material such as corn. Both phones highlight developments worth keeping in mind when considering other mobile phones and their makers.

Samsung says it uses no dangerous metals (lead, mercury, or cadmium) when producing SGH-W510, and that the SGH-F268 and all its accessories contain no BFRs (brominated flame retardants) or PVCs.

An alarm feature alerts you when the SGH-F268 is fully charged, to encourage you to unplug the charger.

Combining the best of both mobile phones is the Samsung E200 Eco, shown in Figure 11-4, which is encased entirely in corn-based bioplastics. It features a built-in alarm that reminds you to unplug the charger when the battery is fully charged.

Figure 11-4:
The E200 Eco is oh-so-corny — and green.

Nokia 3110 Evolve and N79 eco

www.nokia.com

Featuring biocovers made from more than 50 percent renewable materials and a charger that draws 94 percent less power than Energy Star requires, the Nokia 3110 Evolve is a good example of a green mobile phone.

Going one step beyond the Samsung SGH-F268 alarm that reminds you to unplug the charger at full charge, the 3110 Evolve charger notches down power consumption to next-to-nil after the phone is all charged up.

Phoning the future: Nokia Eco Sensor Concept

At the time this book was written, Nokia held the top spot on the Greenpeace *Guide to Greener Electronics* (www.greenpeace.org/electronics). Inventing a mobile phone that taps into wearable sensors that analyze your body's vital signs and your immediate environmental surroundings is what Nokia envisions with its Eco Sensor Concept (www.nokia.com/A4707477).

Charging the Nokia N79 when you take it out of its minimal, ecofriendly box isn't an option — unless you plug in a charger you already own. Nokia, figuring that it's greener to reuse an existing charger, doesn't include one with the N79 eco, pictured in Figure 11-5.

Neither phone was available in the U.S. at the time this book was written, but buyers in the United Kingdom can feel good knowing that Nokia donates 4 pounds sterling to the World Wildlife Fund for each N79 eco it sells.

Figure 11-5: Battery included — but not a charger.

Looking at Green MP3 and Video Players, and Other Entertaining Gadgets

Greenpeace lavished praise on Apple for eliminating PVCs and BFRs from its newest iPods — which is why I'm citing the world's most popular music and video player to kick off this section. The other three music and video players I describe here are also greener choices — two of them get their juice fix from the sun, and the other powers up from good old-fashioned elbow grease.

iPod nano

www.apple.com

Specifically, the latest Apple iPod nano is greener than its predecessors because it

- ✔ Has an arsenic-free glass display
- ✔ Contains no brominated flame retardants (BFRs)
- ✔ Contains no mercury
- ✔ Contains no PVCs
- ✔ Is housed in a highly recyclable metal casing

Add to that list the fact that the iPod nano ships in a minimum-size, recyclable package, and the sum of those parts equals a fine example of a green music and video player choice if you're in the market to buy one. The nano is also a great entertainer for playing games, with downloadable titles such as *Tetris, Pac-Man,* and *Uno.*

Downloading movies and music from the Apple iTunes music store (or ripping CDs you already own) and playing them on the iPod nano, shown in Figure 11-6, uses less energy than spinning the disc equivalents in a CD or DVD player.

Figure 11-6:
Doing away with spinning CDs as a way to listen to music.

Shiro SQ-S solar-powered media player

www.shirocorp.com

Although it isn't readily available in the United States, the Shiro SQ-S solar-powered media player, shown in Figure 11-7, deserves a nod because it's such a bright idea. The gadget gets its charge from a USB cable plugged into your computer, as well as sunlight beaming on its backside when you're out and about. Perhaps other music and video player makers will follow the clever lead of Shiro and start slapping solar panels to the backs of their products.

Figure 11-7:
Sunshine charges the Shiro SQ-S player.

Baylis Eco Media Player

www.ecomediaplayer.com

Winding the Eco Media Player for one minute can provide you with up to 45 minutes of play time to listen to music or FM radio, watch video, or flip through digital photos. The windup gizmo, shown in Figure 11-8, is also a flashlight, recorder, backup device, and emergency mobile phone charger. (Now, that's what I call a multiple-personality product!)

Incidentally, the Eco Media Player is brought to you by the inventor of the world's first windup radio, Trevor Baylis, whose other human-powered gadgets are described in this chapter's final section, "Getting Wound Up Over Green Windup Gadgets."

Figure 11-8:
Wind it up
to listen to
your music.

eMotion Solar Portable media player

http://emotionbuzz.com

Like the Baylis Eco Media Player, the eMotion Solar Portable, from Media Street (see Figure 11-9), can also charge your cellphone or another USB-capable gadget you plug into it. You can play games on the eMotion portable (which you can't do on the Baylis), read e-books on it, or have it read them aloud to you, even while you're listening to soothing music!

Figure 11-9:
Music, video, games, and e-books — busy, isn't it?

Saving Trees by Reading E-Books

Reading e-books on your cellphone, PDA, notebook computer, or dedicated e-book reader — instead of accumulating printed books — helps save trees. It also reduces the other drains on the planet's resources associated with printing and distributing books.

I list in this section mobile and computer e-book (and magazine) reader programs, dedicated e-book reading devices, and the electronic bookstores you can go to browse and download e-books for free or for a price.

Mobile phone and computer e-book readers

Chances are good that you already own an excellent e-book reader without realizing it: your cellphone, smartphone, PDA, or (of course) computer. Browsing, downloading, and reading free and competitively priced e-books on your cellphone, smartphone, or computer is merely a matter of installing an e-book reader program.

Feedbooks

```
http://feedbooks.com
```

The universal e-reading platform Feedbooks is compatible with a wide range of mobile devices, including the dedicated readers listed in the next section and numerous mobile phones and PDAs. Download titles directly to your mobile phone or PDA by opening `http://feedbooks.mobi` with your gadget's Web browser.

Feedbooks also offers a library where you can download thousands of free e-books, publish and share your own content, and create customized newspapers from Really Simple Syndication (RSS) feeds and widgets.

Mobipocket Reader

```
http://mobipocket.com
```

Mobipocket Reader runs on Windows computers and on mobile phones and PDAs that run on the Windows Mobile, Palm OS, Symbian, and Blackberry operating systems. The program is free, but the more than 65,000 titles available on the Web site are not.

Downloading titles to your computer then installing them to read on your mobile device is required for all but the Blackberry version of the program. Downloading books "over the air," directly to your Blackberry, means you can skip the computer "middleman" step.

The Mobipocket Reader Web site also offers news and other RSS feeds. Tapping into them to create your own, custom newspaper can keep you up-to-date on news and other topics when you're on the go.

The Web site also offers dictionaries, medical texts, self-help books, and language-learning titles.

eReader.com and FictionWise.com

The eReader e-book reader program runs on Windows and Mac desktops and notebooks, as well as on many mobile devices running Windows Mobile, Pocket PC, Palm OS, or Symbian operating systems.

The iPhone and iPod touch edition of eReader, shown in Figure 11-10, can download titles directly from your online bookshelf account that you registered with either eReader.com or Fictionwise.com or both.

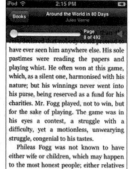

Figure 11-10:
E-books —
a pleasure
on your
iPhone.

eReader on the iPhone is my favorite way to read e-books. The text is beautifully crisp, and the display is large and easy enough on my eyes that I prefer reading on the iPhone to reading on a larger, dedicated reader such as the Kindle 2.

Another reason for this preference is the backlit iPhone display, which is pleasant to read in bed with the lights turned off. Like real books, the Kindle 2 and most other dedicated e-book readers are readable only when the lights are turned on, or in daylight.

Other downloadable e-book reader programs

Other e-book reader programs for computers and mobile devices worth checking out include

- **iSilo:** Runs on Windows computers and many popular mobile phones and devices, including Blackberry, Palm, Pocket PC, Windows Mobile, iPhone, and lots of others. It's at www.isilo.com.

- **Plucker:** The same as in the first bullet, and for Macs too! Check out www.plkr.org.

- **Stanza:** An iPhone and iPod touch reader, with the ability to connect to numerous online bookstores to download free and for-sale books, including Feedbooks, Fictionwise, Project Gutenberg, SmashWords, and a number of mainstream publishers. Visit www.lexcycle.com.

E-book formats and other fun facts

I visited the Manybook.net About page (`http://manybook.net/about`) to see a running count of e-books downloaded in each supported format. My visit revealed the ubiquitous Adobe .PDF format at the top of the electronic bookshelf, and Apple's ahead-of-its-time Newton PDA (circa late 1980s) was at the bottom of the pile, so to speak. The formats and number of downloads (as of this writing) for each one are shown in the following table.

E-Book Format	Downloads	E-Book Format	Downloads
Cellphone (.JAR)	120,391	Mobipocket-mobi	96,266
ePub	178,151	Bookmarklet	154,679
FictionBook	2,778	TCR	1,819
iPhone Books.app	28,268	iLiad PDF	22,129
iPod	83,561	Custom HTML	46,924
iSilo	260,832	Sony (Librie, Reader)	231,676
Microsoft LIT	820	Newton	564
Palm Doc	362,565	Mobipocket	341,086
PDF	1,450,791	eReader	680,812
Plucker	529,274	Large Print PDF	488,081
RTF	300,804	Kindle	264,907
zTXT	17,921	Rocketbook	8,449

The Web site's About page also includes links to a ranking of the top 20 titles downloaded in past years. Visitors downloaded 4,624,184 copies of 22,670 titles in 2008. The top download? *The Art of War,* by Sun Tzu, downloaded 34,057 times.

Dedicated e-book readers

Dedicated e-book readers offer larger displays that have the look and feel of the real paper-based books they replace. This look and feel can provide a more familiar and enjoyable way to get lost in a good book. But dedicated e-book readers have pros and cons, just like any other product. A few things to keep in mind when considering dedicated e-book readers is that they

- ✔ Are generally not backlit, which means you read them in daylight or with the lights turned on
- ✔ Can last weeks on a single charge
- ✔ Let you zoom text up or down to suit your type-size taste
- ✔ Typically let you read other content, such as newspapers, Web-based RSS feeds, blogs, and more
- ✔ Can connect to your computer, wirelessly "over the air," or both, to download e-books and other reading materials
- ✔ May "blink" when you turn the virtual page, which I find distracting. The original Kindle, the Kindle 2, and original Sony Reader are all blinkers, but the latest Sony Reader (selling now) is not a blinker.

Amazon Kindle 2

amazon.com/kindle

As thin as a magazine, lighter than most paperbacks, and capable of browsing and downloading books and other content over the air from Amazon's library of more than 230,000 books, the Kindle 2, pictured in Figure 11-11, is a dream-come-true gadget for serious book lovers.

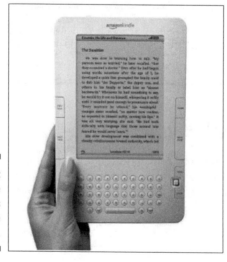

Figure 11-11:
The Kindle 2 screen is easy on the eyes.

Although Amazon's first Kindle was something of a clunker, the new Kindle 2 is a joy to behold — and listen to, thanks to a text-to-speech feature that turns any book into an audio book. The 6-inch black-and-white screen is so sharp that you'll think you're looking at ink on paper — no wonder they call it E-Ink!

Books, newspapers, and blogs are downloaded in fewer than 60 seconds, and the Kindle 2 rechargeable battery lasts up to four days with the wireless feature turned on. Turn it off, and you can keep turning the Kindle 2 virtual pages for up to two weeks.

What's more, Amazon's free Kindle application for the iPhone allows you to continue reading on your smartphone where you left off, in case you forgot to pack your Kindle 2 or decided to leave it behind.

Sony PRS-700BC Reader Digital Book

`www.sonystyle.com/reader`

The Sony Reader Digital Book, shown in Figure 11-12, one-ups other dedicated e-book readers by offering a built-in LED reading light for low-lighting situations. But you can't download e-books to it over the air the way you can with the Kindle 2.

Figure 11-12:
Reading light included.

To find reading material for it, first you download books from Sony's "tens of thousands" of titles and then connect the Reader to your Windows computer (sorry, Mac folks) to make the transfer. A virtual keyboard lets you make notes — or use the included stylus to highlight text on the display.

Iliad Reader

```
http://irextechnologies.com
```

Like the dedicated e-book readers described earlier, the Iliad (shown in Figure 11-13), presents text in a lifelike way — as though you're truly looking at ink on paper — and the 10.2-inch display makes it the largest reader money can buy. The Iliad also does something the other two cannot: It lets you write on the display to make notes, underline text, add comments to documents, or entertain yourself with crossword and Sudoku puzzles.

Figure 11-13: Reading *and* writing are the Iliad's talents.

Besides sketching on the screen, you can also use the stylus to navigate menus and pages, and like the other dedicated readers, the Iliad earns ecofriendly kudos because it consumes power only when you turn the page.

Electronic bookstores

Here is a brief list of electronic libraries where you can go to browse and download books, magazines, and other content:

- **Manybooks.net:** Downloading all the e-books you want from the ManyBooks.net collection of more than 23,000 titles doesn't cost you a penny. That's right, they're all free — and ready to read with your favorite reader program or device. Supported formats include those shown in the nearby sidebar, "E-book formats and other fun facts." Links to assorted e-book conversion utilities and formatting tools can help you adjust your chosen titles to work with your reader program or device.

The owner of the site, Matthew McClintock, maintains it as a service to the Internet community at large, and donations are welcome.

✔ **Read Green Initiative:** The Read Green Initiative (at `http://gore adgreen.com`) offers free access to an alternative, ecofriendly way to read magazines, books, and other publications on your desktop or notebook computer. Visit the Web site to select your free one-year subscription to one of a number of magazines, including *Men's Journal, Elle, Reader's Digest, Car and Driver, Popular Science,* and *U.S. News and World Report.*

The Read Green Initiative is organized and powered by Zinio, the world's largest publisher and distributor of digital magazines, and is supported by a number of well-known publishers and other large companies.

When you purchase additional digital magazine subscriptions, a portion of the proceeds are used to purchase eco unit credits, to buy trees. A visit to Zinio's main Web site (www.zinio.com) is where you can also find links to more than 100 classic novels, textbooks, and other publications.

Getting Wound Up Over Green Windup Gadgets

Earlier in this chapter, I described the Baylis Eco Media Player, which you can charge by winding its built-in crank. Sold by and named after the man who invented the windup radio, Trevor Baylis, his company also sells a slew of other human-powered gadgets and gizmos:

```
www.tclproducts.co.uk/baylisnextgeneration.html
```

Listed in this section is a smattering of crank-to-charge products made by Baylis and other human-powered gadget makers:

✔ **Baylis LED Eco Safety Station:** Having a flashlight on hand in case the lights go out is always wise — especially when your elbow grease charges the battery inside. The station comes with a trio of Eco Mini Pro Torch flashlights which, when cranked for a minute, provide 25 minutes of light. Keep winding and you can attain a total charge of up to five hours.

✔ **Baylis Mini Eco Radio (see Figure 11-14):** The windup radio has come a long way since Trevor's original invention — as epitomized by this product. Wind the crank to charge the combination AM/FM radio, flashlight, and emergency cellphone charger, or let the built-in solar panel soak up some rays to help keep the gizmo charged.

Figure 11-14:
It's a flash-
light and
radio, all in
one.

✔ **Slik-Stik walking stick:** Invented by Baylis protégé Denise Anstey, a dis- abled woman who was dissatisfied with poorly designed walking sticks, the Slik-Stik has a built-in crank to charge superbright LED lights that shine a forward beam and a footfall flashlight for safe footing in the dark. Other James Bond-like features include a panic button that sounds an alarm if you need assistance, and another press can activate the Slik- Stik's high-intensity red strobe lights, when you're trekking near high- traffic roads and crosswalks.

✔ **Freeplay Jonta:** Advertised as the last flashlight you'll need to buy, this heavy-duty windup torch has superbright LED lights, and a rugged case to take hard knocks.

✔ **Katio Voyager KA500 (see Figure 11-15):** Designed to serve during emergencies and disasters, a built-in USB jack lets you plug in and charge your iPod, cellphone, digital camera, or another gadget — after, of course, you charge up the Voyager by cranking the handle or letting the sunlight shine down on its built-in solar panel. An efficient LED lamp can be used for low-lighting situations such as reading, or amped up for fuller flashlight functioning.

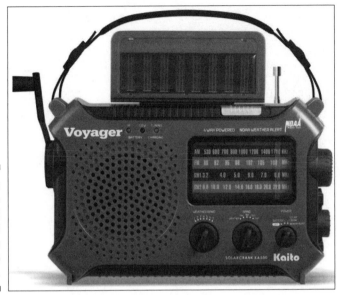

Figure 11-15: Stay connected and informed when the lights go out.

Chapter 12

Getting Green Gadgets for on the Go

. . . .

In This Chapter

▶ Learning the art of hypermiling

▶ Using efficiency gizmos in your car

▶ Getting around more efficiently with GPS and mobile-phone apps

▶ Working out with green fitness gadgets

▶ Charging up with portable power chargers and extenders

▶ Going places with green garments, bags, and cases

. . . .

The choices and options I focus on in this chapter are all about gadgets for on the go. Whether it's GPS-savvy gizmos to help you plot the most direct route between points A and B (saving on gas along the way), or harnessing the recharging power of the wind or sun by wearing gadgets on your body that do just that, getting out of the house with greener gadgets is what's in store here.

Lastly, I take you on a tour of some superstylin', ecofriendly, gadgetcentric garments, gizmo cases, and notebook bags — items that help you keep all those other gadgets safe and dry.

Driving Your Car More Efficiently

Want to save gas, money, and time? You can — by employing efficient driving habits and smartly plotting your course. The term *hypermiling* refers to the practice of driving more efficiently and safely by anticipating traffic and road conditions and adjusting speed accordingly. That means braking less by allowing more space when slowing to a stop and then *slowly* increasing speed when you start moving again.

As the Hypermiling.com Web site puts it, *hypermiling* can reward you with fuel-efficiency savings that lower not only your car's carbon footprint but also how much you spend at the pump. The term *hypermiling* was coined by Wayne Gerdes, whom hypermilers consider the father of the, ah, *movement* (no pun intended!). Gerdes is known to get an average of 50 miles out of every gallon of gasoline he pumps into his Honda Accord, thanks to hypermiling techniques.

Making modifications to their cars and installing gadgets to track their vehicle's fuel efficiency vitals and other factors is another thing hypermilers do to achieve greater savings. I discuss those types of gadgets in the later section "Tricking Out Your Car with Efficiency Gizmos."

Visit these Web sites to find out more about driving more efficiently, reducing how much you spend at the pump, and, subsequently, lowering your car's carbon footprint:

- ✔ www.fueleconomy.gov: Operated by the United States Department of Energy/Energy Efficiency and Renewable Energy and the U.S. Environmental Protection Agency, the site offers tips, mileage calculators, news and feature stories, and tools to help you find the lowest gas prices in your region.

- ✔ www.epa.gov/fueleconomy: The United States Environmental Protection Agency's official subsection of its Web site treats all things fuel economy — with links to news, guides to increase your car's fuel efficiency, and other, related content.

- ✔ http://ecomodder.com: The site bills itself as "an automotive community where performance is judged by fuel economy rather than power and speed." The site offers more than 100 hypermiling tips, a discussion forum, and a garage where fellow hypermilers post their vehicles' current mileage, thanks to modifications they've made to their cars (and future mods they intend to make).

- ✔ www.cleanmpg.com: Check out news, reviews, member mileage logs, and a forum for discussing topics such as ways of increasing fuel economy to attain better mileage (MPG) and to lower the emissions produced by your car.

Tricking Out Your Car with Efficiency Gizmos

Maintaining, monitoring, and motoring along with the help of eco-oriented auto gadgets can help you save gas and money, and in the case of the second pair in the following list, save yourself from distractions and possible mishaps.

If matching smaller, more energy-efficient auto surround systems with the latest compact, fuel-efficient hybrids sounds like a good idea to you, take a look at the following sidebar, "Driving music to greener ears."

The following gadgets are examples of different ways you can green your ride:

✔ **Kiwi "drive green" computer:** Plug the PLX Kiwi computer into your car's service port and then start driving like a hypermiler, thanks to the gizmo's series of lesson plans designed to help you optimize your driving behavior to maximize fuel efficiency.

The PLX Kiwi monitors your car's vitals and your driving style, and the lessons teach greener motoring techniques that focus on smoothness, drag, acceleration, and deceleration. PLX estimates that you can increase your fuel efficiency as much as 33 percent. Visit www. plxkiwi.com.

✔ **Iqua Vizor SUN and LG solar Bluetooth car kit:** Soaking up the sun through the front windshield is how these two Bluetooth speakerphone kits get their charge. If your mobile phone can dial calls by listening to your voice, one of these kits can cut the distraction — and danger — normally associated with fiddling with your phone while driving.

The Iqua model clips to your car's sun visor — perfect for picking up your voice but a little counterintuitive because you must set it on your dashboard so that the sun can reach its solar panel when it's time for a recharge. Iqua estimates that you can talk for as long as 20 hours between charges. Check it out at www.iqua.com.

The LG solution mounts to your windshield, giving you one hour of talk time for every 2 hours of exposure, for an estimated 16 total hours of talk time. Go to www.lge.com to find out more.

✔ **Coffee cup power inverter:** Parking the PowerLine power-inverting cup in your car's drink holder, shown in Figure 12-1, provides two 120-volt AC outlets to juice household gear such as TVs, video game consoles, or other devices you would normally plug into a wall outlet. A USB port can keep your mobile phone or other portable gadget charged up so that you're good to go when you get where you're going. Visit www.powerline.com.

Figure 12-1:
Don't try
drinking
from this
cup!

✔ **Accutire digital programmable tire gauge:** Maintaining the correct pressure in your car's tires can go a long way toward helping you achieve better fuel efficiency. Checking your tire pressure with the Accutire digital tire gauge (http://measurement-ltd.com) takes the guesswork or inaccuracy out of old-fashioned mechanical gauges, and the built-in LED flashlight makes using it at night a breeze.

✔ **CarChip Pro:** Skipping in-car displays (such as the ScanGauge II, at the end of this list), the CarChip Pro plugs into your car's on-board diagnostics port (ODB), typically located beneath the steering wheel or dashboard.

As you drive, the CarChip Pro (www.davisnet.com) reads and stores data from your car's on-board computer, continuously logging driving and engine performance. You read your car's results by unplugging the CarChip Pro from your car and plugging it into your computer's USB port and running the included program.

✔ **Spotlight rechargeable flashlight:** Put your car's cigarette lighter to greener, healthier-living use by swapping in this tiny but superbright rechargeable flashlight. The shining little wonder can burn for as long as two hours before you need to plug it back in for a recharge. Go to www.12vspotlight.com.

✔ **ScanGauge II 3-in-1 automotive computer:** Staying on top of your car's vital statistics can help you squeeze out more miles per gallon between fill-ups. The ScanGauge II (www.scangauge.com) taps into your car's every efficiency-related factor to provide real-time feedback such as miles per gallon, fuel/distance to empty, horsepower, cost per mile and trip, and troubleshooting data so that you can fix your ride when the Check Engine light appears.

Driving music to greener ears

Making its debut performance in the Chevrolet Volt, the Extended-Range Electric Vehicle from General Motors is the new Bose Energy Efficient Series audio sound system.

Bose (www.bose.com) claims the following numbers for this in-car sound gear, compared to typical sound systems:

- ✔ 30 percent smaller
- ✔ 40 percent lighter
- ✔ 50 percent less energy usage

Bose achieves the series' design goals by using smaller and more efficient components. To cut energy consumption in half, Bose employs high-motor-force speakers, advanced switching amplification, and proprietary control circuitry. Because the components are smaller and lighter, overall vehicle mass is decreased, which can help increase fuel efficiency. The Bose Energy Efficient Series sound system meets the demands of smaller, more energy-efficient vehicles while providing quality sound — and that's music to any energy-conscious driver's ears.

Tapping into GPS and Mobile Phone Applications for Green Getting-around

A global positioning system (GPS) navigator in your car can help you get where you're going in the most fuel- and time-efficient manner. To find out more about GPS issues, check out *GPS For Dummies,* 2nd Edition, by Joel McNamara (Wiley Publishing). You can use a GPS navigator to calculate your route in multiple ways: by getting directions based on factors such as taking the fastest or shortest route and skipping toll highways and roads. You can also map out routes for walking or biking.

Most portable GPS navigators come with hardware for mounting them on your car's dashboard or to the windshield. (Note, however, that a windshield mount can tip off thieves that your gadget might be in the glove box, as the following sidebar "Stop that GPS thief!" points out.) if you don't have GPS, don't feel left out. Pull on up to the nearby sidebar, "Picking up poor man's GPS — sort of," to learn about mobile apps and Web sites you can use even if you don't have a GPS device.

The GPS mapping programs bundled with mobile phones (such as T-Mobile's G1 or Apple's iPhone) don't typically offer spoken turn-by-turn directions or some of the other features found on dedicated navigators. They do offer scalable color maps and point-to-point directions, as shown in Figure 12-2. Of course, you can always add the turn-by-turn direction capability to your mobile phone — for a price — as I describe in the upcoming section, "Talking mobile phone GPS navigator apps."

Figure 12-2: Getting you there, step by step.

Stop that GPS thief!

Newsflash: GPS navigators have taken the top spot as the number-one item snatched from cars. According to the Federal Bureau of Investigation, portable-navigation-snatching rose 700 percent between 2006 and 2008, where nearly 25,000 of the good-direction-givers were illegally separated from their rightful owners.

A 2007 study cited that spotting a suction-cup mount on the inside windshield motivates many a thief to break in and grab GPS navigators tucked in glove boxes or beneath seats (thoughtfully grabbing anything else they can get their hands on as well, of course).

Removing your GPS navigator's windshield mount can make it seem less noticeable, however the suction-cup mark left behind may be an even bigger lure because it means you're hiding something the thieves are looking to get their hands on. Wiping away the suction cup mark is one option, as is switching to a friction mount that's easy to remove from the dashboard and secret in the glove box with your navigator if you still prefer to leave it behind when you exit the car.

Picking up poor man's GPS — sort of

Downloading or tapping into one or more of these free mobile-phone mapping programs and Web sites can help you find directions even if you don't have GPS:

✔ **Google Maps** (`http://google.com/m`): A mini-version of Google Maps is part of a suite of several Google Mobile apps, including Gmail, Calendar, Earth, Photos, Translate, and YouTube.

✔ **MapQuest 4 Mobile** (`http://mapquest.com/mq4m`): This freebie mobile phone application provides an easy-to-use interface for finding directions, maps, aerial imagery, and traffic information.

✔ **MapQuest for Mobile Web** (`mapquest.com`): Get the same stuff available in MapQuest 4 Mobile (see preceding bullet) without running an application by accessing MapQuest from your mobile phone's Web browser.

✔ **MapQuest Send to Cell:** Plan your trip using any using either of the two MapQuest methods above, then click the Send to Cell button to send the results to your mobile phone.

✔ **YellowPages.com** (`m.yellowpages.com`): You can access this mobile edition with your phone's Web browser or download the mini-app version to run on your phone.

Talking mobile phone GPS navigator apps

Buying and installing GPS navigator programs on your mobile phone or PDA can give your trusty gadget the ability to say directions out loud. You can run the programs on mobile phones that don't have built-in GPS by purchasing an optional (and external) Bluetooth GPS receiver.

Mobile GPS navigator applications that like to be seen *and* heard include

✔ **AmAze:** This free GPS navigation program has turn-by-turn voice directions, for a variety of GPS-equipped smartphones and PDAs, including Blackberry, LG, Samsung, Sony Ericsson, and Windows Mobile. Visit `http://amazegps.com`.

✔ **ALK Copilot Live 7:** Provides natural voice directions in 20 languages on a number of Pocket PC or Windows Mobile smartphones. Check out `http://alk.com`.

✔ **MapQuest Mobile Navigator:** Voice-guided GPS navigation service is offered by several of the major wireless carriers for about $50 per year.

✔ **Voice TeleNav GPS Navigator:** This one is available from all major mobile carriers for around $10 per month for unlimited service. TeleNav (`http://telenav.com`) provides turn-by-turn driving directions, both onscreen and by voice, on a number of popular GPS-equipped mobile phones, including Blackberry, HTC, Motorola, Palm, and other models.

Portable GPS navigators

Here are three portable GPS navigators that can literally tell you how to get where you want to go in the most efficient way:

- ✓ **TomTom GO 930:** Not only does the TomTom GO 930, shown in Figure 12-3, say out loud where and when to turn, but you can also tell *it* an address you want to visit by speaking aloud. The Map Share feature lets you update your maps according to up-to-the-minute changes (such as road closings or under-construction hours) that other drivers can see, and you can see their updates. Visit www.tomtom.com.

Figure 12-3:
Speak and
ye shall find.

Getting traffic updates requires the purchase of the optional RDS-TMC receiver, which is standard equipment in the pricier GO 930T. Cueing you to get in the correct lane before upcoming turns is one of the gadget's special talents, and built-in Bluetooth means you can pair your mobile phone with the GO 930 and use it as a handsfree speakerphone. (That's what I'm talkin' about!)

- ✓ **Garmin Nuvi 880:** As with the TomTom GO 930, you can tell the Garmin Nuvi 800 where you want to go by simply saying so, out loud. Thanks to the gizmo's multipersonality design and small form factor, the Nuvi 800 (www.garmin.com) is one GPS navigator you're not likely to leave behind when you get out of the car.

That's because it also plays MP3 music and audio books, converts currency and measurements, displays photo slide shows, and can keep you entertained with a slew of games, including Sudoku, Solitaire, and Video Poker. Pairing your mobile phone with the Nuvi 880's built-in Bluetooth capability automatically copies your phone book, making it easier for you to keep your eyes on the road to make and take calls without taking your hands off the wheel.

✔ **Magellan Maestro 4370:** Taking a page from your mobile phone's speed-dial function, the Magellan Maestro 4370 OneTouch feature can quickly pull up directions for favorite destinations (such as restaurants or businesses) with, well, a single touch of your finger.

Staying on top of traffic conditions is easier if you have help from the RDS/TMC receiver built into the gadget's bundled car charger. AAA reviews of hotels and restaurants make it a cinch to call and make a reservation, using the Maestro 4370's Bluetooth handsfree function, without even touching your mobile phone.

Like the Garmin Nuvi 880, the Maestro 4370 also plays music, and it one-ups the Nuvi by entertaining you with video you can load on it — after you park the car, of course! Check out `www.magellangps.com`.

GPS and green mobile phone apps

In addition to the GPS navigation applications mentioned a few pages back, the following seven mobile phone apps that also tap into GPS can help you minimize your car's carbon footprint — and your own:

✔ **Carbon-Meter:** Coming soon for Google Android and Blackberry smartphones, the iPhone version of Carbon-Meter rewards your ecofriendly activities and efforts with coupons and specials sponsored by local advertisers, as shown in Figure 12-4. Run, walk, or bike your way to increase your ecosavings — and your savings account! Visit `www.viralmesh.com/carbon-meter`.

✔ **Ecorio:** Running on a Google Android-based mobile phone near you, Ecorio (`http://ecorio.org`) taps into the phone's GPS feature to track your personal carbon footprint. Choosing your mode of travel — car, bus or train, or bike — determines how seriously green you are about getting around.

Ecorio suggests carpool options by matching up drivers and passengers, lets fellow greener-gadgeteers keep tabs on one another (in the same town or across the country), and offers an option to buy carbon offsets by way of Carbonfund.org.

✔ **greenMeter:** This iPhone and iPod Touch application can help you lower your car's effect on the environment by weighing parameters such as your vehicle's tonnage and the price of gas against how you drive. Tapping into the iPhone's built-in accelerometer to gauge the car's rate of forward acceleration, greenMeter calculates vehicle readings such as miles-per-gallon fuel efficiency and carbon footprint. Visit `http://hunter.pairsite.com/greenmeter`.

Figure 12-4:
Getting
there the
greener
way.

✔ **iNap:** As someone who has more than a few times missed a bus stop because the motion lulled me into a nap, the iPhone app iNap is a wake-up call to staying awake on the bus.

Tapping into the iPhone's GPS radio, iNap tracks my location and sounds an alarm as I'm nearing my final stop. Unfortunately, GPS reception doesn't reach underground to the subway, so for those treks I'm on my own as far as catching myself catnapping.

✔ **ShopSavvy:** If you're using a phone that runs the Google Android platform, you're in luck when it comes to savvier shopping. Point your phone at the bar code of any product, and ShopSavvy searches for the best price at stores near you, thanks to the gadget's GPS location finder, which keeps track of where you are and what's in the vicinity.

Pick the closest location with the lowest price, and save time and gas now that you're not running around all over the place looking for the best deal in town. Check it out at www.biggu.com.

✔ **UbiGreen:** Presently a research project and not yet something you can hold in your hand, UbiGreen (http://dub.washington.edu/projects/ubigreen) gauges how you get around to calculate how much CO_2 you saved during the week. Glancing at the UbiGreen background running on your cellphone, as shown in Figure 12-5, can help put your best foot forward as you take steps to reduce your carbon footprint.

✔ **Tracky:** Aimed at helping you navigate during off-road activities such as hiking, biking, skiing, driving, and camping, Tracky displays a large compass for staying on course, as shown in Figure 12-6. You can also let the program guide you to points of interest by voice — speaking of which, it's time to talk about getting in touch with other greener gadgets and gizmos for the great outdoors. Visit www.trackthisout.com.

Figure 12-5:
Just one
look, that's
all it takes.

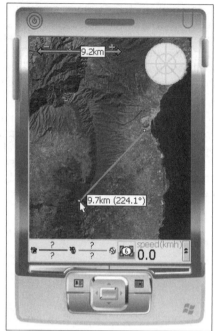

Figure 12-6:
Staying the
off-road
course.

Tracking Green Gadgets for Fitness and Outdoor Activities

When you head out for a run, bike ride, or camping trip into the wild, you probably take a gadget (or two) along with you. You can maximize your performance and comfort — while minimizing your carbon footprint — if those gadgets are of the green variety.

Although some of these products get their charge from the sun or elbow-grease — and can be used to recharge your other gadgets — none is solely designed for recharging per se. (Those gadgets get their own day in the sun in the next section, "Staying in Charge with Portable Power Chargers and Extenders.").

In this section I show you a gaggle of green gadgets for various outdoor activities and purposes:

✔ **BodyGard Survivor 12-in-1 self-powered emergency companion:** One of the BodyGard Survivor's list of features is its carrying strap. That may be stretching things a bit, but I still wish I had had one of these items when I was a Boy Scout.

Winding the hand crank charges the battery, which powers the gadget's flashlight, panic alarm, FM radio, and red emergency flasher. Set the motion-activated security alarm to scare off things that go bump (or roar) in the night outside your tent. To give your MP3 player or cellphone a much-needed boost, plug them into the charging outlet. Nontechnical amenities include a signaling mirror and a compass. Visit www.swisstechtools.com.

✔ **2C Solar Light Cap and Everlite powered LED headlamp:** The Solar Light Cap (http://solarlightcap.com), shown in Figure 12-7, can keep your head cool by day and give you a light to read or work by at night. A solar cell on the upper bill soaks up sunlight to charge the cap's built-in battery. Come darkness, press the button to turn on dual LED lights — which can run as long as 24 hours on a single charge when used at dimmer levels. Switched to full brightness, the cap's lights can last as long as four hours.

Figure 12-7:
Solar charged light to brighten your night.

Another solar light to wrap your head around — or to wrap around your head — is the Everlite solar headlamp (http://newlite.com). Six hours of sunlight on the solar panel provides 12 or more hours of bright LED light. Being unbound rather than sewn in, such as the 2C Cap, makes the Everlite headlamp a more flexible solution for the rest of us.

✔ **Goblin Aero 150 MPG:** The Goblin Aero (www.goblinmotors.com) is a *velomobile*, which you peddle like a bike — or switch on the power-assist system to take a load off as you cruise under sunny or rainy skies, thanks to the protective screen and skins. Goblin estimates you get up to 150 MPG from its ultra-efficient gasoline engine, or opt for the EcoSpeed electric drive system to cut the Aero's carbon emissions to zero.

✔ **Solar Rechargeable Lantern AM/FM weather radio:** Set the Solar Rechargeable Lantern (www.solarhome.org), shown in Figure 12-8, in the sun for 8 hours, and enjoy up to 12 hours of light while listening to tunes, news, or weather reports on a built-in radio. The solar panel folds away when you're not charging the lantern; a wall charger and car-lighter-plug charger are included so that you can charge up before heading into the wild.

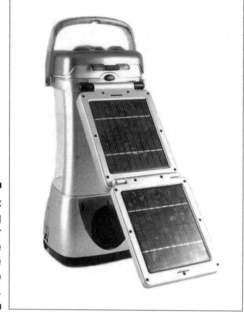

Figure 12-8:
Capturing
sunlight for
campfire
story-time
light to
read by.

Staying in Charge with Portable Power Chargers and Extenders

Portable power chargers and extenders can help you keep your gadgets charged and usable when you're away from a power source that you can plug in to. The ones I describe here are ecofriendly because they rely on the sun (or wind) for a charge, or on good old-fashioned elbow grease to wind built-in cranks to charge them. They can then in turn charge your gadgets. In other words, these gadgets turn natural energy or your energy into energy you can use to power your other gadgets:

- **Solio Magnesium Edition solar charger:** Unfold the "petals" of the Solio Magnesium Edition portable solar charger (www.solio.com), shown in Figure 12-9, and you see three solar panels that soak up the sun to give renewed recharge life to your gadget. Use the Solio to recharge MP3 players, cellphones, digital cameras, handheld video-game players, and many other gadgets. Fully charged, the Solio can recharge a typical mobile phone more than twice, or provide more than 20 hours of MP3 music.

Figure 12-9:
Getting
charged
up from the
sun.

✔ **Gaiam SideWinder cellphone charger:** Attach the adaptor for your cell-phone to the Gaiam SideWinder and get cranking for up to six minutes of talk time after two minutes of winding. It's at www.gaiam.com.

Although the SideWinder isn't meant for full-charge service, its tiny size makes it perfect for camping or other situations when power is out of reach and you need to reach out and call someone.

✔ **Freeplay Weza foot-powered portable generator:** Pump your foot on the pedal to charge the Weza portable power generator. The portable powerhouse can also can be charged from other sources — including solar, wind, and AC power when plugged into a wall outlet.

Designed to jump-start a boat or car battery in a pinch, the foot-powered device can also recharge smaller gadgets such as your iPod, cellphone, or other powered gizmos. Visit www.freeplayenergy.com.

✔ **HY Mini wind-powered charger:** Relying on the wind, rather than on you, is how the HY Mini wind-powered charger generates power to juice up your MP3 player, digital camera, mobile phone, and other gadgets.

What, no wind today? No worries. Connect the HY Mini (www.hymini.com) to your bicycle's handlebars or strap it to your upper arm with optional accessories and get pedaling or running to make some wind of your own as you go about your merry, green way.

- **Brunton SolarRolls:** The Brunton SolarRolls, shown in Figure 12-10, are available in sizes powerful enough to charge a satellite phone or your laptop's battery — or smaller gadgets such as mobile phones, MP3 players, digital cameras, or camcorders. Famed mountaineer Ed Viesturs reportedly brought one along when he climbed the Annapurna summit in the Himalayas, where snow could do no harm to the SolarRoll because it's waterproof. Visit www.brunton.com.

Figure 12-10:
The Brunton
Solar-
Rolls —
wasabi sold
separately.

- **Energizer rechargeable solar charger:** The pink Energizer Bunny has gotten greener with the company's handy Energizer Solar battery charger (www.energizer.com). Flip open the lid to expose the solar panel when the sun's up — or plug it into a wall outlet to charge it up after sundown.

  The charger charges AA and AAA rechargeable batteries, and the USB-out port can recharge gadgets that can connect that way, such as iPods, digital cameras, cellphones, and portable GPS navigators.

- **nPower PEG** (http://greennpower.com): Pop the nPower PEG into your backpack (or attach it to your hip or leg), plug in your gadget, and presto — instant power, brought to you by *you*! Harvesting kinetic energy (in this case, up-and-down bodily movement) as you move about, the nPower PEG charges portable electronic gizmos at the same rate as a wall charger, which means an hour of walking can bring your iPod or other gadget's charge to about 80 percent.

I sing the body electric

Max Donelan (shown kneeling in the photo) is an assistant professor of kinesiology at Simon Fraser University near Vancouver, British Columbia. As chief science officer and director of Bionic Power Inc. (www.bionic power.com), he and his team developed the Biomechanical Energy Harvester, a wearable technology that unobtrusively generates electricity from the natural motion of walking and uses it to charge a wide range of portable battery-powered devices.

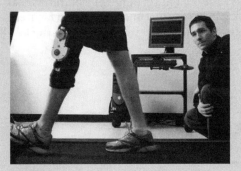
Bionic Power

Weighing 3½ pounds, the Biomechanical Energy Harvester prototype would be too heavy to wear comfortably for more than a little while. Mr. Donelan said his team is aiming to bring the weight to just under 2 pounds, or 900 grams — the magic

number he came up with after working with athletic-brace companies, which discovered that pro football players could perform without hindrance when a brace weighed less than a kilogram.

Mr. Donelan envisions early adopters of his product as people whose lives literally depend on portable power, such as military personnel or public-safety workers and first responders. Simply put, if you can *be* the recharger, you can create all the battery juice you want.

The idea came to Mr. Donelan and his colleague and friend Art Kuo about a decade ago, after reading an article about energy harvesting. Because of their main scientific interest in how people walk, the team thought they could get a lot more power from the body by focusing on the knee joint, essentially harnessing the energy for free without putting undue demands of the wearer. He compares the concept to regenerative braking in hybrid cars.

Although he believed he would be the only person who would walk around all day with the contraption on his body, Mr. Donelan said many of the people he has spoken to about the device said they would not only wear it but would also wear it conspicuously. Mr. Donelan calls it the *Prius effect,* to make it plainly known to others that the wearer is generating her own power.

Leafing Through Green Garments, Bags, and Cases

Green gadget choices don't have to stop with the gadgets themselves. Cases, holders, backpacks, and other toting choices have become part of the whole green gadget ecosphere, thanks to the growing selection of green accessory products.

Although the companies listed in these bullets typically offer other choices to match the wide-ranging gamut of gadgets in our lives, I have chosen a small batch of ecofriendly products to describe here:

- ✔ **ScotteVest Solar recharging jacket:** Gadget-geek jacket maker ScotteVest (http://scottevest.com) has made a gizmo-savvy garment that's designed to keep your mobile phone and other portable gadgets charged on sunny days. Its secret is a big solar panel on the back. You can also detach the panel and set it in the sun when the weather's too hot for full coverage. The panel charges a battery that's secreted inside the jacket. Tons of additional hidden compartments and tunnels for routing your headphone wires can keep you in charge and in style at the same time.

- ✔ **Voltic solar backpacks and bags:** Solar bags in the Voltic line (www.voltaicsystems.com) come with built-in rechargeable batteries that store the energy the panels soak up from the sun, as shown in Figure 12-11. The bags' overall greenness is increased by the fact that the fabric is made from recycled plastic bottles.

Figure 12-11: Solar charging meets backpack.

- ✔ **Eclipse Solar Gear:** The company offers a wide selection of backpacks, messenger bags, laptop and camera cases, and even a solar fishing-tackle bag. Although you can carry your notebook in one of the Eclipse messenger bags, the company says that the solar panel can't generate enough energy to charge it. It can, however, charge your cellphone, MP3 player, digital camera, or camcorder. Visit http://eclipsesolargear.com.

✔ **Tread mobile phone cases:** The Better Energy Systems line of eco-friendly mobile phone cases are made from recycled tires from Colombian cargo trucks. The cases are of biocompatible butyl rubber, which is the same material used in joint replacements and chewing gum. Check out `www.tread.com`.

Original Good Rumor Has It mobile phone cases: Treading on slightly softer fabric grounds, the Rumor Has It cases (at `www.originalgood.com`) are made from recycled wedding saris that are hand-embroidered by artisans from New Delhi and Gujarat who employ their unique embroidery skills to earn a sustainable living. If fair trade is your favored way of doing business, buying one of these cases demonstrates that your actions speak louder than the words you say into the cellphone it's protecting.

Chapter 13

Adding Green Gadgets around the House

*W*hat could be more fun than shopping for new, green consumer electronics? Couple that fun with the satisfaction of replacing dying and not-so-green high-tech gear with green new models, and you have a win-win situation. And that's what this chapter is all about. Chapters 14 and 16 can help you get rid of your unwanted gear the responsible way. (That would make a win-win-win situation.)

For starters, I tell you about some of the gadgets you can buy to monitor and manage your household's "bigger picture" energy usage. Next, I take you on a tour of the latest products that exemplify just what it means to be gadgetry greener in the house. I describe new, more energy-efficient HDTVs, savings-savvy timers, and even motion-detecting gizmos that automatically turn lights on or off. There's something here for everyone — and every room — in the house.

Considering Green Gadgets for Every Room in the House

Some energy-saving gizmos, such as the smart power strips I write about in several other chapters, are right at home in every room in the house. Plugging your powered gadgets and other consumer electronics into a smart power switch can make it easier to completely power off several "energy vampires" at once.

The power-switching gadgets in this list can be used separately, or mixed and matched for greater control over turning the devices you've plugged into them on and off:

- ✔ **Universal TrickleSaver:** Powering off the DVD player, video game console, and other components connected to your TV is the magic act the TrickleSaver (`http://tricklestar.com`), shown in Figure 13-1, performs when you turn off your set. So long, energy suckers!

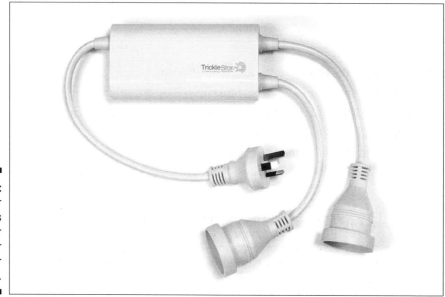

Figure 13-1:
Let your gadgets and gear pull their own power plugs.

Turn your TV on, and the undead come back to life. Talk about getting the bigger picture!

- ✔ **Westek indoor power strip timer:** The Westek indoor power strip timer can turn on and off lights and other items plugged into it, depending on times you tell it to do its switching thing. The timer controls four of the power strip's eight outlets, and a hinged protective cover prevents accidental timing mishaps. Visit `www.amertac.com`.

- ✔ **Belkin Conserve:** Bending over to reach a power strip that's on the floor and hard to reach is why many people don't bother turning off power strips. Coming to your back's rescue is the Belkin Conserve, at `http://belkin.com`.

Press the remote control to instantly turn on or off the devices plugged into six of the strip's eight outlets. The remaining pair of outlets stays on all the time so that you can keep on around the clock certain devices — such as your cable or DSL modem and WiFi router.

Monitoring and Controlling Household Energy Usage

A home energy monitor provides real-time feedback about how much energy your home's powered parts are using. These gizmos typically display power usage in terms of actual kilowatts, and estimate what it's costing you on your monthly electric bill. Studies have shown that energy monitors can help motivate you to reduce your dwelling's total power consumption 4 to 15 percent.

Connecting an energy monitor may be as simple as plugging your individual power-consuming devices into a handheld model to gauge their usage one by one, or as involved as opening your circuit breaker box to clamp sensors around the incoming power lines and connect wires to two breaker points (as shown in Figure 13-2). For this type of energy monitor installation, you might want to hire an electrician to do the job.

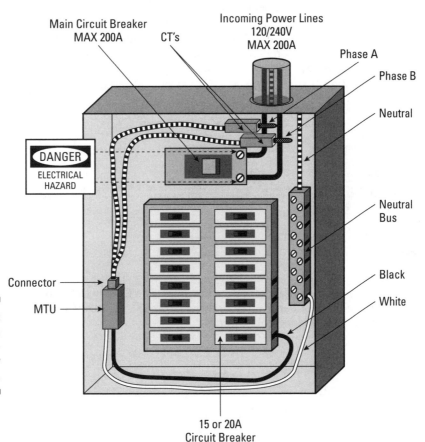

Figure 13-2: Getting a grip on better energy savings.

WARNING!

Only a professional electrician or Do-It-Yourself type who has experience with electrical systems — and the good sense to cut the main power — should attempt to install the kind of energy monitor sensors shown in Figure 13-2.

Some portable energy monitors gauge power usage on a gadget-by-gadget basis, which can help you determine how each one contributes to your home's energy consumption. Then you know which gadgets to use more efficiently or possibly replace with a more efficient one. The two portable and whole-home energy monitors described here illustrate how installing and using one of these gizmos in your home can help you stay on top of your energy usage:

- **Kill A Watt:** Wondering just how much power that room heater or printer is drawing when it's turned on — and turned off? Plug your gadgets or any other electrically powered item into the Kill A Watt, and instantly find out how many watts it draws, and how much it contributes to your monthly electric bill. Visit www.p3international.com.

- **The Energy Detective:** Skipping the plug-it-in approach, The Energy Detective, shown in Figure 13-3, taps directly into your home's circuit breaker and displays how much total power you're using — and paying for — in real time. Turning on and off appliances and other gadgets reveals how much each is adding to your overall load. Go to www.theenergydetective.com.

Figure 13-3: Gauge your home's total energy usage in real time.

To read about my experience installing The Energy Detective to monitor my home's power consumption, have a look at the nearby sidebar, "Investigating my home's balance of power."

Turning Things On and Off Automatically

Gadgets that turn the lights on and off automatically when you enter and leave a room, or a thermostat that heats or cools only when you're home, can go a long way toward reducing your monthly electricity bill. Some of these energy-saving automatons are simple to use. Others require the installation services of a professional electrician.

The products I highlight in the following list illustrate a number of green options that remember or sense when to cut the power so that you don't have to. (How's that's for green gadget *re-thinking?*)

- **Honeywell 5-2 day programmable thermostat:** Swapping your manual thermostat with the Honeywell 5-2 day programmable thermostat lets you set heating and cooling temperatures — and then forget them.

  Set it to turn up the heat or air conditioner a few minutes before you wake, turn it down when you head off to work, kick it up a few notches when you're home again, then adjust the temperature again at bedtime for a comfortable and energy-efficient night of sleep. Sleeping in on the weekend? No worries — setting the Honeywell to keep you warm or cool beyond your usual wake up time is par for the course. Go to `http://yourhome.honeywell.com`.

- **GreenSwitch:** Leaving the job to the GreenSwitch power control system makes unplugging as easy as hitting a wall-mounted or remote power switch.

  Only the outlets you set by power zones turn off when you hit the switch, and your home's air conditioning and heating are automatically set to the unoccupied mode for more energy savings. Professional installation is required and can take as little as an hour before you're on the smart- switching road to energy recovery. Visit `http://green-switchteam.com`.

- **Motion-detecting lights and switches:** Having lights automatically turn on or off when you enter and leave the room saves energy and frees your hands for carrying laundry or other things. Simply screw the Motion Bulb into a light socket and presto, instant sensing as you come and go.

  Drawing only 20 watts when on, one Motionbulb (`www.motionbulb.com`) can last up to 5 years — which saves you from replacing about 10 ordinary light bulbs.

- **The SensorPlug motion-sensing outlet:** This product can provide automatic on and off switching when you walk in and out of a room for table and floor lamps, radios, and anything else you plug into it. Check it out at `http://sensorplug.com`.

Investigating my home's balance of power

Warning: Don't try installing The Energy Detective at home, folks. Unless, that is, you're versed in working with electricity — and you've cut the power completely to your circuit breaker before you begin.

With that out of the way, I can tell you that installing The Energy Detective (www.the energydetective.com) to monitor my tiny home's power consumption was not difficult. However, I was a wee bit nervous about screwing sensor wires into my circuit breaker (see Figure 13-2) even though I cut the main power to the box. To reiterate, paying an electrician can reduce the chances of accidentally frying yourself when poking around in your home's circuit breaker. (Is there such a thing as intentionally frying yourself when . . . wait, let's not go there!)

Here are the steps I took to install The Energy Detective:

1. Turned off main circuit breaker power switch.

2. Removed circuit breaker panel cover.

3. Mounted the Measuring Transmitting Unit (MTU) using double-sided tape..

4. Connected black wire to a 20 amp circuit breaker in the panel.

5. Connected white wire to neutral bus in the panel.

6. Clamped the pair of Current Transformers (CT) over incoming power lines, making sure to align sides with red dot in same direction to maintain proper polarity.

7. Connected CT cable to MTU.

8. Taped slack lengths of wires against back of circuit breaker panel because I'm a bit of a neat freak.

9. Turned on the main circuit breaker switch and noted the green LED on the MTU was flashing once per second, which meant it was picking up the flow of power through the cables.

10. Set the MTU's "house code" on the TED Receiving Unit Display (RUD) so that it was certain to track my home's electricity and not my neighbor's (in the unlikely event that they also happen to be using a TED).

11. Looked at the TED display and saw that, low and behold, the little sucker was tracking my home's real-time power consumption.

12. Turned off the main circuit breaker switch and reinstalled the panel cover.

13. Turned on the main circuit breaker and observed my house's base consumption rate* of around .100 kilowatts, which increased when I turned on my

- Printer by printing a page, waking it from standby mode = 1.110 kilowatts

- Standup 1500 watt radiator set to Max mode at the highest setting = 1.500 to 2.500 kilowatts

- Ecofriendly tankless instant hot water heater = 10.000 to 18.000 kilowatts

- Electric oven = 3.750 kilowatts

- Xbox 360 and 32-inch HDTV = .310 kilowatts (to my surprise there was no jump in consumption when I spun the DVD drive by popping in a movie)

- Toaster oven = 1.350 kilowatts

- Microwave oven = 1.770 kilowatts

- Ecofriendly washer/dryer all -in-one while running hot water cycle = 18.550 kilowatts, 1.170 kilowatts during wash cycle without hot water flowing in, and around 1.400 during drying cycle, which can take 1 to 3 hours, depending on load

✔ Refrigerator turning itself on to adjust interior temperature = 260 kilowatts

✔ Writing desk lamp = .120 kilowatts + sofa reading lamp = .140 + third room lamp = .160

✔ Front porch light = .140 kilowatts + side house light = .160 kilowatts

✔ Vudu Video Store in a Box movie player + 32-inch HDTV = .270 kilowatts

✔ Backup hard drive turning itself on to run Time Machine program to back up MacBook = .110 to .120 kilowatts

✔ The Energy Detective alone with all other appliances, lights, and energy vampires cut off = .20 kilowatts

*Plugged in active and standby (energy vampire) appliances and devices when gauging .100 kilowatt baseline consumption rate include power strips with powered-on MacBook charging iPhone and Bluetooth headset via USB, active cable broadband modem, active WiFi network router, active HDMI port-switching box, HDTV in standby mode, printer in standby mode, TiVo in recording mode, Xbox 360 in standby mode; always-on appliances that include refrigerator, oven range and microwave oven, washer/dryer combo unit, LCD display thermostat, HVAC, instant-on hot water heater; and nonstandby appliances that include desk and room lamps, overhead lights, toaster oven, and coffee maker.

Controlling Your Entire House with Home Automation Systems

Home automation involves the automatic — and, through your computer or another device, remote — control of various functions within your home. Home automation systems can make your household green because they can manage energy usage on your behalf, automatically adjusting your home's thermostat or turning appliances off based on your schedule. They can also turn lights on and off, control your home entertainment system, and automatically water your plants when you're on vacation.

An automated security system might include sensors that can detect intruders or fire and smoke and then trigger your home automation system to dial for help, flash the lights, and sound an alarm. In addition, most home automation systems allow you to control the following:

✔ Intercoms and video cameras

✔ Heating and air conditioning

✔ Coffee makers

- Pet watering and feeding
- Outdoor sprinklers
- Garage doors and gates
- Pool heaters and hot tub pumps
- Water pumps (to bail a flooded basement or other space)

Home automation systems communicate by sending unique data signals through your home's power lines, turning your home's wiring into a virtual network of sorts. For a slightly more technical explanation, pop over to the nearby sidebar, "How home automation talks itself to sleep." Controlling your home automation system when you're away from home can be accomplished by running a mobile application, such as the one by Crestron for the iPhone, shown in Figure 13-4, or by tapping into your system by way of the Web.

Generally, you can easily install basic home automation gizmos and computer programs (such as the popular X10 system) to control lights and your living room's home theater. More sophisticated home automation systems for monitoring and controlling window blinds, heating and air conditioning, and fire, smoke, and security alarm systems typically require professional installers.

How home automation talks itself to sleep

Devices plugged into receiver boxes or outlets communicate back and forth with preprogrammed or real-time commands you send from your PC, remote, or cellphone. So telling the night light in Junior's room to go to sleep at a predetermined time is merely a matter of sending the signal through your home's electrical lines.

In addition to the radio frequency (RF) signals running through your home's power wire "network," home automation systems typically connect to your home network's router by way of Ethernet or WiFi, which is how you access and control everything with your PC, home automation remote control, or cellphone.

A number of communications protocols are what your home's lights, appliances, and other connected devices use to talk with each other and your PC, remote control, and cellphone. Some send and receive commands through your home's electrical wiring, as described above.

Some remote controls beam infrared (IF) signals to control device the way typical TV remotes do, while others use RF signals that don't require a line of site between the remote and the device.

One popular protocol, X10, is named after the company (www.x10.com) that, in 1974, invented the home automation system bearing the same name.

A professional electrician or Do-It-Yourself type who has experience with electrical systems should install home automation control systems that require connecting directly into your home's circuit box or wiring inside the walls.

Figure 13-4:
Empowering
home power
control on
the go.

In this list, I highlight various home automation product makers and resellers:

- **X10:** X10 is a longtime maker of home automation modules, remotes, and other gizmos for controlling lights, indoor climate, security systems, and other powered appliances and devices. Visit `www.x10.com/home page1.htm`.

- **Control4:** Control4 (`http://control4.com`) manufactures wired and wireless home-automation products that can be installed in any home in just a few hours, without the need for extensive or expensive remodeling. Product line can integrate lighting, audio, video, landscape, and climate control into a single cohesive system.

- **INSTEON:** Using both the power lines in the home and radio frequency communication, INSTEON adds remote control and automation to lighting, appliance, and home control applications of all types. Visit `www.insteon.net`.

- **Crestron:** Total Home Technology Solution (`www.crestron.com`) eliminates the need to walk from room to room to adjust drapes, lights, temperature, and audio/video components. From an easy-to-use color touch panel, a remote, or a customized keypad, a single touch can make the lights dim, the shades close, the high-definition TV turn on, and your favorite movie begin.

- **Z-WAVE:** The Z-Wave wireless "ecosystem" lets all your home electronics talk to each other (and to you) by way of remote control. It uses simple, reliable, low-power radio waves that easily travel through walls, floors, and cabinets. The Z-Wave control can be added to almost any electronic device in your house, even devices that you wouldn't ordinarily think of as "intelligent," such as appliances, window shades, and home lighting. Go to `www.z-wave.com`.

- **Elan Home Systems:** This company makes innovative multiroom systems that integrate your stereos, telephones, and televisions to create an entire home entertainment experience. Check it out at `http://elanhomesystems.com`.

- **Hawking Technology:** The HomeRemote Pro Home Control lets you secure, monitor, and control your home remotely by using a computer or cellphone Web browser. Using the broadband connection in your home, the HomeRemote Pro Internet Gateway (`http://hawkingtech.com`) communicates with the HomeRemote Pro servers to allow remote control of your home lighting, appliances, doors, garages, window shades, thermostat, and much more.

The following Web sites can help you choose the right system for gaining ultimate control over your home's overall power usage and energy consumption:

- ✔ **Electronic House:** An excellent source of authoritative news reporting, reviews, roundups, and features covering a variety of products and consumer electronics categories, including home automation and home theater. Visit http://electronichouse.com.

- ✔ **Remote Central:** News, reviews, and features on all things remote control, as well as a discussion board covering topics relating to lighting, home control, and automation technologies and systems, including modules, switches, controllers, remotes, applications, and troubleshooting. Go to www.remotecentral.com.

- ✔ **Smarthome and Smarthome blog:** Get the latest product news from home automation retailer Smarthome (www.smarthome.com). Its blog (http://blog.smarthome.com) offers product highlights from the store's wide selection of products, including home automation and lighting control, security and surveillance systems, and home theater products, such as speakers, remotes, and audio/video distribution.

Looking at Green HDTV, Music, Movie-Watching, and Audio Products

When you choose energy-efficient gear for the living room, den, or basement home theater, you entertain yourself while lowering your monthly electric bill. The outstanding performers chosen for this section exhibit a large number of green consumer electronics features. Use this list to help you outfit your domicile with new home theater and entertainment gear:

- ✔ **Toshiba Regza 46XV545U:** The Toshiba 46-inch Regza 46XV545U gets rave reviews for its supersharp, high-definition picture quality — and it's no slouch when it comes to being green, too.

  Built-in sensors automatically adjust the backlight to consume less power in low-light or nighttime settings; and the auto-brightness setting can shave the cost to power the big screen to less than $4 a month, based on five hours of daily viewing. Visit http://toshiba.com.

- ✔ **Vizio VECO320L:** Drawing nearly 44 percent less power than traditional 32-inch LCD HDTVs, the Vizio VECO320L offers two HDMI ports for plugging in your DVD player, video game console, or cable box.

  Although I don't list prices in this book, I can report that, at the time I wrote this, this set was priced below $500 — that means it can save you bucks and energy, in one fell swoop. Go to www.vizio.com.

✔ **Sony Bravia VE5:** Sensing when you're no longer in the room and watching, the Sony Bravia VE5 HDTV can turn itself off to save energy. Come back in, and the HDTV turns itself on again.

Sony says the set draws 40 percent less power than other LCD models — and nearly zero watts when it's powered off in Standby mode. What's more, a light sensor can automatically adjust the picture brightness to match the room's mood, drawing even less energy when the lights go down and it's time to start the show. Check it out at `www.sonystyle.com`.

✔ **Knoll Eco-System GS8 Audio amplifier:** Whereas amplifiers and bass-booming speakers are notoriously famous for being hungry power eaters, the Knoll GS8 amplifier (at `http://knollsystems.com`) can save you as much as $100 on your bill when compared to typical amps.

The amplifier's smart-sensing technology determines which of the box's four pairs of stereo channels are in use, delivering only to those channels needing it. Comparable amplifiers without the same smarts consume about 14 times (40 watts) as much power when idling, but the GS8 draws only 4 watts. Sounds green to me!

✔ **Sony's BDP-S350 Blu-ray:** Powering on the Sony BDP-S350 Blu-ray player and opening the tray to pop in a movie takes only six seconds when the quick-start option is turned on.

But turning it off can lower the player's energy vampire draw to less than a third of a watt, which translates to just over thirty cents a month to operate based on five hours of daily use. Leaving the quick-start option on decreases startup time but increases the estimated monthly cost to about a buck. Visit `www.sony.com`.

✔ **EZ Power Wind-Up Remote Control:** Thirty twists to the dial of the EZ Power Wind-Up Remote Control fully charges the gizmo for as much as seven days of use.

The remote can control as many as six components, including TVs, cable boxes, and DVD players, which means fewer rechargeable batteries to power the six unneeded remotes. Available only in the United Kingdom at the time of this writing, diehard green home theater buffs willing to spring for overseas shipping can get their hands on one from Amazon UK. Go to `http://amazon.co.uk`.

✔ **Netflix Player by Roku:** Energy-saving Blu-ray players are better than old-school players for helping to save the environment, but don't forget how much energy is expended to produce, pick, and return rental-store DVDs — or ship them through the mail the Netflix way. Skipping the disc completely is how the Netflix Player by Roku, shown in Figure 13-5, offers the green way of watching movies in your home. Go to `www.roku.com`.

Sign-on to your Netflix account on your computer, browse a selection of more than 20,000 Watch Instantly titles and click the ones you want. Then grab a bowl of popcorn and press Play on the Roku's remote to start watching within about a minute after the movie begins streaming to your TV over the Internet. Look, Ma — no more DVD juggling!

Figure 13-5:
So long,
DVDs —
hello
streaming!

Watching green TV shows

Choosing and using green home entertainment gear sets the perfect stage for tuning in to these green-thinking TV shows:

✔ *The Green,* **Sundance Channel:** A regularly scheduled series of programs — including *Big Ideas for a Small Planet,* and *The Ecoists* — dedicated entirely to the environment, plus additional multimedia content focusing on ecology and green living on the series' companion Web site. Visit www.sundancechannel.com/thegreen.

✔ *It's Easy Being Green,* **Fine Living Network:** An entertaining and informational look at the growing green lifestyle and the latest trends in sustainable goods, services, and technologies, with appearances by eco-conscious celebrities; hosted by the noted organic chef, author, and green lifestyle consultant Renee Loux. Go to www.fine-living.com/fine/its_easy_being_green.

✔ *Find & Design,* **A&E:** Part treasure hunt, part decorating show, *Find & Design* shows viewers how to bargain like an expert and design like a pro armed with a modest amount of cash, a list of flea markets, and tag sales. Visit www.aetv.com/findanddesign.

✔ **Planet Green:** Planet Green (http://planetgreen.discovery.com) is the first and only 24-hour ecolifestyle television network with a robust online presence and community. Launched in June 2008, the show offers more than 250 hours of original green lifestyle programming. And, their mission extends online at http://planetgreen.discovery.com and its sister site, www.treehugger.com.

✔ *Backyard Habitat,* **Animal Planet:** Teaches you how to make the planet a better place for animals, one back yard at a time. It also builds on the National Wildlife Foundation's ongoing Backyard Wildlife Habitat program, which for more than 30 years has inspired people to make a home for wildlife right outside their back door. Check it out at http://animal.discovery.com.

✔ **Torrent HDMI cables:** Unlike most HDMI cables you can buy to connect your HDTV, DVD player, video game console, and other hi-def devices, the Torrent (http://torrent-inc.com) line of cables are free of harmful substances, such as polyvinyl chloride (PVC) and other environmentally unfriendly stuff.

✔ **The Home Security Television Simulator:** Unlike timers that just turn lights on and off, the Home Security Television Simulator, shown in Figure 13-6, mimics the flickering glow of a television to trick potential burglars into thinking someone's home and watching the TV. Visit http://hammacher.com.

The phony baloney boob tube mimics scene changes, fades, swells, and color shifts of a TV as perceived from outside using a bright multicolor LED display diffused with an opalescent lens. Consuming only 2 percent of the power a real TV uses, the dummy set is smart enough to turn itself on at dusk and off four to seven hours later.

Figure 13-6:
The TV lights are on but nobody's home!

Movie downloads give DVDs the boot

Watching pay-per-view, downloadable, or streaming TV episodes and movies is greener than renting from the local video store because you save on gasoline and time, and eliminate the resources used to make and ship the discs from store to store and from shipping center to mailbox. If you want to enjoy your flicks and feel the satisfaction of going green, you have plenty of choices to download movies (legally, mind you).

Own an Xbox 360 or TiVo HD? Activating either by visiting www.netflix.com/activate

provides you the same access to your Netflix Watch Instantly titles without having to shell out extra bucks for the Roku player. The Xbox 360 Live Video Marketplace also offers hundreds of standard definition (SD) and high-definition (HD) movies and TV shows for purchase or rental. The TiVo HD can also tap into thousands of film and TV titles available from Amazon's Video on Demand store (www.amazon.com/vod).

Sony's PlayStation Video Store (www.store.playstation.com) gives PS3 players another way to download and watch movies rather than spinning a Blu-ray disc in the video game console. Video downloaded from the PlayStation Video Store can be transferred from the PS3 to the PSP portable handheld gaming system for on-the go-entertainment.

At the time of this writing, Vudu's Video Store in a Box (www.vudu.com) led the download-able movie player pack with the largest library of HD titles. Like the PlayStation 3 or Xbox 360, movies and TV shows are stored on a built-in

hard drive. The remote control features a simple scrolling wheel design for browsing titles and starting, pausing, fast-forwarding, rewinding, and stopping movies and shows.

Download movies and TV shows from the Apple Music Store (www.apple.com/itunes) right to your iPod or iPhone. Watching the same titles on your Windows or Mac computer is another option — or move the movie party to the big screen in the living room with Apple's Apple TV video, music, and photo player.

Fiddling with Other Ecofriendly Home Gadgets

In this section, I give you a handful of wacky, weird, and way out there household gadgets for most every room in the house. And when I say, "way out there," I mean some of these gadgets can help you conserve water and energy outside the house.

✔ **Bedol Water Powered Clock:** Powered by a splash of water and a dash of salt, the Bedol water-powered clock, shown in Figure 13-7, keeps perfect time with no batteries. Electrodes inside the gizmo harvest energy from the water — though the maker suggests adding a squeeze of lemon juice to enhance the water-power drawing efficiency, which translates to fewer fill-ups. Go to http://bedolwhatsnext.com.

Figure 13-7: Chasing time with a sip of water, a dash of salt, and a squeeze of lemon.

✔ **ECOlight water-powered shower light:** The Sylvania ECOlight, shown in Figure 13-8, converts incoming water pressure to energy to shine the spotlight on you when you're singing in the shower. Visit www.sylvania onlinestore.com.

Figure 13-8: A bright approach to more efficient showering.

A built-in sensor changes the color of the LED light based on water temperature, which means no more freezing cold or scalding hot surprises when you step under the stream.

✔ **Solar-powered holiday lights:** Sucking up sunlight by day is how the solar-powered holiday lights shown in Figure 13-9 recharge the included batteries to shine brightly at night. A full day of light can power the 26-foot long string of 60 lights for around eight hours, and because they're self-contained, there's no need for extension cords like ordinary, power-sucking holiday lights. Visit www.shopgetorganized.com.

Figure 13-9: Solar-powered holiday lights worth caroling over.

✔ **EasyBloom Plant Sensor:** Planting the EasyBloom Plant Sensor in your garden (shown in Figure 13-10, on the left) can provide precise monitoring of sun, soil, temperature, and humidity — factors which help determine and adjust watering, light, and soil levels and conditions.

Fortunately, the EasyBloom (`http://easybloom.com`) does all the figuring so that you don't have to, thanks to "plant doctor algorithms." The accompanying program runs when you plug the garden gizmo into your computer's USB port, as shown in Figure 13-10, on the right.

Figure 13-10:
Helping gardeners get green thumbs.

Part V
Ridding Yourself of Gadgets the Green Way

The 5th Wave   By Rich Tennant

©RICHTENNANT

"I can be reached at home on my cell phone, and I can be reached on the road with my pager and PDA. Soon I'll be reachable on a plane with e-mail. I'm beginning to think identity theft wouldn't be such a bad idea for a while."

In this part . . .

When you want to replace that old PC of yours with a newer, ecofriendlier notebook, don't just dump the PC in the trash. Instead, find out whether it can be of use to someone else. You can give it to a relative or friend. If no one you know wants your cast-off gadget, you can donate it, trade it in, or auction it.

No matter how you decide to get rid of the gadget, however, be sure to erase your personal information from it first. Protecting yourself against potential identity theft (or just plain embarrassment) is an important topic, which is why I dedicate an entire chapter to it.

A possible scenario is one in which a hopelessly useless gadget has reached the end of its life cycle. If that's your scenario, I give you some information on locating a nearby or nationwide recycler, corporate take-back program, or other gadget "e-waste" processing facility.

Chapter 14

Donating, Gifting, and Selling Unwanted Gadgets

*T*his chapter's title says it all, and you've come to the right place if you want to get rid of gadgets or other electronics devices you think someone else can use. I say, "think" because the item you want to get rid of that seems valuable to you — that old IBM PC in the garage that boots up from floppy disks — in reality has reached the end of its useful lifecycle.

Selling the original Macintosh you used in college, on the other hand, is a viable option — even if it's only because the person who buys it wants to turn it into an aquarium rather than use it as a computer.

In this chapter, I help you figure out whether the gadgets and gear you're thinking of discarding are useful to anyone. If so, I help you weigh your many options to donate, gift, trade in, or sell your stuff.

 Wiping your personal information from gadgets, cellphones, computer hard drives, and digital cameras before selling or giving them away can protect you against potential identity theft — or just plain embarrassment. Chapter 15 has all the information you need to erase your personal information from your gadgets.

If you determine the things you want to get rid of are hopelessly useless, don't fret. Chapter 16 details what steps to take to dispose of your stuff the green way to ensure they're properly reused or recycled.

Determining whether an Unwanted Gadget Is of Use to Anyone

The first step in deciding whether your gadget is of use to someone is figuring out whether the items you want to get rid of are useful. The following new (or nearly new) gadgets in working condition are almost always useful to others:

- ✔ Computers
- ✔ Cellphones
- ✔ iPods and MP3 players
- ✔ Digital cameras and camcorders
- ✔ Home entertainment gear

Sometimes damaged but still-working (or easily repairable) gadgets and gear are of use to others. For instance, getting rid of a reasonably up-to-date computer with a broken monitor makes sense. But giving away or trying to sell the broken monitor doesn't make sense.

Used but still-working gadgets and gear can be useful, and so can broken or damaged electronics that have useful parts — like my first-generation iPhone shown in Figure 14-1. The night before I was to appear on TV to show off the (then) new iPhone 2.0 software, I accidentally knocked my iPhone off my desk and onto the hardwood floor. In spite of a spider web of cracks, the screen still responded to my touch and the iPhone worked. The next morning, I wound up paying a woman $100 to get to the front of a line of hundreds to buy a new iPhone 3G, and then raced up to Manhattan to make the 5 p.m. airing on Fox News. I wound up selling the original iPhone for more than $200.

Running down the following checklist can help you determine whether your potential electronic giveaway, donation, or for-sale item is valuable to another person.

Repeat after me: "My unwanted gadget or other electronic device is"

- ✔ New or nearly new, and in working condition
- ✔ Not so new but in nice shape and in working condition
- ✔ Kind of old but something I'm certain others would find of use
- ✔ Really old but something I see others selling for a pretty penny on eBay, which means I can probably sell mine, too
- ✔ New, but not working because a part is broken or not working and needs replacement or repair, to make it good as new again
- ✔ Not so new but in nice shape but not working because of a broken part or needed repair that will make it useful again

Figure 14-1:
My smashed but working iPhone fetched more than $200.

If you answer Yes to any of these questions, you can ask yourself the next question: To give away or to sell?

I help you decide which way to go in the next section, but before I get ahead of myself, consider the following potential caveats even if your *yes* was *indubitably, undoubtedly, unequivocally YES!*:

✔ What you may consider "kind of old but something I'm certain others would find of use" may not be seen as useful at all by certain organizations that accept donations such as used PCs.

✔ Sending used computers that have at least a Pentium III processor (or newer) is often a requirement among many organizations that accept computer donations but donating anything older is of no use.

✔ Saying no to the two preceding points means that your gadget or other electronic device likely falls into the "hopelessly useless" category known as *e-waste*.

✔ Don't despair! The adage "One man's trash is another man's treasure" can prove true for your e-waste when you drop it off or send it to a reputable recycler who can properly process and extract reusable bits and pieces.

Weighing the Risks and Rewards of Donating, Gifting, and Selling Unwanted Gadgets

Giving away your gadgets or other unwanted electronics can reward you with that good feeling you get for doing something thoughtful and helpful for another person or group.

Selling, auctioning. or trading in your unwanted stuff for cash or credit toward a new purchase can also satisfy your green sensibilities — literally and figuratively!

Either way, you're honoring the three Rs, by

✔ **Reducing** the amount of resources required to create, ship, and maintain new electronic stuff.

✔ **Reusing** a gadget or device you don't want but someone does.

✔ **Recycling** a still-useful product by keeping it in service and out of the recycling bin — or worse, in your local trash stream or a toxic waste dump overseas.

The following pluses and minuses of giving away versus getting cash can help you decide how to say goodbye to your unwanted gadgets and gear:

✔ **Give:** Giving an unused computer, cellphone, or other gadget to a friend, a family member, a coworker, or another person you care about, or just plain like, or even a total stranger, can give you that good feeling you get by doing something nice for someone else without putting a price tag on it.

✔ **Donate:** Gives that same good feeling of just plain giving, but can also give back monetarily at tax time in the form of a deduction you can claim on your filing form — providing the recipient of your donation is a not-for-profit 501(c)(3)-status charity, foundation, or other organization. (For more on the fine print of donation deductions, check out the nearby sidebar, "Deducing donation deductions.")

Deducing donation deductions

According to the Internal Revenue Service IRC Section 170, giving your unwanted computers and other gadgets to 501(c)(3) organizations, such as public charities and certain private foundations, can entitle you to deduct up to 50 percent of your adjusted gross income from your itemized tax return. Donating your stuff to 501(c)(3) organizations that are private foundations generally entitles you to deduct up to 30 percent of your gross income. Corporations can deduct all donations to 501(c)(3) organizations up to an amount equal to 10 percent of their taxable income.

The deduction for electronics donations is the fair market value — the used value in the current market. Shipping costs may also be deductable, so remember to ask for a receipt!

✔ **Trade in:** Getting rid of your gadgets by sending them to one of several Web-based trade-in companies can fatten your wallet with cash, or earn you credit toward the purchase of new gadgets and gear the company sells. Besides the inconvenience of having to ship your stuff and wait for your check or credit to show up, trading in carries the potential — albeit, remote — chance that your item gets damaged, stolen, or lost on its way to the trade-in company.

✔ **Sell locally:** Listing your unwanted electronics in your local paper's classified section or online on a local community listing such as craigslist (www.craigslist.org), can add greenbacks to your wallet, without the potential inconvenience of shipping or other risks associated with online trade-in or auctioning options.

✔ **Auction:** Auctioning your gadgets and electronics on such Web sites as eBay, Bonanzle, or eBid, can bring in cash, but potential risks and inconveniences can outweigh the benefits if you're not careful about how you list your item, and who you let bid. When it comes to eBay, it's all about reputation, baby: yours (the seller), theirs (the buyer), and the shipping service you choose to shuttle the goods between the two of you. Eliminating these risks by choosing the "local pickup" option and completing the transaction in person can ensure you get your money and the buyer gets their goods — assuming someone in your area wants what you're auctioning. Listing items that nobody bids on before the auction ends can cost you a goodly sum in fees if you're auctioning high-ticket items such as computers and other pricier goods.

Choose the option that sounds like the best fit for you and then read more about your choice in the following three sections. You'll be on your way to saying "so long" to your unwanted gadgets in no time.

A few things to keep in mind when getting rid of gadgets and other electronic devices are

- **Receipts and warranties:** Finding the original receipt and evidence of an extended warranty you may have purchased for a gadget you're getting rid of can be helpful to the person on the receiving end, should the gadget require service or repair after you let it go.

- **Manuals, installation discs, and packaging:** Locating and including manuals, quick start guides, installation discs, cables, original packaging, and anything else that came with the gadgets you're getting rid of can be helpful to the person you're giving to. Plus, you'll free up clutter and materials in your house you would otherwise wind up recycling later.

Giving the Gift of Unwanted Gadgets

What more is there to say about giving unwanted gadgets to friends, family members, coworkers, or anyone you know who can benefit from your unwanted gadgets?

Not much, except what you already know if you're the giving type; that your action helps another person. For us gadget-giving types, that's a nice feeling, and reward enough.. (I'm a prodigious giver-away-er of unwanted gadgets.)

Well now, wait; there *is* something else to say on the subject. Giving your identity and other personal information away with gadgets that store that kind of stuff doesn't feel so nice. You can read all about the subject in Chapter 15.

Doing Good by Donating Computers and Other Gadgets

Although donating computers, cellphones, and other gadgets to a local group you're familiar with is one option, it's often more helpful to send your unwanted digital stuff to one of many organizations that matches your give-aways with others who can benefit the most from them.

The most commonly donated electronic goods are

- **Computers:** Organizations that take back computers generally refurbish the system by reinstalling or upgrading the operating system and repairing faulty hardware, if necessary. The computers are then sent to schools, community groups, assistance programs, and even international organizations that work with developing countries that have little or no access to computers and the democratic power of the Internet. Other useful computer-related donations include printers, monitors, keyboards and mice, operating systems and applications (with valid registration codes), and USB memory devices.

✓ **Cellphones:** Several organizations gladly accept unwanted cellphones so victims of domestic abuse, the elderly, or other persons in need can call 911 at no charge. Cellphones can also be reset to provide free or limited service for those in need, or sold to raise funds for not-for-profit groups, charities, or causes.

✓ **Digital cameras and camcorders:** Various organizations accept digital camera and camcorder donations to provide schools, groups, and clubs the tools that give those in need the opportunity to explore creative photography and filmmaking.

✓ **Entertainment equipment:** TVs, DVD players, even VHS players can be useful to schools and other organizations where learning is the first order of business.

The following organizations are difficult to categorize by product type because many of them accept all kinds of high-tech stuff, including computers, printers, cellphones, and accessories.

Reading more about each can help you gain greater familiarity with which may offer the best fit to receive your gadget generosity:

✓ **Call to Protect:** This national philanthropic program is aimed at combating domestic violence. All donated phones are sent to the group's partner, ReCellular, where they're either refurbished and sold, or recycled. One hundred percent of the net proceeds generated by the sale of the refurbished phones are used for grants to national organizations working to end family violence. All phones donated that are obsolete or damaged are recycled according to strict environmental standards. The site links to ReCellular's Free Data Eraser, which provides instructions for securely erasing many cellphones before getting rid of them. Visit www. wirelessfoundation.org/calltoprotect.

✓ **Cell Phone Trade-Ins:** This site lets you dispose of your cellphone and help those in need, or just pad your wallet a little bit with cash. The service also welcomes iPod trade-ins. Either way, check the site to see whether your phone or iPod model is one they want. If so, you can print a prepaid label to mail your unwanted gadget to Cell Phone Trade-Ins, and soon thereafter, you'll get a check in the mail if you opted for cash. Go to http://cellphonetradeins.com.

✓ **Collective Good:** This mobile devices recycling service makes a donation on your behalf in exchange for your unwanted cellphone, pager, or PDA. Charity choices include The United Way, The Red Cross, Friends of the Congo, and several others. Go to www.collectivegood.com.

- **Computers for Schools:** Computers for Schools (`www.pcsforschools.org`) provides a low cost alternative for achieving technology in the classroom, and welcomes contribution of quality computer equipment and support dollars from donors across the nation to accomplish their refurbishing work.

- **eBay Rethink:** The eBay Rethink Initiative (`http://pages.ebay.com/rethink`) brings together industry, government, and environmental organizations to offer ways to donate, sell, reuse, and recycle unwanted gadgets and gear. Donations through eBay Giving Works allow you to donate part or the entire final sale price to the nonprofit of your choice. I talk about selling your unwanted digital stuff on eBay later in this chapter.

- **Freecycle Network:** Freecycle Network (`www.freecycle.org`) is a grassroots nonprofit movement of people who are giving (and getting) stuff — including electronics — for free in their own towns. It's all about reusing and keeping good stuff out of landfills. Local groups are moderated by a local volunteer group — or what Freecycle refers to as "them's good people." Membership is free.

- **Goodwill:** Encourages businesses and individuals to donate their new and used computers. Typing your address into the Goodwill locator (`www.goodwill.org`) can point you to the nearest drop-off site for your unwanted computer and peripherals. Just like yours truly, Goodwill recommends you securely erase your personal information from your unwanted computer's hard drive, the basics of which I cover at the end of this chapter, and more fully in the next chapter.

- **National Cristina Foundation:** A not-for-profit foundation dedicated to the support of training through donated technology. The foundation matches donated computers and other technology products with charities, schools, and public agencies in all 50 states, Canada, and in many countries around the world. Check it out at `www.cristina.org`.

- **Plug-In To eCycling:** A partnership between the U.S. Environmental Protection Agency (EPA) and consumer electronics manufacturers, retailers, and service providers, Plug-In To eCycling (`http://epa.gov/epawaste/partnerships/plugin/index.htm`) offers you more opportunities to donate or recycle — eCycle — your used electronics. The site offers links to numerous partners, including the major mobile phone carriers AT&T, T-Mobile, Sprint, and Verizon (whose HopeLine program provides wireless phones to victims of domestic violence).

- **Recycles.org:** A service project aimed at area businesses, residents, schools, and nonprofit organizations interested in recycling and reusing computers. The organization's Web site serves as a regional and nationwide exchange board directly connecting your unwanted computers with nonprofit organizations in need. You fill out a form describing what you want to get rid of and then respond to requests that come in to choose where your unwanted stuff winds up.

✔ **ReUseIt Network:** The ReUseIt Network (`http://reuseitnetwork.org`) is an online forum for connecting local community members who are getting rid of items they no longer want with those who can use castoff electronics — and most anything else you can think of (except drugs), such as sofas, bikes, and even horse manure. The site organizes groups by state.

✔ **TechSoup:** This computer and software technology philanthropy service for nonprofits is the exclusive U.S. distributor of Microsoft product donations. TechSoup (`http://techsoup.org`) helps connect nonprofits and libraries to over 240 products from 25 donating partners. The site can help you find a refurbisher who will ensure that equipment they send to nonprofits and schools works and runs legal copies of software.

Finding the TechSoup refurbisher section is a bit confusing; here's how to get there:

Go to `http://techsoup.org`, click the Learning Center tab, and then select Hardware from the In Learning Center section on the left side of the page. Select the Ten Tips for Donating a Computer article, scroll to "Determine if your old computer can be reused," and then click Donate Hardware in the paragraph that follows.

TechSoup says refurbishers will also make sure anything you donate that they don't use — e-waste — will be disposed of properly.

Note: If your computer is older than five years, TechSoup advises you send it to a commercial recycler.

✔ **Wirefly:** Wirefly's dot-com sister site claims that it sells more cellphones every day than any other online authorized dealer. So it's only fitting its dot.org site offers a trio of options for getting rid of your unwanted cellphone: recycling for charity, donating (via Cell Phone Trade-Ins), and paying you cash. Charities include the ASPCA, Livestrong, Sierra Club, and several others. Visit `www.wirefly.org`.

Trading In or Selling Gadgets for Greenbacks

Trading in your unwanted gadgets and gear can reward you with cash or credit to apply toward the purchase of something new. Most trade-in programs expect your unwanted gadget to be in good condition, though some will take back damaged goods, such as a working iPhone or Palm smartphone with a cracked screen that otherwise operates as it should.

In this section, I offer you some general information about dealing with trade-in sites and how the process works. I also list several manufacturers and dedicated trade-in companies so that you can find one that fits your needs.

Most of the trade-in Web sites promise to securely wipe out your computer's hard drive; however, doing the job yourself can give you a greater sense of security that your personal identity information is truly gone for good. To learn more about *disk wiping,* check out Chapter 15.

The basics of the trade-in process

How much can you get back in cash or credit? More than you might imagine. Visiting many of the trade-in Web sites I tell you about in a minute, I was pretty floored to find out many of the products I plugged into the quote calculators yielded cash or credit values in the hundreds of dollars.

Before you take the plunge into the trading game, keep these points in mind:

- **Big-ticket items:** Trading in big-ticket items such as TVs isn't a common practice — however, the trade-in Web sites EcoNEW and VenJuvo do accept HDTVs. Both are included in my list of trade-in Web sites, later in this chapter.

- **Set-up fees:** Most retailers will take away your old TV at no cost to you when you buy a new HDTV. Others might charge you a setup fee to deliver, turn on, and connect your other entertainment gear to your new big screen before hauling off the old one. Ask about any such fees before sealing the deal.

- **Recycling:** Trade-in Web sites typically promise to responsibly recycle gadgets or other electronics they deem hopelessly useless — which means your e-waste won't wind up in a toxic dump overseas. Before spending your hard-earned green, however, check with your retailer to find out whether they recycle items they take back.

- **Mix-and-match trades:** Many computer manufacturers offer trade-in programs that include taking back products from other makers in exchange for cash or credit toward the purchase of a new computer or peripheral — how convenient.

Trade-in programs that offer cash or credit for your unwanted digital stuff vary in what they take back. Here's a rundown of the products you can send to trade-in programs:

Desktop and notebook computers	Camcorders
mobile phones	Multimedia projectors
iPods and MP3 players	Home audio receivers
PDAs and handheld computers	Car audio receivers

Video game consoles	Computer servers
GPS navigation devices	HD-DVD players
Cameras (digital and nondigital)	

The process of trading in your unwanted gadgets and gear typically goes something like this:

1. **Visit the trade-in service's or reseller's Web site to see whether they take back what you want to get rid of.**

   Some take back many different things, others just specific products, such as cellphones or iPods.

2. **Click drop-down menus to select your product and specifics.**

   Information you can provide includes the model, how much memory it has, and what condition it's in.

3. **Generate a quote based on what you enter in Step 2 to find out the estimated value of what you're getting rid of.**

   Figure 14-2 shows how much this iPod would fetch.

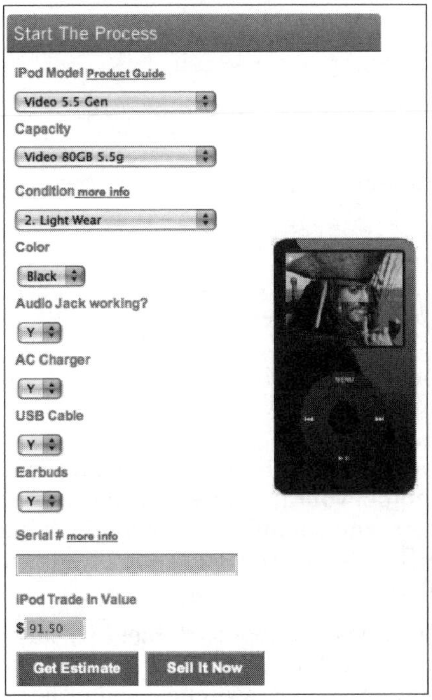

Figure 14-2: Estimating your used iPod's trade-in value.

4. **If the price sounds right to you, register with the trade-in Web site.**

   Registering generates a shipping label (sometimes prepaid, sometimes not) for sending in your stuff and generally wraps up by having you choose whether you want cash or credit.

5. **Wait for your check or credit to come through, then spend or apply toward new purchase.**

Finding a trade-in site for you

Some trade-in programs are run by the computer manufacturers, although several of the computer companies partner with branded versions of DealTree's EZTradein.com trade-in Web site (see Figure 14-3). EZTradein.com also takes back a heck of a lot of other electronics stuff, as you'll soon see.

Trading in your old computer and peripherals is an option offered by these computer manufacturers:

- ✔ **Apple:** www.apple.com/environment/recycling; for education and business customers
- ✔ **Dell:** http://dell.eztradein.com
- ✔ **Gateway:** http://gateway.eztradein.com
- ✔ **HP:** www.hp.com/united-states/tradein
- ✔ **IBM:** www-935.ibm.com/services/us/index.wss/offerfamily/financing/a1030525
- ✔ **Sony:** http://sony.tradeups.com
- ✔ **Toshiba:** http://toshiba.eztradein.com

The Sony trade-up program, shown in Figure 14-4, also takes back PDAs, smartphones, camcorders, and digital cameras.

Trade-in Web sites that give you cash or credit in exchange for your unwanted electronics include the following:

- ✔ **EZTradein.com:** Welcomes trade-ins from the preceding list, and pays you seven days after receipt of your unwanted gadgets and other electronics. EZTradein partners with a number of computer manufacturers, as well as Best Buy, TigerDirect.com, Buy.com, and other consumer electronics makers and retailers.
- ✔ **Sony:** Accepts copiers, desktops, notebooks, tablet PCs, large flat panel displays, monitors, PDAs, smartphones, printers, professional audio, cameras, camcorders, storage devices, switches, and projectors. Visit http://sony.tradeups.com.

Figure 14-3:
EZTradein
accepts
all kinds of
unwanted
electronics.

Figure 14-4:
Trade up the
old for the
new with
Sony.

✔ **Gazelle:** Gazelle (www.gazelle.com) lets you trade in most of the typical stuff — computers, iPods, digital cameras — and also video games and Blu-ray movies. Unlike most other trade-in programs, Gazelle thoughtfully provides a prepaid mailing box to ship your stuff. As of this writing, the site reports an average payment to customers is $115. Gazelle sends payment by way of PayPal, check, or Amazon.com gift card.

✔ **GameStop:** Find the store nearest you to drop by and trade in video game consoles, games, and accessories for store credits or cash. Opting for credit earns you more — and you can use the credit either in-store or on the GameStop Web site (www.gamestop.com).

✔ **Consumer Electronics Recycling:** Accepts trade-ins of working or broken cellphones, smartphones, PDAs, iPods, and Zune media players, and assuming that your gadget is in the condition you said it was, the company sends your check in as little as one or two business days. That's fast money! Visit www.cerecycle.com.

✔ **Small Dog Electronics:** Trading in your unwanted Mac or iPod earns you credit toward the purchase of any new product or products from Small Dog Electronics (www.smalldog.com/tradein).

✔ **MyBoneYard:** MyBoneYard (myboneyard.com) is one of the few trade-in Web sites to take smaller size flat panel displays. You can also trade in desktops, notebook computers, and a variety of laptops and monitors, but MyBoneYard doesn't accept models from IBM, Dell, and Sony. Additionally, it accepts smaller-sized plasma TVs. MyBoneYard appears to be the least lucrative; receiving payment — in the form of a prepaid Visa credit card — can take three to ten weeks.

✔ **EcoNEW:** Choosing a gift card from three partners — Sam's Club, Office Depot, or Navy Exchange stores (for our men and women in the armed services) — is your only way to get paid for your unwanted computers, camcorders, and other gadgets. EcoNEW (http://econewonline.com) also accepts LCD HDTV trade-ins, which is uncommon in the trade-in biz.

✔ **FlipSwap:** Trade in your iPod or cellphone for in-store credit or a check sent to you or a charity of your choosing if you prefer. Or type your zip code to locate a nearby FlipSwap partner retail store to walk in with your trade in and walk out with a little more green in your wallet. Visit www.flipswap.com.

✔ **NextWorth:** Specializing in iPod and iPhone trade-ins only, NextWorth (http://nextworth.com) partners with Amazon (giving you gift card credits for your unwanted player or phone) and with J&R electronics (www.jr.com) for online or instant in-store credit if you happen to be in Manhattan and opt to drop by.

✔ **BuyMyTronics:** Trade in your iPod, cellphone, PDA, video game machine, laptop, digital camera, or camcorder and get a check in the mail a few days after BuyMyTronics (http://buymytronics.com) verifies that what you sent is as you described. Opting for electronic funds transfer by way of PayPal instead of the mail makes your exchange of unwanted gadget for e-cash all the more green.

One unusual trade-in service is www.techforward.com, which requires you to purchase what's called a Guaranteed Buyback plan when you purchase a new computer or other electronic device. With the Buyback plan, you know exactly what TechForward will pay you when you get rid of your gadget or PC in as little as six months, to as long as two years, from the time of initial purchase.

Selling Your Old Electronics on Craigslist

Selling your unwanted gadget or other electronic device by listing it in your local paper or on an online listing site, such as Craigslist (www.craigslist.org), isn't much different from selling anything — be it a couch, article of clothing, or vintage GI Joe with Life-Like hair (eh hem).

These tips will help you get started:

✔ **Do comparative pricing:** Check your local paper to see whether others are selling items like the gadgets you want to get rid of, and then price accordingly.

✔ **Be descriptive:** When you list unwanted gadgets, a colorful description can grab a potential buyer's eye better than being too simple or vague. For instance, a listing such as "Pretty in Pink Palm Centro for Your Valentine" is more attention getting than "Palm Cellphone."

Signing up to list items for sale on Craigslist, shown in Figure 14-5, is free. Craigslist.org is the big umbrella Web site beneath which the service's hundreds of regional sub-sites live.

Choosing the region closest to you may seem like the obvious thing to do; however, if you live close to a city, you might want to choose it instead to reach more potential buyers. For instance, say you live in Jersey City and take the train into Manhattan every day. Listing your original iPhone you've replaced with the latest model in the Big Apple not only attracts more potential buyers, it makes it easier for you to exchange the device with the buyer on your lunch break or on your way to or from work.

Selling my HDTV on craigslist

Selling my too-big LCD HDTV on craigslist when I moved into my tiny new home saved me the fees and astronomical shipping cost I would have had to charge a buyer if I were to sell it on eBay. Even if I sold it locally by way of eBay, I would still incur eBay's fee for the commission it takes on a sale in addition to the fee to list the item in the first place.

The buyer of my HDTV happened to live just a few blocks away, a young woman whose parents came along with her to check out the set. They were nice people and I knocked $50 off the price because I can relate to saving money at that age (and at my age!).

Sensing I could trust the buyer, I had no qualms about giving out my address so they could come by and see the set. On the other hand, when I've sold smaller unwanted gadgets, I've asked the buyer to meet me in a public place, such as a bookstore cafe.

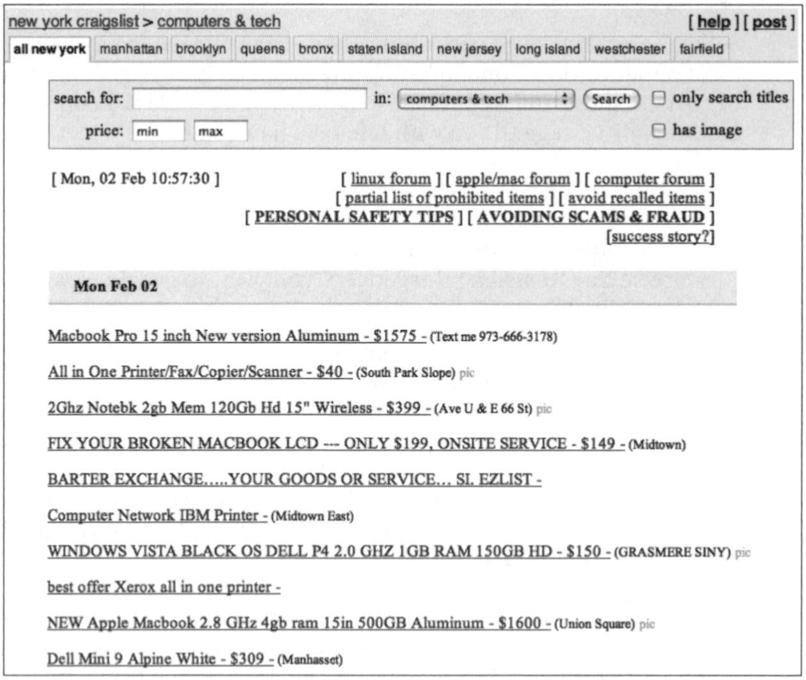

new york craigslist > computers & tech   [**help**] [**post**]

| all new york | manhattan | brooklyn | queens | bronx | staten island | new jersey | long island | westchester | fairfield |

search for: _____ in: computers & tech ⬦ (Search) ☐ only search titles

price: [min] [max]   ☐ has image

[Mon, 02 Feb 10:57:30]   [linux forum] [apple/mac forum] [computer forum]
                              [partial list of prohibited items] [avoid recalled items]
                    [PERSONAL SAFETY TIPS] [AVOIDING SCAMS & FRAUD]
                                                        [success story?]

Mon Feb 02

Macbook Pro 15 inch New version Aluminum - $1575 - (Text me 973-666-3178)

All in One Printer/Fax/Copier/Scanner - $40 - (South Park Slope) pic

2Ghz Notebk 2gb Mem 120Gb Hd 15" Wireless - $399 - (Ave U & E 66 St) pic

FIX YOUR BROKEN MACBOOK LCD --- ONLY $199, ONSITE SERVICE - $149 - (Midtown)

BARTER EXCHANGE.....YOUR GOODS OR SERVICE... SI. EZLIST -

Computer Network IBM Printer - (Midtown East)

WINDOWS VISTA BLACK OS DELL P4 2.0 GHZ 1GB RAM 150GB HD - $150 - (GRASMERE SINY) pic

best offer Xerox all in one printer -

NEW Apple Macbook 2.8 GHz 4gb ram 15in 500GB Aluminum - $1600 - (Union Square) pic

Dell Mini 9 Alpine White - $309 - (Manhasset)

Figure 14-5:
Selling locally on Craigslist can help you earn more for your unwanted gadgets.

That strategy worked for me when I listed my original Xbox 360 in Philadelphia rather than the tiny Jersey Shore beach town where I live. Because I'm always up for the one-hour drive to Philly to hang out with my best friend, I had many more responses and offers to buy my Xbox 360 than when I originally tried selling it closer to home. On the other hand, listing my HDTV locally and finding a buyer was no trouble at all because it appealed to a wider potential buying audience. See the nearby sidebar, "Selling my HDTV on Craigslist."

Auctioning Unwanted Gadgets on eBay and Other Auction Web Sites

Auctioning your unwanted gadgets and other electronic stuff on the big daddy auction site of them all — eBay — can reach the world's largest audience of potential buyers. (See Figure 14-6.)

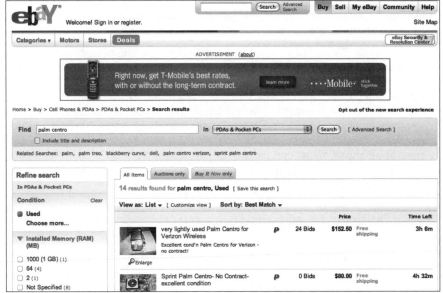

Figure 14-6: eBay is the Big Kahuna of online auctions.

Selling my unwanted gadgets and other tech-related stuff on eBay has been a mostly positive experience. However, as I explain in the sidebar "How I lost $1500 by not playing by the rules," understanding every eBay rule and policy can prevent a similar screw-up from happening to you when you're selling anything for more than a few bucks.

The following nuggets of advice can help make selling your unwanted gadgets and digital stuff more profitable:

✔ **Know your competition.** Search for the same product you're selling, and pay attention to how high the bids are for the auctions that are ending the soonest. Also, select the "Completed Auctions" check box in the left column to narrow down the final prices the same gadget sold for. Price your gadget a little lower or around the same price that many other sellers landed for the same gadget to increase your likelihood of closing a sale.

How I lost $1500 by not playing by the rules

I was new to eBay at the time, and I didn't know not to send an item to an address other than the verified one, which would have protected me against the fraud I endured. Here's the story: I listed an unwanted notebook computer on the site. No one bid on it, but when the auction ended, I received an e-mail from a guy offering the Buy It Now price of $1200 — and he said he would pay up to $300 to cover shipping the notebook to South Africa.

I said yes; however, I wouldn't ship the computer until I had withdrawn the full amount from my PayPal account, which allows me to withdraw $500 per day with the debit card the electronic funds service offers members. Three days later, I had the money in hand; it didn't seem like it should matter that the guy asked me to ship the computer to what he said was his work address, rather than the verified home address PayPal listed for the buyer.

I shipped the computer by way of UPS, tracked it online, and saw that it arrived about a week later. That was the last I thought of it until a few months later, when my PayPal account suddenly appeared $1500 in the red. The service sent me notification that the transaction was being investigated, and when I e-mailed the buyer, he said it was just an error and I shouldn't worry, it would get cleared up.

The long and short of it: The guy had stolen a credit card to pay me, and when the owner of the card eventually discovered the illegal charge, they notified PayPal, which in turn hit me with what's called a chargeback. The moral of the story? Shipping only to a buyer's confirmed address can protect you from losing your shirt.

- ✔ **Think twice about Buy It Now and Reserve Prices.** Attaching a Reserve Price to your unwanted gadget can turn off potential buyers — especially if you set a high Buy-It-Now price. Deciding whether to use the Reserve Price option can spell the difference between turning away bidders and getting lots of potential buyers bidding on your item.

- ✔ **Avoid padding your shipping costs.** Hiking your shipping charge beyond what it costs to ship your unwanted gadget can turn off potential buyers and limit your chance of making a sale. Offering free Priority Mail or other relatively fast but affordable shipping service for smaller gadgets can increase your chance of attracting a winning bidder.

- ✔ **Choose the proper category.** Choosing the most accurate category for your item can make the difference between lots of people bidding on it versus fewer bids because potential buyers didn't find it. Selling an iPod in the MP3 Players category attracts buyers, but choosing the iPod category specifically ensures that the right group of potential buyers sees your unwanted iPod.

- ✔ **Remember that a picture is worth a thousand words.** Posting a clear, detailed picture of your gadget and any accessories that come with it shows potential buyers your item is for real and in (hopefully) nice condition. Skipping a photo or using a stock image limits your chance of selling your items.

✔ **Allow PayPal protection.** Allowing potential buyers to pay for your item with PayPal can increase your chance of selling your item. Protect yourself from scam artists by requiring bidders to have a PayPal account and ship only to a winner's confirmed address to help assure potential buyers that you're an honest seller.

✔ **Build a feedback rating.** Successful eBay sellers have one critically important thing in common: a positive feedback rating. Build your own positive feedback rating by accurately listing your items, communicating with bidders and buyers, shipping on time, and leaving accurate feedback.

✔ **Enlist eBay-savvy friends.** If auctioning only one or a few gadgets is all you have in mind, consider having an eBay savvy friend, family member, or trusted coworker with a positive rating sell your unwanted item on your behalf, then reward their efforts by allowing them to keep a share of the sale price.

Getting into the nitty gritty of selling your gadget on eBay is beyond the scope of this book — but not beyond the scope of *eBay For Dummies,* 5th Edition, by Marsha Collier (Wiley). Read that book if you're planning to sell lots of unwanted gadgets and other things to become a top-notch selling pro.

The best-known auction Web site, eBay isn't your only option. Considering what makes the other online auction Web sites different from eBay can help you choose the one best suited for getting rid of your stuff:

✔ **Bonanzle:** Bonanzle (`www.bonanzle.com`) refers to itself as an online marketplace for buying and selling items faster while having more fun, stating its specialty is "helping you buy and sell items that aren't shiny, new, and mass-produced." Posting items is free, and Bonanzle charges low final offer value fees that range from fifty cents for items under $10, and $1, $3, and $5 for items under $50, $100, and $1000. Anything more than that costs sellers only $10.

✔ **eBid:** Charging no listing fee and a final value fee of only 3 percent to basic free members, the growing eBid member base (`http://ebid.net`) makes it worth taking a look at. eBid eliminates the final value fee for members who pay for Seller+ privileges for as little as $1.99 per week to $59.99 per year. At the time of this writing, eBid.net has a lifetime Seller+ membership offer for $49.99.

✔ **PlunderHere:** PlunderHere (`www.plunderhere.com`) says that its goal is to become the "go to" marketplace for buyers and sellers. With no fee for listing items and a small final value fee from .01 to 2.5 percent, it may well be where you go to sell your gadgets. PlunderHere also charges small fees for listing options, such as adding video, or for featuring your item on the site.

✔ **Overstock.com Auctions:** Overstock.com Auctions (`auctions.overstock.com`) states that its listing, upgrading (if applicable), reserve price, and end of auction final value fees are 33 to 50 percent lower than "our major competition." Hmm, I wonder who they're talking about? Anyway, fees are based on a percentage of the selling price, and the service's feedback rating system is similar to "The World's Biggest Auction Web Site Whose Name We Shall Not Speak" — which can make for more reliable buyers.

✔ **Wigix:** Wigix (`www.wigix.com`) calls itself a "socially-driven marketplace," where you can communicate with others to negotiate prices. Unlike eBay, Wigix doesn't charge you to list an item. And making money without selling anything by perfecting item descriptions in Wigix's catalog can earn you a slice of the revenue pie. Selling a gadget for under $25 is free, and Wigix takes a commission of only $1.50 from both buyer and seller for items sold up to $100. Wigix takes an additional 2 or 3 percent commission for items selling over $1000.

Chapter 15

Erasing Your Personal Information before Getting Rid of Gadgets

. . . .

In This Chapter

▶ Obliterating your personal information

▶ Considering trust in determining how to prepare a giveaway

▶ Deauthorizing password-protected computer programs before giving away your PC

▶ Deleting user account files on your computer

▶ Restoring factory settings

▶ Getting rid of deleted files on hard drives for good

. . . .

*I*n Chapter 14, I explain how donating, or "gifting," your unwanted computer or mobile phone is a greener action than tossing the device in the trash. Maybe you prefer to make some extra bucks by selling items rather than giving them away. Either way, hooray! The planet thanks you — and so will the lucky recipient or organization on the receiving end of your act of kindness if you're giving without taking cash in return.

Before waving bye-bye to an old notebook computer or digital camera, you can protect your identity from possible theft by potentially unscrupulous buyers or benefactors. To protect your identity, you can erase the many bits of personal data stored on built-in memory devices, memory cards, and hard drives.

This chapter explains how to wipe out personal identity information from gadgets you're tossing so that your bank account or other aspects of your personal privacy aren't wiped out or exposed.

Deleting Your Personal Stuff — The Short Way and the Long Way

Wiping personal information is easier on some devices than on others. Gadgets without hard drives — such as mobile phones and smartphones and personal digital assistants (PDAs) — are typically easy to wipe clean. You might think that eliminating personal information from an unwanted computer should involve only the task of dragging files and folders to the Recycle Bin or Trash, and then emptying those receptacles. So long, and thanks for all the memories, right? Not so.

Although documents and other files tossed into the Recycle Bin or Trash appear to vanish after it's emptied, some or most of the information stays on the hard drive. It's stored in a hidden format that seems inaccessible to us mere mortals but is in reality easy pickings for hackers, tech-savvy types, and nosy, entry-level service technicians.

Choosing a *disk wiping* option is the most thorough way to securely erase the hard drive on your soon-to-be-discarded computer. Unlike the basic formatting process, disk wiping overwrites the drive with gobbledygook, a process that techies refer to as *zeroing*.

The trade-off to wiping the disk is that completing the job can take many hours or an entire day or more, depending on the level of security you choose. That's because the drive is wiped many times in a row. The larger the number of wipes, the stronger the guarantee that even the faintest recollection of you is truly a thing of the past.

For a more thorough take on the ins and outs of disk wiping, check out the Apple description of how the Mac's Disk Utility, shown in Figure 15-1, gets the cleanup job done, at http://support.apple.com/kb/TA24002?viewlocale=en_US. The Disk Utility options are few, but many are the hours you wait after choosing the more secure 7-Pass or 35-Pass Erase options.

When you dig into a gadget's settings, you often find an option to erase and reset the gizmo, as shown in Figure 15-2. For example, after you press the Erase All Content and Settings button on the iPhone and it restarts, it has no recollection that you ever existed.

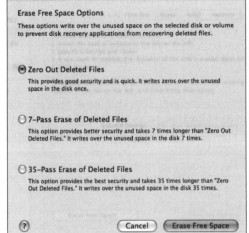

Figure 15-1: The more secure the disk-wiping option, the longer you wait for it to complete.

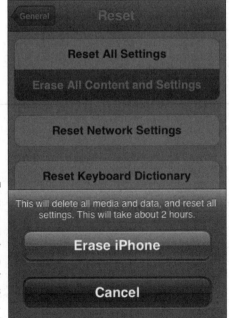

Figure 15-2: Press the red button and your relationship with your iPhone is history.

On some cell phones or PDAs, erasing personal data and settings is often accomplished by tapping a few keys or holding down a button or three while powering on the gadget. Voilà! The gadget then has straight-from-the-factory freshness and is ready to start a new personally rewarding relationship with a fresh face (and fingertips) — just like it was when you turned on the gadget for the first time.

Saying "sayonara" to gadgets and computers that have built-in or attached hard drives requires that you give them special consideration and take certain steps to ensure that the recipient doesn't also wind up scoring your personal or sensitive information in exchange.

Determining how to prepare a computer before disposing of it comes down to one thing: trust.

Considering Trust to Decide How to Erase Personal Information

Giving an unwanted computer to a trusted family member or friend who isn't likely to install a snooping utility to scan the hard drive for previously deleted information is generally assurance enough for most people that past memories once living on the computer will remain so forever.

If you donate or sell a computer to a stranger or someone not quite close enough to you to call a friend or trusted acquaintance, you have to decide which approach to take before turning over the goods: quick and relatively easy or complex and time consuming.

To know you is to trust you

Preparing a computer before giving it away to someone you trust requires a few steps before you're ready to give it away:

1. Back up files and media that you want to keep.

2. Reclaim rights to the programs and media you want to keep (see the later section "Deauthorizing Computer Programs before Giving Away Your PC").

3. Create a new user account for the soon-to-be owner (for this step and Step 4, see "Deleting Your User Account Files without Reformatting the Hard Drive," later in this chapter).

4. Delete your user account.

5. Run optional disk cleanup programs for additional security (see "Completely Erasing Deleted Files and Hard Drives," at the end of this chapter).

I want to trust you, but I'm just not sure

Restoring a computer by using the factory restore discs generally supplied with most computers is the easiest way to wipe out and restore the hard drive to factory freshness. Performing a factory restore requires these steps:

1. Back up the files and media that you want to keep.

2. Reclaim rights to the programs and media you want to keep (see "Deauthorizing Computer Programs before Giving Away Your PC," later in this chapter).

3. Restart the computer with its factory restore discs (see "Restoring Computers to Factory-Fresh Condition," later in this chapter).

4. Choose the Reformat option, if it's available, and run the restore process.

5. (Optional) Install drivers and bundled programs.

6. (Optional) Run system updates.

7. (Optional) Reinstall and update additional programs.

Depending on how much time you're willing to invest in your giveaway, you might want to reinstall any programs that were added after you originally purchased or acquired the computer. Ditto for however many tens or possibly hundreds of hardware drivers and operating system and third-party program updates, upgrades, and patches you downloaded to keep all your programs up-to-date.

Finders keepers

How risky is selling or giving away a computer without first wiping the hard drive of private information? Very, according to a 2003 study conducted by two MIT graduate students.

Sifting through data left on 158 hard drives, the students uncovered more than 5,000 credit card numbers as well as financial and medical records, personal e-mail messages, and digital pictures of the (ahem) "adult" variety.

One hard drive purportedly contained a year's worth of banking transaction information — from the automatic teller machine it previously served before the students got their hands on the drive.

The students said around 60 percent of the drives had been formatted but not securely wiped, which enabled the students to recover files deleted from the drive's previous owners' documents folder with a simple disk recovery utility.

Zapping cellphones and smartphones in seconds

If the gadget you're giving away is a mobile phone, smartphone, or MP3 player that has no built-in hard drive, erasing your past is a cinch.

Restoring most mobile phones to factory freshness generally requires keying in a series of symbols and numbers and then pressing the Call button to carry out the wipeout.

On the other hand, you zap a Palm smartphone and PDA by holding down a button while powering on the device. On some devices, choosing an option from the device's Settings menu erases and restores the gadget to factory freshness.

Check the manual's index for the word *resetting* or *restoring* or *erasing,* or search the Web for your particular device and the phrase *factory restore* or *factory reset.*

On the other hand, you might decide to restore the computer's hard drive to minimal factory freshness and leave to the new owner the task of all that extra reinstalling and updating.

Deauthorizing Computer Programs before Giving Away Your PC

Before you get rid of a computer, you have to deactivate or deauthorize programs that require a password or a registration code to use or enable them to open files or media. Apple iTunes, for example, lets you play purchased music on as many as five computers, and it's your job to keep track of which computers you authorized to play the music you paid for.

Wiping out a hard drive before deauthorizing iTunes means saying goodbye to one of those keys to your purchased music kingdom. (See the following sidebar, "Deauthorizing iTunes," for more details.)

Sometimes, *authorizing* and *deauthorizing* go by different names — including activating and deactivating, authenticating and deauthenticating, and locking and unlocking. Whatever you call the process (see Figure 15-3), the purpose is always the same: To give you the right to manage usage rights to products or media that are rightly yours.

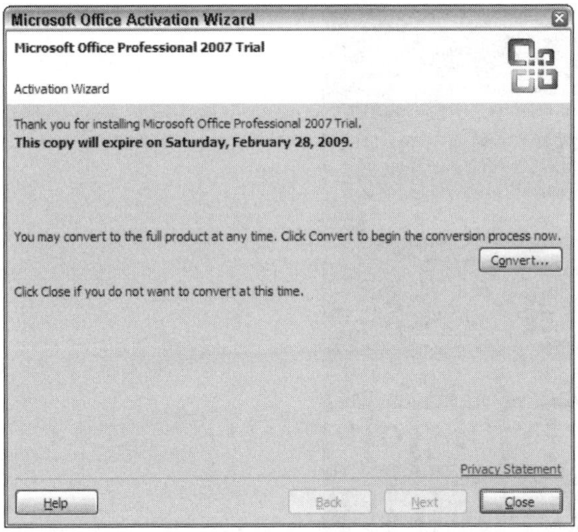

Microsoft Office Activation Wizard ⊠

Microsoft Office Professional 2007 Trial

Activation Wizard

Thank you for installing Microsoft Office Professional 2007 Trial.
This copy will expire on Saturday, February 28, 2009.

You may convert to the full product at any time. Click Convert to begin the conversion process now.

Convert...

Click Close if you do not want to convert at this time.

Privacy Statement

Help   Back   Next   Close

Figure 15-3:
Apple calls it authorization, and Microsoft calls it activation.

Many programs — such as Microsoft Office, for instance — use a similar per-computer or per-device protection scheme, so be sure to deactivate or, in the case of Office, uninstall those programs before getting rid of desktop and notebook computers.. This way you'll be able to reinstall programs you've deactivated on your new computer using the program's installation disc (or in many cases, downloading the latest version), and then activating with the registration code you received when you originally purchased the program.

Like their bigger-box cousins, running programs on gadgets sometimes require you to authorize them, as shown in Figure 15-4, and in some cases, deauthorize them if you intend to download and use them on a different device.

Making a list of the programs that require deactivation or deuthorization can prevent potential headaches (and spending) in the future.

Print, or e-mail yourself, a copy of any receipts containing activation codes you may need the next time you install or use the programs.

Figure 15-4:
After you
download
an iPhone
application,
your autho-
rization is
required to
install and
run it.

Launch each program on your list and deactivate or deauthorize accordingly. Here are some examples of programs, utilities, and games that require authorization or activation to use them:

- ✔ Adobe Photoshop
- ✔ Bioshock
- ✔ iTunes
- ✔ Microsoft Office
- ✔ Norton Antivirus
- ✔ Mark/Space Missing Sync
- ✔ Nero
- ✔ Spore

Deauthorizing iTunes

I cite Apple iTunes in this sidebar to demonstrate how to deauthorize a program on your computer. Why iTunes? Because it's the world's most popular program for buying music online, chances are good that you're using it too! And I'm guessing that you, like me, would rather not accidentally give up the right to play music or videos you purchased for your own listening and viewing pleasure.

You can use your iTunes account and media you've purchased (movies, TV programs, music) on up to five computers. Apple lets you deauthorize all five computers once per year if you've authorized all five uses but aren't accessing iTunes on five computers. The option isn't available unless all five uses are active, and it doesn't appear if you used the option already but have yet to pass the one-year mark.

To deauthorize iTunes on a Mac or Windows computer, follow these steps:

1. **Open iTunes.**

2. **Choose Store⇨Deauthorize Computer.**

3. **Select Deauthorize Computer for Apple Account and enter your Apple ID and password.**

   If you see the alert (shown in the figure), you know you have successfully deauthorized iTunes.

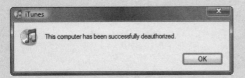

Warning: Deauthorize iTunes on your computer before upgrading RAM, adding a new, built-in hard disk or another system component, or reinstalling Windows. Changes such as these can cause iTunes to treat your upgraded computer differently from the one you originally authorized, so be sure to deauthorize to avoid the potential need to use a second usage slot on the same — albeit somewhat different — system.

To deauthorize every computer all at once and reset the usage count to zero:

1. **Open iTunes.**

2. **Click iTunes Store in the left column.**

3. **Click your account name in the upper-right corner.**

   If the button is labeled Sign In, click it and sign in to your iTunes account, and then click the Account button again to display your account information.

4. **Enter your password.**

5. **Click the Deauthorize All button.**

6. **Click Deauthorize All Computers button.**

Note: You don't see the Deauthorize All button if you authorized fewer than five computers or if you already used the option within the past 12 months.

Deleting Your User Account Files before Getting Rid of a Computer

The steps necessary to delete your personal user account files and information before giving a computer to someone you trust varies between Macs and Windows PCs.

As I explain at the beginning of this chapter (see "Deleting Your Personal Stuff — the Short Way and the Long Way"), deleting your user account files — items such as documents, photos, videos, and music — makes them *appear to disappear* from the hard disk.

You can recover some or most of the files by using a disk recovery utility such as Active@ UNDELETE, shown in Figure 15-5. Running a disk wiping utility erases all traces of your deleted user account files but doesn't erase the computer's operating system or programs. (See the section "Completely Erasing Deleted Files and Hard Drives," at the end of this chapter.)

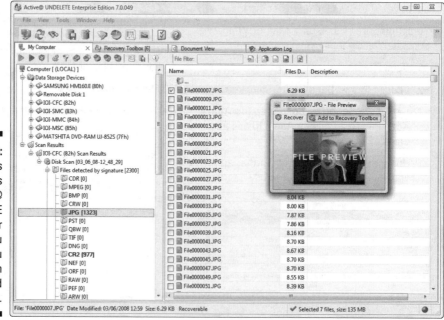

Figure 15-5:
Utilities
such as
Active@
UNDELETE
can recover
files you
thought you
deleted from
your hard
disk.

Deleting your Windows XP user account and creating a new one

To follow the step-by-step instructions in this section, you must turn on the Classic View for your Windows computer's Control Panel (if it isn't already on). With Classic View turned on, we're both on the same page, so to speak, which means you won't stumble when following the steps. To turn on Classic View, choose Start⇨Control Panel, and then click the Classic View link.

To get your Windows XP computer ready to give away, create a new user account for the new owner and delete your user account by following these steps:

1. **Choose Start⇨Control Panel⇨User Accounts.**

   The User Accounts control panel appears.

2. **Click the Create a New Account link.**

   The Name the New Account box appears.

3. **Type the name of the computer's intended owner, and then click Next.**

   If you don't know who's getting your giveaway, type a generic name, such as My PC.

   The Pick an Account Type screen appears with the account type you want — Computer Administrator — already selected, as shown in Figure 15-6.

4. **Click the Create Account button.**

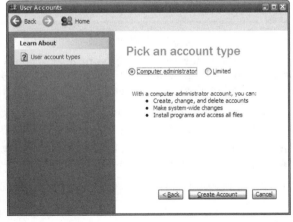

Figure 15-6:
The default
Computer
Admin-
istrator is
the account
type you
want.

The User Accounts control panel appears, showing the new user's account and your account (and any others your computer may have).

To delete your user account, you must log out of your account and log in with the new one.

5. **Save any open documents or files and close all open programs.**

6. **Choose Start⇨Log Off.**

    The Windows log in screen appears.

7. **Click the new user's icon to log in.**

8. **Choose Start⇨Control Panel⇨User Accounts.**

    The User Accounts control panel appears.

9. **Click your user account icon.**

    The Change Account box appears.

10. **Click the Delete the Account link.**

    The Delete Account dialog box opens, as shown in Figure 15-7.

Figure 15-7:
Decide
whether
to keep or
delete the
old files.

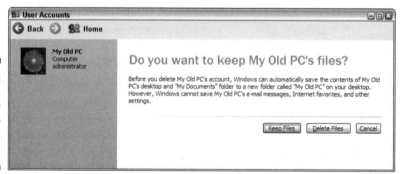

11a. **To save your files in a folder named after your user account to the Desktop (so you can back up your files to an external hard drive or discs before you give away the computer), click the Keep Files button.**

    Windows might spend a few seconds or many minutes moving your user account folder to the desktop, depending on how many files you have.

11b. **If you already backed up your personal files and you're certain that you didn't forget anything, click the Delete Files button.**

    A warning box appears asking if you are sure you want to delete the user account.

12. **Click the Delete Account button.**

    It can take windows a couple of seconds or several minutes to delete your files.

13a. **If you chose Delete Files in Step 11b, Windows moves the contents of your user account folder to the Recycle Bin; right-click the Recycle Bin and then choose Empty Recycle Bin. Then click Yes to confirm your choice.**

    Or

13b. **If you chose Keep Files in Step 11a, Windows leaves the contents of your user account folder on the Desktop.**

14. **Copy your user account folder to a backup hard drive or other backup device, and then drag the folder to the Recycle Bin.**

15. **Right-click the Recycle Bin and choose Empty Recycle Bin; then click Yes to confirm your choice.**

Deleting your Windows Vista user account and creating a new one

To follow the step-by-step instructions in this section, you must turn on the Classic View for your Windows computer's Control Panel (if it isn't already on). With Classic View turned on, we're both on the same page, so to speak, which means you won't stumble when following the steps. To turn on Classic View, choose Start⇨Control Panel, and then click the Classic View link.

To get your Windows Vista computer ready to give away, create a new user account for the new owner and delete your user account by following these steps:

1. **Choose Start⇨Control Panel⇨User Accounts.**

    The User Accounts control panel appears.

2. **Click the Manage Another Account link.**

    The User Account Control warning box appears.

3. **Click the Continue button in the User Account Control warning box.**

    The Manage Accounts control panel appears.

4. **Click the Create a New Account link.**

    In the Create New Account dialog box that appears, you can enter the computer owner's name and choose between a standard user or administrator account.

5. **Type the name of the computer's intended owner, as shown in Figure 15-8.**

   (If you don't know who's getting your giveaway, type a generic name, such as My PC).

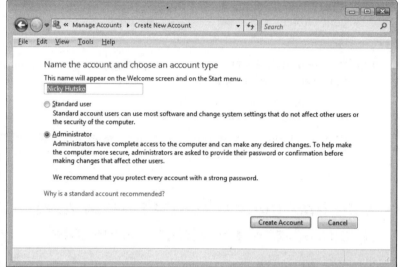

Figure 15-8:
Entering the computer owner's name in the text box.

6. **Select the Administrator option and then click the Create Account button.**

   The Manage Accounts control panel appears, showing the new user's account and your account (and any others your computer may have).

   To delete your user account, you must log out of your account and log in again with the new account.

7. **Save any open documents or files and close all open programs.**

8. **Choose Start➪Arrow➪Log Off.**

   The Windows log in screen appears.

9. **Click the new user's icon to log in.**

10. **Choose Start➪Control Panel➪User Accounts.**

    The User Accounts control panel appears.

11. **Click the Manage Another Account link.**

    The User Account Control warning box appears.

12. **Click the Continue button in the User Account Control warning box.**

    The Manage Accounts box appears.

13. **Click to select your user account icon.**

    The Change an Account box appears.

14. **Click the Delete the Account link.**

    The Delete Account box appears, asking whether you want to keep or delete the old files, as shown in Figure 15-9.

Figure 15-9:
Choose
whether
to keep or
delete the
old files.

15a. **To save the files that are in your user account folder to the Desktop so that you can back them up before you get rid of the computer, click the Keep Files button.**

    The Confirm Deletion box appears. Go to Step 16.

15b. **If you already backed up your personal files and you're certain that you didn't forget anything, click the Delete Files button.**

    The Confirm Deletion box appears.

16. **Click the Delete Account button.**

    If you chose Keep Files, it can take a few seconds or several minutes for Windows to move the contents of the user account that you're deleting to a folder on the Desktop. Go to Step 17a.

    If you chose Delete Files, go to Step 17b.

17a. **If you chose to Keep Files, copy your user account folder to a backup hard drive or another backup device, and then drag the folder to the Recycle Bin, right-click it, choose Empty Recycle Bin, and then click Yes to confirm your choice.**

    And you're done.

17b. If you chose Delete Files, it can take Windows a few seconds to many minutes to delete your account and files from your hard disk.

Note: Your deleted files will not appear in the Recycle Bin.

Deleting your Mac user account and creating a new one

To prepare your departing Mac to give away, create a new user account for the new owner and delete your user account by following these steps:

1. **Click the Apple menu and choose System Preferences.**

   The System Preferences box appears.

2. **Click the Accounts icon to open the Accounts panel.**

   The Accounts panel appears.

   *Note:*If the lock icon in the lower-left corner of the screen is locked, click it and type your password, and then press Return.

3. **Click the plus sign (+) button above the lock icon.**

4. **On the New Account panel that appears (see Figure 15-10), click the drop-down menu button and select Administrator.**

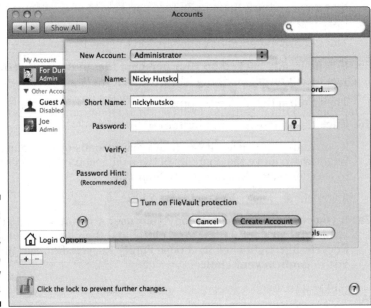

Figure 15-10: Fill in the necessary informationto create a new account.

5. **Type the name of the computer's intended owner, and then press the Tab key to have the Mac automatically generate the new user's Short Name, also shown in Figure 15-10.**

   If you don't know who's getting your computer, type a generic name, such as My Mac.

6. **Click the Create Account button, and then click OK to dismiss the warning about creating a new account without a password.**

   Let the new owner come up with a password!

   The Accounts preference panel appears, showing your account and the new account (and any other accounts your Mac may have).

   To delete your user account, you must log out and log back into the new account.

7. **Click the Apple menu and choose Log Out.**

   The Mac log in screen appears.

8. **Click the new user account's icon to log in.**

9. **Click the Apple menu and choose System Preferences.**

   The System Preferences box appears.

10. **Click the Accounts icon.**

    The Accounts panel appears.

    Note: If the lock icon in the lower-left corner is locked, click it and type your password, and then press Return.

11. **Click your Account icon in the left column, then click the minus sign (–) button above the lock icon.**

    You're asked whether you're sure that you want to delete the user account, as shown in Figure 15-11. You must also decide what to do with the your Account's Home folder, which contains your personal files.

12a. **If you want to back up your files before deleting them, select either Save the Home Folder in a Disk Image or Do Not Change the Home Folder, and then click OK.**

   If you need a refresher course in the details of making a backup copy of your files, check out the nearby sidebar, "Save yourself."

12b. **If you've already backed up your user account files and don't need to save them, select Delete the Home Folder option, and then click OK.**

   Your Mac may take a few seconds or several minutes to either delete your Home folder or create a disk image of it, depending on how many files it contains.

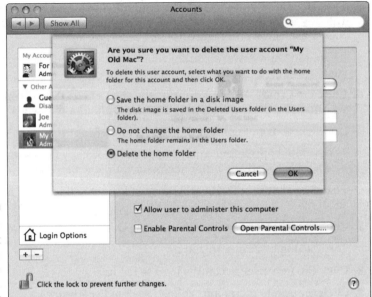

Figure 15-11:
Decide what
to do with
the Home
folder.

Save yourself

You have two ways to save your files so that you can back them up to an external drive or to another backup device after you remove your user account:

✔ Save the files as a compressed disk image file that occupies less backup space and can be decompressed at any time if you need to reclaim some or all of your files.

✔ Leave the files intact so that you can copy some or all of them to a backup drive before you delete the folder.

Both choices leave the saved file or folder in the Users folder.

To open the Users folder, choose Finder⇨ *Macintosh HD*⇨Users. (Replace *Macintosh HD* with whatever you named your hard disk.)

After backing up your user folder or compressed disk image file, you can drag it to the Trash then right-click on it and choose Empty Trash; then say a final farewell to your former file-based self.

Restoring Computers to Factory-Fresh Condition

Factory freshness means that no personal data is on the gadget or computer, and all its custom settings are reset to the defaults that the manufacturer chose at the factory. Restoring a Mac or Windows computer is relatively quick and easy — as long as you're still in possession of the operating system recovery discs.

The steps for restoring Macs and Windows computers to factory freshness are generally alike, and they go something like this:

1. Insert the original system recovery (or separately purchased Mac OS X or Windows XP or Vista operating system) installation disc in the CD or DVD drive and power on or reboot the computer

2. Hold down the C key on the Mac keyboard to start from the disc rather than the hard disk; in Windows, you press any key when prompted about booting from the disc.

3. Choose the option to erase the hard disk quickly (and insecurely) or slowly (more secure) before restoring the operating system and bundled applications.

4. Pour a favorite beverage and read a book or go for a long walk, and return an hour or so later to a newly restored computer that has no recollection of you and is more than happy to take up with a new owner, thank you very much.

5. Hand over the computer to its new owner — and don't forget to include the recovery discs so that the new person can perform the same amnesiac wipeout in the future!

Only the quick-and-dirty versus slow-and-secure formatting choices need additional explanation, so choose your system, grab those system discs, and let's rock and recover!

Formatting and restoring a Windows hard drive

You restore a Windows Vista or XP PC to factory freshness as described in the preceding set of steps. However, which formatting options you choose from depends on the make and model of the computer you're preparing to give away and on its recovery discs.

Some computers are shipped with several discs for restoring not only the Windows operating system but also additional programs that come bundled as part of the package. Some computers require you to burn your own set of recovery discs with a bundled disc burning utility, as shown in Figure 15-12.

Figure 15-12:
Restoring
factory
freshness
with discs
you burn.

Because the steps to recover a Windows Vista or XP PC with the bundled factory restore discs vary by make and model, you might need to poke around to find options for how the hard drive is formatted before installing the operating system.

Alternatively, you can skip the manufacturer's recovery discs entirely and restore the computer by using the Windows Vista or XP installation CD. It either came with the computer or you purchased it later on.

Choosing the Windows-only method guarantees that you have the option of selecting the longer, full-formatting option.

If your factory restore discs don't offer a secure formatting option, you can first perform the first steps of a Windows-only restore, followed by the factory restore process. Why the double take? The first pass lets you choose the longer and more secure method of wiping out the hard disk before installing Windows — which you'll skip because you use the factory restore discs to do that job.

Windows XP

Boot the Windows XP installation disc and format your hard drive by following these steps:

1. **Insert the Windows XP disc into the CD drive and then restart your computer.**

   If your version of Windows XP came with a floppy disk, insert it into the floppy drive and then restart your computer, and when prompted, insert the CD and press Enter.

2. **Press any key when you see the prompt** Press any key to boot from CD or DVD.

   The Windows XP setup screen appears and begins loading the setup files it needs to run the installation. This step can take a few minutes.

3. **When the Windows XP Installation Welcome screen appears, press Enter.**

   The licensing agreement appears.

4. **Press F8 to agree to the licensing agreement.**

   Your computer's hard drive partition (or partitions) appears.

5. **Press the arrow keys on your keyboard to select the C: hard drive partition (if it isn't already selected), as shown in Figure 15-13.**

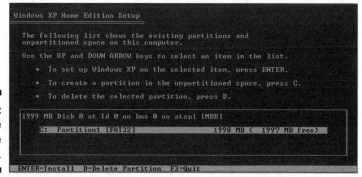

Figure 15-13:
Select the
C: hard drive
partition.

6. **Press the D key to delete the partition, and then press the L key to confirm your choice.**

7. **If your computer lists additional partitions, repeat Steps 6 and 7 until you've deleted all the partitions.**

   A single unpartitioned space appears in the list after you've deleted the hard drive partition (or partitions).

8. **Press C to create a new partition.**

   A partition sizing screen appears.

9. **Press Enter to create the new partition with the maximum size possible (already filled in by the installation program).**

   Windows creates the new partition.

10. **Press Enter to choose the newly created partition (if it isn't already selected).**

11. **Choose Format the Partition by Using the NTFS File System and then press Enter to continue. (If NTFS isn't listed as an option, choose FAT32.)**

Do *not* choose the Quick option, because it only prepares the hard disk for Windows XP and does not erase all your previous personal files and settings.

12. **Press F to format the hard drive.**

A progress indicator appears as the hard drive is formatted. This step can take several minutes or longer if the hard drives is very large.

13. **When the hard disk format is complete, follow the prompts that appear in order to install Windows XP, or cancel the installation if you want to reboot with the factory recovery discs and restore the system to factory freshness.**

Windows Vista

Boot the Windows Vista installation disc and format your hard drive by following these steps:

1. **Insert the Windows Vista installation disc and power on or reboot the computer.**

2. **Press any key when you see the prompt** Press any key to boot from CD or DVD.

The Windows Vista installer program displays a progress indicator as it loads the installation files, and then the Windows Vista installer country selection window appears.

3. **If the defaults are not the choices you want, click the drop-down menus to change your language, date and time, and keyboard choices, then click the Next button.**

4. **Click the Install Now button.**

Windows will ask you to please wait while it loads the installation files, and then the Windows Vista Product Activation window appears.

5. **Type the Windows Vista product key code, then click the Next button.**

Skip typing the product key if you're running the Windows Vista installation only to format the hard drive before you reboot with the factory recovery disc or discs to restore the computer. Click No when prompted a second time to enter your product key.

6. **If you're prompted to select the version of Windows Vista you're installing, choose the one that matches the installation disc, and then click the Next button.**

The Windows Vista licensing agreement appears.

7. **Click the check box to accept the license terms, and then click the Next button.**

   The Upgrade and Custom installation window appears.

8. **Click the Custom button.**

9. **Click the hard drive partition and then select the Drive Options link.**

   A number of options appears below the hard drive partition.

10. **Click the Delete button, and then click the OK button on the warning message.**

    The hard partition will be deleted and the unpartitioned hard drive appears with the title "Unallocated Space."

11. **Click New to create a new partition, and then choose NTFS Format (if it isn't already selected).**

    The partitioned hard drive appears.

12. **Select the Format option, and then click the Next button.**

    The Windows Installer will format the hard drive. This step can take several minutes or longer if the hard drive is very large.

13. **Click Next if you want to continue installing Windows Vista and follow the prompts, or click the Close box to cancel the installation so that you can reboot with the factory recovery discs and restore the system to factory freshness.**

Formatting and restoring a Mac hard drive

Choosing the most thorough hard drive formatting option is the key to securely erasing personal information from a Mac that you're giving away.

To format and restore a Mac hard drive, follow these steps:

1. **Insert the Mac System Recovery or OS X Install disc into your Mac's disc drive.**

2. **Power on your Mac, and then immediately press and hold the C key to boot the Mac from the disc.**

   When you hear the DVD drive spinning around and see startup indicator you can let go of the C key.

   The language selection screen appears.

3. **Choose your language, and then click the arrow button in the lower-right corner.**

4. **When the Welcome screen appears, click the Utilities menu at the top of the screen and choose Disk Utility.**

   The Disk Utility program appears.

5. **Click Macintosh HD in the top-left column, and then click the Erase tab.**

   Disk Utility hard disk erase options appear.

6. **Click the Security Options button, and then choose one of the three erase options shown in Figure 15-14.**

   The Zero Out Deleted Files option is the fastest way to wipe your Mac's hard disk, but it's not as thorough or secure as the 7-Pass Erase or 35-Pass Erase options, which can take several hours to more than a day to complete.

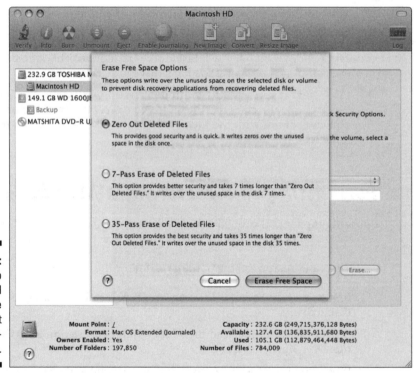

Figure 15-14: The Zero Out Deleted Files is the fastest but least thorough option.

7. **Click the Erase Free Space button in the lower-right corner, and then click the Erase button to acknowledge the warning and begin the disk wiping process.**

   A progress indicator appears.

8. **When the disk wiping is done, choose Disk Utility⇨Quit Disk Utility.**

   The Disk Utility returns you to the Mac OS X Installer Welcome screen.

9. **Click Continue on the Welcome screen, and then follow the prompts to restore the Mac's OS X operating system and applications.**

Completely Erasing Deleted Files and Hard Drives

Deleting files removes them from being seen, but some or most of the files remain on the hard drive in a hidden format — even if you empty your Recycle Bin or Trash. Although mere mortals can't easily recover the hidden files, hackers, tech-savvy types, and nosy entry-level service technicians can.

If you have a hopelessly useless computer that you're sending to a recycler rather than to a new user, it's extremely important that you wipe the hard drive. Doing so prevents anyone who's handling the computer on its way to the grave from potentially recovering your personal files or information from the drive.

Disk wiping utilities remove all traces of hidden files left behind on a drive's free space after deleting your user account — or an entire hard drive before running one of the computer recovery methods described earlier in this chapter.

Wiping Mac hard drives is easy, thanks to the Disk Utility program included with every Mac.

Although Microsoft doesn't include a disk wiping program in Windows, you can find several that are free to download.

Wiping Windows hard drives

To wipe your Windows computer's hard drive before restoring it to factory freshness, see the earlier section "Formatting and restoring a Windows hard drive."

If you can't find the Windows XP or Windows Vista installation disc to wipe out the hard drive on a computer you're sending to a recycler, worry not — all is not lost. Running one of the free disk wiping utilities in the following list can wipe your hard drive clean before you dispose of it.

You don't have to completely reformat your hard drive and reinstall everything before you give it away; you can just wipe the free space on it after you create a new user account and then delete yours. That way, the new owner gets a like-new experience — with OS and all the programs still on the computer — but no traces (not even hidden ones) of your personal files, which you've deleted. You can do so by using one of these free utilities:

- **Darik's Boot And Nuke (DBAN):** Creates a bootable floppy, CD, or USB storage device to start up your computer and wipe built-in or attached hard drives. See `www.dban.org`.

- **CMRR Secure Erase:** Available at `cmrr.ucsd.edu/people/Hughes/SecureErase.shtml` and has the same function as DBAN (see preceding bullet).

- **No File Recovery:** Wipes free space without erasing the Windows operating system, programs, and other files you want to keep on the hard drive. See `www.softdd.com/no-file-recovery`.

- **Active@ Kill Disk:** Similar to No File Recovery (see preceding bullet), with the option to create a bootable floppy, CD, or USB storage device to start up your computer to wipe free space or the entire drive. The free version offers only a single-pass wipe. See `www.killdisk.com`.

- **Eraser:** Similar to the programs in the preceding two bullets and available at `www.heidi.ie/node/6a`.

All the disk wiping utilities in the preceding list offer multiple levels of disk wiping thoroughness, from relatively fast and fairly secure to slow as molasses and safe from even the CIA's savviest tech wizard.

Wiping Mac hard drives

To completely wipe your Mac's hard drive before restoring the computer to factory freshness, see "Formatting and restoring a Mac hard drive," a little earlier in this chapter.

You might, instead of restoring your Mac to factory freshness, have deleted your user account files and created instead a new account for the intended recipient of your Mac (see "Deleting Your User Account Files before Getting Rid of a Computer," earlier in this chapter). If so, you can run Disk Utility to ensure that deleted files are securely erased without wiping out the operating system and installed applications.

To securely wipe deleted files from your Mac's hard disk, follow these steps:

1. **Click the Desktop to switch to the Finder; then press Command+Shift+U to open your Mac's Utilities folder.**

   Note: You find the Utilities folder in your Mac's Application folder, in case you prefer to navigate to it with your mouse.

2. **Double-click the Disk Utility icon to launch it.**

   The main Disk Utility screen appears and displays your Mac's built-in hard disk and any other disks in the left column.

3. **Click the disk labeled Macintosh HD (or whatever you may have renamed your Mac's main startup hard disk), and then click the Erase tab.**

   Disk Utility hard disk erase options appear.

4. **Click the Erase Free Space button.**

   The Erase Free Space Options box appears.

   The Zero Out Data option is the fastest way to wipe your Mac's hard disk, but it's not as thorough or secure as either the 7-Pass Erase or 35-Pass Erase option, which can take several hours to more than a day to complete.

5. **Click the Erase Free Space button in the lower-right corner; then click the Erase button to acknowledge the warning and begin the disk wiping process**

6. **When the disk wiping is done, choose Disk Utility⇨Quit Disk Utility.**

Chapter 16

Recycling and Properly Disposing of Hopelessly Useless Gadgets

. . . .

. . . .

*I*n Chapter 14, I talk about how it's greener to donate, gift, or sell your unwanted cellphone or computer instead of tossing it in the trash. But even when your intentions are good, some out-of-service electronics — such as that decades-old PC clone in the garage that ran on floppy disks — are so out-of-date they're more hindrance than help.

Ditto for that reasonably modern smartphone that slipped from your hand and blew apart in four directions when it hit the pavement. Either way, opting to recycle — or *e-cycle* — hopelessly useless or expired electronic stuff — or *e-waste* — is still the smarter, greener choice over dumping dead electronics in the garbage. Chapter 1 discusses why burying dead gadgets and other electronic devices has a hazardous effect on not only local environments and the people living in them but also on the planet and worldwide population.

As the saying goes, "One man's trash is another man's treasure," especially when the trash we're picking over is of the electronic variety. Although a fried PC's number-crunching days may be long over, a number of recyclable elements retrieved from its insides — such as gold, copper, and aluminum — may have already found new life inside that spanking new notebook computer propped open on your seatback tray table.

If you're reading this chapter, you've come to the last option in the reduce-reuse-recycle mantra for being green. In the following pages, I explain how to securely erase personal information from gadgets or computers and help you decide whether they should be left whole or separated into parts before shipping or dropping off to one or more environmentally responsible recyclers or corporate e-cycling programs.

Understanding E-Waste and E-Cycling

E-waste refers to an electronic device or gadget that has these characteristics:

- ✔ It has reached the end of its lifecycle.
- ✔ It's broken beyond repair.
- ✔ It's still working but isn't worth upgrading, selling, or giving away.

E-cycling is the process of properly disposing of e-waste.

E-waste from around the world that isn't e-cycled often winds up in China, where it's cheaper to dump than properly dispose of.

The environmental organization Greenpeace estimates that 20 to 50 million tonnes (metric tons) of electronics are discarded every year — enough e-waste to fill a train of containers to encircle the entire planet!

Computers and gadgets have hundreds to thousands of components, many of which contain toxins such as lead and mercury, and hazardous chemicals such as brominated flame retardants.

Some researchers estimate up to 75 percent of unwanted electronic devices and gadgets are in storage because many people are uncertain how to properly dispose of their unwanted e-waste.

An e-waste recipe for disaster

Environmental watchdog organization Greenpeace (www.greenpeace.org/electronics) cites the following elements and factors as the most common and harmful ingredients in the world's hazardous e-waste recipe for disaster:

✓ **Brominated flame retardants (BRFs):** Used in circuit boards and plastic casings, some BFRs don't break down easily and wind up building up in the environment. Learning disorders, memory impairment, impact on the thyroid and estrogen hormone systems, and resultant behavior problems after exposure in the womb are cited as potential effects caused by exposure to BFRs.

✓ **Tetrabromobisphenol (TBBPA):** Another brominated flame retardant, it's linked to neurotoxicity. As much as 1000 metric tons of TBBPA went into the manufacturing of 674 million cellphones in 2004.

✓ **Cathode ray tubes (CRT):** Approximately 10,000 metric tons of lead went into the total worldwide sales of CRTs in 2002. Although CRTs are increasingly a thing of the past, exposure to the lead contained in discarded CRTs has been linked to intellectual impairment in children, as well as blood, reproductive, and nervous systems disorders in adults.

✓ **Cadmium:** The highly toxic cadmium bioaccumulation is used in older CRTs, rechargeable batteries, and contacts and switches. Exposure to it primarily affects the kidneys and bones.

✓ **Mercury:** Used to produce flat-screen displays, mercury is linked to brain and central nervous system disorders, especially during the early stages of development.

✓ **Chromium hexavalent compounds:** Chromium hexavalent compounds are used to produce metal housings and are highly toxic and carcinogenic.

✓ **Polyvinyl chloride (PVC):** A plastic that is used for insulation on wires and cables in some electronics. When produced or disposed of by incineration or burning, PVC releases chlorinated dioxins and furans. These toxins are highly persistent in the environment and are toxic in even low concentrations.

Fortunately, public awareness of e-waste and e-cycling is on the rise, as more states, cities, communities, and individuals do the right thing when it comes to collecting and properly processing and disposing of discarded electronics. Here are just two examples:

✓ California defines unwanted televisions and monitors as hazardous materials; dumping them in the trash is against the law.

✓ As of July 1, 2009, New York City's Electronic Equipment Collection, Recycling and Reuse Act permits New Yorkers to return used electronics to the manufacturer for recycling. In summer of 2010, tossing e-waste in the trash will be illegal for New Yorkers.

Many municipalities collect household hazardous waste, such as dead computers and VCRs, and a growing number of public and private organizations offer local, statewide, national, and international programs to collect, accept, and properly process and dispose of e-waste.

An increasing number of computer, cellphone, and consumer electronics manufacturers offer take-back e-cycling programs to accept not only their own brand of once-new-now-e-waste products, but also products made and sold by competitors. Some of the programs are free, and others require you to pay a processing fee, cover the cost of shipping, or both.

Finding E-Cyclers

The World Wide Web is the most useful tool for finding companies, organizations, and services to collect, process, and dispose of your e-waste.

Visiting your local city, town, or state government's Web site is a good place to start.

Reputable or not?

With public awareness about the harmful environmental effects caused by companies and recyclers who export e-waste overseas on the rise, finding ones that "do the right thing" matters.

Helping take some of the guesswork out of finding responsible recyclers is the e-Stewards program (www.e-stewards.org). Formed by The Basel Action Network and the Electronics TakeBack Campaign, the e-Stewards Web site lists national and mail-in recyclers that meet super-stringent criteria for globally responsible recycling.

However, until many more qualifying e-Stewards recyclers are within reach of the nation's population, your other e-waste disposal options are many — possibly even on the street where you live.

Local or from a distance?

If you live in a city or large town, an e-waste recycler or drop-off location is probably close by — such as the lumber company two blocks from my house that accepts small e-waste items such as rechargeable batteries and discarded cellphones.

The state-run New York City Web site (www.nyc.gov), for instance, explains everything city dwellers need to know about recycling and e-cycling in the Big Apple, including street-side pickup rules and schedules, drop-off locations, and lists of manufacturers and retailers that offer take-back e-cycling programs and services, with Web site links to learn more.

New York City law requires stores that sell rechargeable batteries (or products containing them) to take back dead rechargeable batteries for recycling, no purchase necessary (see Figure 16-1). That means tiny hardware stores and big-name cellphone and consumer electronics superstores alike must accept your gift of dead recyclable cells — no wonder Manhattan is called the world's melting pot!

Considering what kind of unwanted gadgets and useless electronics you're disposing often determines where you can drop off or ship your e-waste.

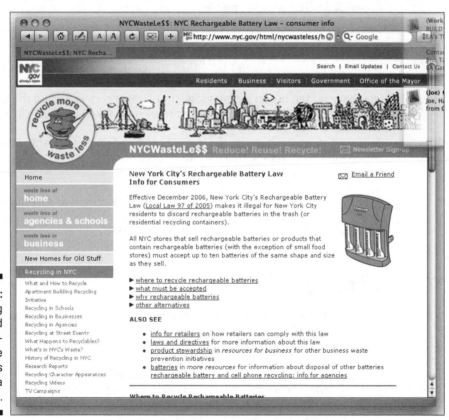

Figure 16-1: Trashing dead rechargeable batteries in NYC is a no-no.

Let your fingers do the walking, er, typing

Near the start of this chapter, I state that the Web is your best friend when it comes to finding an e-cycler, and I'd like to add that the good ol' Yellow Pages are also a useful resource in your quest to get rid of hopelessly useless gadgets and gear. However, I'm not talking about those thick tree-stealing Yellow Pages taking space atop the 'fridge or tossed in the coat closet. I'm referring to the virtual version: `www.yellowpages.com`.

Mobile versions optimized for cellphones and smartphones make it easy to find a recycler near you — literally, if your device has built-in GPS to mark your exact location on the map like the version for the iPhone. Tap the recycler's listed address and the iPhone opens the built-in Google Maps program and displays the location and even directions to get there from your location.

Finding the same visually helpful maps is just as easy with your computer and Web browser. Go to `http://maps.google.com`, type your zip code to home in on your location, type **recycle** in the Search field, and then click Search Maps.

Small stuff is usually easier to unload than bigger items such as TVs, computers, and burned out VCRs. Now that gadget and computer makers, and retailers, have gotten hip to the message that being green is a good thing in the public's eye, more and more corporations offer take-back recycling services.

Some are close by, such as the Radio Shack or Apple Store at the local mall, and others — including Dell, HP, and Apple — offer mail-in take-back programs.

Either way, finding an e-cycler with a good track record of responsible e-waste disposal begins with a visit to one or more Web sites run by e-cycling-friendly organizations and corporations.

Finding a local e-cycler

Finding a responsible e-cycler in your city or town starts with a visit to your computer and the Internet. The following list highlights some starting points to find an e-cycler near you:

> ✔ **Your state or city Web site:** Most states follow the `.gov` Web site address format. For instance, typing `www.nj.gov` will take you to my home state's Web site, where a search on *recycle* turned up links to a directory of statewide recyclers.

Visiting `www.usa.gov/Agencies/State_and_Territories.shtml` provides links to every U.S. state's Web site. You can find a complete list of cities, counties, and towns at `www.usa.gov/Agencies/Local_Government/Cities.shtml`.

Accessing cities and towns with the .gov domain isn't as common as statewide .gov domain Web site addresses. The Web address `www.nyc.gov` takes you to the Big Apple's Web site, while the City of Los Angeles's Web site is accessed by typing either the not-so-obvious Web address `www.ci.la.ca.us`, or the somewhat more intuitive lacity.org.

✔ **The Rechargeable Battery Recycling Corporation Call2Recycle database:** Looking to immediately unload some dead recyclable batteries before you get into the rest of this e-waste and e-cycling business? Point your Web browser to `www.rbrc.org` to search Rechargeable Battery Recycling Corporation's Call2Recycle database for a drop-off center near you.

Chapter 3 is the place to go to learn more about the pluses of replacing disposable batteries with rechargeable cells.

✔ **The Environmental Protection Agency (EPA):** Checking your state's environmental agency Web site for electronics recyclers is another option. Go to `www.epa.gov/epahome/state.htm` to access the Environmental Protection Agency's directory of state agencies. (See Figure 16-2.)

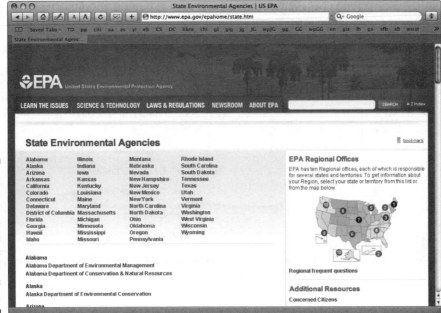

Figure 16-2: Visit the national EPA Web site to find your state's environmental agency's Web site.

Many state and city Web sites also link to national recycling organizations and programs. For instance, type what you're getting rid of and your zip code on Montana's Where to Recycle Web page (`www.deq.mt.gov/Recycle/Where-to-Recycle_New.asp`), and a list of nearby e-cycling organizations and facilities opens, compliments of Earth911.com, which calls itself "your one-stop shop for all you need to know about reducing your impact, reusing what you've got and recycling your trash."

Searching for locations to discard a dead cellphone near my ZIP code led me to a list of nearby recycling facilities, including office retail superstore Staples (`www.staples.com/recycle`) — a nationwide corporation (which happens to provide the perfect segue to my next topic).

National and corporate e-cycling programs

Shipping or dropping off your useless gadgets, computers, and other high-tech gizmos to nationwide organizations, recycling partners, and corporations is fast becoming a practical and reasonably convenient way to get rid of e-waste.

Accessing Web sites for more information about participating organizations and companies sometimes leads you right back to where you started — your own city or town, or one nearby.

Cashing in e-waste the EZ way

Planning to buy a new gadget to replace the one you're getting rid of? As I mention in Chapter 14, a number of Web-based companies let you trade in your dead or unwanted gadgets and other electronic stuff for cash. One such trade-in Web site is EZtradein.com. Use the site's Trade In Estimator to see whether trading in your outdated, dying, or dead item can kick back cash or a Best Buy gift card. EZtradein.com accepts

- Audio and video components
- Camcorders
- Cameras
- Car audio
- Cellphones
- Computers
- Game consoles
- GPS navigation gear
- Monitors
- MP3 players

Choosing an environmentally responsible e-cycling service or program based on e-waste product category is easier with a visit to the Web site myGreen-Electronics.org, which is operated by the Consumer Electronics Association (CEA).

As of this writing, the companies and organizations listed on myGreenElectronics.org take back useless (and in some cases, reusable) computers and peripherals, dead cellphones, spent inkjet cartridges, and lifeless rechargeable batteries.

Itching to jump onto the Web instead of flipping through a list? Check out the EPA's Plug-In to eCycling program (`www.epa.gov/epawaste/partnerships/plugin/partners.htm`) for links to more than 20 manufacturers and retailers committed to collecting, reusing, or recycling old electronics. In addition to the manufacturers and retailers described below, the Plug-In Partners program includes Intel, Sharp, Wal-Mart, Samsung, and others.

Check myGreenElectronics.org and each listed company or organization's own Web site for additions or changes.

Apple

`www.apple.com/environment/recycling`

Apple offers recycling and trade-in programs through its retail stores, and through partnerships with other organizations:

- ✔ For customers in the United States, Apple offers a free recycling program for old computers and displays with the purchase of a new Mac.

- ✔ At Apple retail stores, you can recycle your iPod for free. The program offers environmentally friendly disposal and a 10 percent discount on the purchase of a new iPod.

- ✔ The free recycling program at Apple takes back iPod players or any cell phone from any manufacturer.

- ✔ A trade-in program for education and business customers in the United States has already diverted more than 270 tons of e-waste from landfills since August 2005.

- ✔ A recycling partnership with the city of Cupertino, California, has recycled more than 340 tons of electronics. All electronics products — from any manufacturer — are accepted free of charge.

- ✔ Apple also participates in recycling programs in Asia, including national programs in Japan and Taiwan.

Dell

```
www.dell.com/recycle
```

Dell offers programs to help you repurpose or recycle unwanted computers and peripherals, including

- ✔ **A donation option for old computers:** At Dell Recycling, consumers can donate their computers to the National Cristina Foundation (`www.cristina.org`) to help disabled and economically disadvantaged children and adults in your community. The foundation will even pick up your computer at your doorstep.

- ✔ **Environmentally friendly methods:** Dispose of hopelessly useless computers, keyboards, mice, monitors, and printers, even if it's another brand.

Gateway

```
www.gateway.com/recycle
```

The Gateway Web site states the company is "committed to providing consumers and businesses with environmentally safe options for the disposal of used PCs." However, the company relies on partnerships with other organizations to handle or refer customers to various trade-in and recycling options.

- ✔ For residents of California, Maine, Maryland, Texas and Washington, Gateway suggests that you review your state's specific electronic waste recycling legislation (`www.gateway.com/about/corp_responsibility/elec_waste_recycling_leg.php`) to learn about collection options in your area.

- ✔ Perfect for home users or small businesses with fewer than 10 units, Gateway's Trade-In & Recycle Program (`www.gateway.eztradein.com/gateway`), powered by Dealtree, offers you cash for your old technology. For products with no value, Gateway will ship and recycle them free of charge.

- ✔ Gateway also provides a list of recycling organizations and services. To find it, click the Recycling Options link under the More Options heading.

Hewlett-Packard

```
www.hp.com/recycle
```

HP's recycling program is 20 years strong and spans 40 countries. In addition to recycling, HP offers a variety of product end-of-life management services including donations and trade-ins.

Global recycling services include

- ✔ **HP Inkjet or LaserJet cartridges:** Cartridge boxes contain return materials (available for some products and countries). Order postage-paid return shipping materials online or find other return options.

- ✔ **Hardware products:** HP has an online ordering tool through which you can request recycling services.

Additional North American recycling services include

- ✔ **Rechargeable batteries:** HP has contracted with RBRC (`www.rbrc.org`) which provides over 32,000 retail drop-off locations in the U.S. and Canada.

- ✔ **Cellphones:** Any brand. Free for customers in California who purchase a new HP phone product.

- ✔ **HP/Compaq mercury lamp assemblies, user replaceable:** It's free for customers in Connecticut and Massachusetts.

Panasonic

`www.panasonic.com/environmental/index.asp`

Panasonic's commitment to sustainability dates to its founder, Konosuke Matsushita, who believed it was important to put people (and the environment) before products:

- ✔ As a service to all Panasonic mobile computer individuals and organizational customers, Panasonic, through its partner PlanITROI (`www.planitroi.com/web/panasonic/Touchbook.htm`), offers three interconnected, retired IT asset solutions covering product remarketing, reuse, or recycling.

- ✔ Each option for Panasonic's Toughbook mobile computers offers the assurance that the units will receive proper, environmentally sound disposal at their end of useful life. All units handled under the PlanITROI recycling process are managed in accordance with U.S. Environmental Protection Agency EPEAT standards. The process is free of charge, and all units are handled in accordance with U.S. Department of Defense standards for data removal.

- ✔ Panasonic provides a link to RBRC (`www.rbrc.org`) to help visitors find nearest location to get rid of dead rechargeable batteries.

Sony

```
www.sony.com/recycle
```

Sony offers a nationwide program by partnering with Waste Management's (`www.wm.com`) network of recycling centers around the country. The recycling centers allow consumers and businesses to recycle all Sony products free throughout the United States. The program also accepts all makes of consumer electronics, recycling any non-Sony product at market prices. Other programs include

- **Green Glove delivery program:** When you select premier in-home delivery with any 32"" or larger Bravia LCD television, Sony will remove, package, and haul away your old TV from any room in your house for recycling.

- **Camera and camcorder trade-in program:** Trade in that old camcorder or camera and receive Sony credit to apply to new Sony camcorder or camera purchase online at SonyStyle.com

- **Battery recycling program:** Drop off dead Sony rechargeable batteries at any Sony Style store. Battery recycling bags included with some VAIO PCs let you drop off batteries at a Sony Style store drop box near you.

Toshiba

```
www.toshiba.com/recycle
```

Toshiba offers free recycling of all Toshiba notebooks, gigabeat MP3 players, and packaging, as well as low-cost recycling options for other manufacturer laptops and consumer electronics products. A trade-in partnership with Dealtree (`toshiba.eztradein.com/toshiba`) gives Toshiba customers the opportunity to trade in their laptop or other consumer electronic product for its cash value.

Cellphones, ink cartridges, batteries, and other stuff

For rechargeable batteries, cartridges, and so on, made by Apple or HP, see the earlier sections about those companies. For mobile phones, rechargeable batteries, and other gadgets made by everyone else, take a look at this list:

- **Best Buy:** Consumers can drop old cellphones, inkjet cartridges, and rechargeable batteries for recycling into a drop box in the entryway of each store. The same drop box provides envelopes and labels for people who wish to send in their old inkjet and toner cartridges from home. Best Buy (`www.bestbuy.com/recycle`) also offers free take-away of an unwanted appliance or TV when purchasing a new replacement.

- ✔ **Motorola:** Offers free cellphone recycling programs that are productive fundraisers for K-12 schools (visit (www.motorola.com/recycle). Also provides a link to the EPA's Plug-In to eCycling program (www.epa.gov/epawaste/partnerships/plugin/partners.htm) — which in turn links to program pages of several manufacturers and retailers committed to collecting, reusing, or recycling old electronics.

- ✔ **MyBoneYard:** Offers a simple three-step process to safely recycle your unused electronics in an environmentally friendly way — and maybe even get a little extra green in your wallet! After registering and supplying information about the make and model of your unwanted gadget, MyBoneYard (www.myboneyard.com) e-mails you a prepaid shipping label to send in your device.

- ✔ **Nokia:** Connect to Recycling program is an innovative take-back initiative focused on recycling and safe disposal of products. Keeping Nokia products out of landfills advances human technology and respects the environment. Visit www.nokia.com/environment.

- ✔ **ReCellular:** The world's largest collector, reseller, and recycler of wireless devices and accessories. Based in the United States, with facilities in Brazil and China, the company collects more than 75,000 cell phones at more than 40,000 locations each week. Also administers recycling programs for many wireless service providers, retailers, and manufacturers. Go to www.recellular.com.

- ✔ **TechForward:** Offers a twist on the conventional online trade-in service by allowing you to lock in the future value of your newly purchased products for a fee. After locking in a guaranteed buyback plan, you receive trade-in values for your product for six months to two years from the day you commit. At any point, you can trade in your product for the quoted value. The buyback guarantee also assures that the product is reused or recycled, rather than thrown out. Check it out at www.techforward.com.

- ✔ **Wireless — The New Recyclable:** A wireless industry program to facilitate environmentally sound practices among carriers and manufacturers, as well as to educate consumers about how to recycle their wireless devices. Program participants allow you to drop off your used wireless phones and accessories at their retail stores, regardless of the device's model. Other programs have mail-in options. Go to www.recyclewirelessphones.com.

- ✔ **The U.S. Postal Service:** The USPS (www.usps.com/green/recycle.htm) provides special bags in 1,500 post offices to recycle ink cartridges, BlackBerries, PDAs, and MP3 players free — postage included!

Erasing Personal Information

In Chapter 15, I explain how getting rid of personal information before disposing of unwanted computers and gadgets protects your identity from possible theft by potentially unscrupulous buyers or benefactors. Permanently erasing contacts, phone numbers, pictures, e-mails, and other personal information from cellphones, smartphones, and other portable gadgets is generally fast and simple.

Rather than leave the task of permanently erasing my identity to the unknown, I always perform the "disk-wiping" process described in Chapter 15. However, skipping the disk-wipe steps in favor of a heavy hammer (I'm serious!) is an option if you're willing and able to physically remove the hard drive from the desktop or notebook. Removing a few screws or turning a couple of knobs on the side or back of many desktop PCs provides easy access to the insides. Removing a few screws from the underside of most notebooks usually provides access to the hard disk (see Figure 16-3).

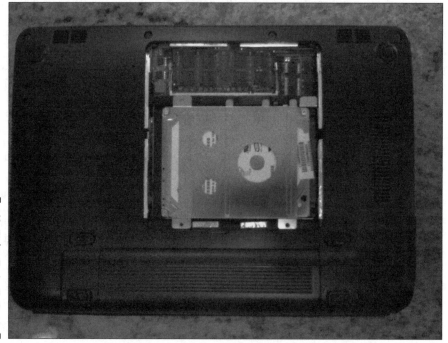

Figure 16-3:
Unscrewing a door underneath your note-book often reveals the hard drive.

You smash up a hard disk to make it unreadable the same way in either case:

1. **Remove the hard drive from the computer.**

   If you're not sure how to identify which part is the hard drive, ask a techie friend to show you.

2. **Place the hard drive on a solid surface such as a workbench or concrete floor.**

3. **Hammer the heck out of the hard drive, making sure to whack all sides and edges to ensure structural damage to the disk inside.**

4. **(Optional) Use a heavy-gauge screwdriver or similar pointed tool to hammer holes through the hard drive and ensure it's truly unreadable.**

5. **When you're satisfied your handiwork has rendered the hard disk unreadable, put down the hammer.**

   Be sure to collect any loose bits that may break away, to include with the computer, smashed hard drive, and any other parts or peripherals you're dropping off or shipping to a recycler.

Hammering the heck out of a hard drive not only renders it unreadable, it's also surprisingly gratifying — especially when the hard drive taking the beating crashed, causing you a little digital heartbreak of your own.

Deciding Whether to Break Down E-Waste or Leave It Whole

Disassembling or breaking down gadgets, electronics, or computers into parts and pieces is rarely necessary before dropping off or sending these unwanted things to recyclers or e-cycling programs.

Call or check the recycler's or take-back program's Web site for Frequently Asked Questions (FAQ) or guidelines to determine whether you need to break down what you're getting rid of.

Keeping useful parts

Sometimes it's wise to break down or remove certain parts from some gadgets. Removing the memory modules from a relatively new notebook that drowned in the swimming pool, for instance, can save money and boost performance on the replacement system — assuming the memory modules still work.

Repurposing an internal hard drive to work as an external backup device for another computer is another option, thanks to kits such as the one shown in Figure 16-4. It turns an unused PC hard drive into a useful external backup drive.

Figure 16-4:
The Samba
turns an
internal
hard drive
into an
external
drive.

Consider keeping these parts to reuse, give away, or sell:

- ✔ **Hard drives** (desktop and notebook PCs)
- ✔ **Internal memory modules** (desktop and notebook PCs)
- ✔ **Removable memory cards** (digital cameras, camcorders, PDAs, cellphones, and notebook computers)
- ✔ **Cellphone and smartphone SIM cards** (transfer yours to the new mobile phone you're acquiring to replace the one you're getting rid of)

Peripherals and other parts and pieces

Getting rid of unwanted computers and other gadgets often means also disposing of related stuff such as printers, mice, keyboards, installation CDs, manuals, and ink and toner cartridges.

Most take-back programs accept these things when you drop off or send in a computer. Check before you say goodbye.

Tossing out-of-date manuals with your weekly paper recycling is fine — just be sure to break down manuals with plastic covers and binders, and recycle separately. Ditto for plastic installation disk binders, sleeves, and packaging.

Information about inkjet and laser toner cartridge recycling and disposal programs offered by the major printer manufacturers can be found on their respective Web sites.

- ✔ **Brother:** www.brother.com
- ✔ **Canon:** www.canon.com
- ✔ **Epson:** www.epson.com
- ✔ **Hewlett-Packard:** www.hp.com
- ✔ **Kodak:** www.kodak.com
- ✔ **Lexmark:** www.lexmark.com
- ✔ **Samsung:** www.samsung.com

Buying a new printer to replace the old one? Visit your new printer manufacturer's Web site to learn about inkjet and toner cartridge recycling programs — or give the gift of renewed life to your spent cartridge by refilling it yourself with a refill kit from www.4inkjets.com. The refill kits (see Figure 16-5) cost substantially less than new inkjet or toner cartridges, and usually you can refill most toner cartridges two or more times. Cha-ching!

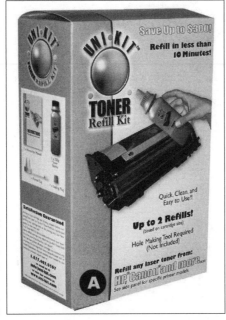

Figure 16-5:
Refilling spent inkjet and toner cartridges costs less than buying new ones.

Part VI
The Part of Tens

In this part . . .

The first chapter in this part serves up ten cool PC add-ons that can give your desktop or notebook that oh-so-ecofriendly touch. The second chapter takes you on a tour of the top ten finalists from the 2009 Greener Gadgets Conference design competition. The third chapter is where to get ten green gadget buying tips. And in the fourth and final chapter, you'll find answers to ten frequently asked questions about green gadgets.

Chapter 17

Ten Cool Green PC Peripherals and Accessories

● ●

*T*ricking out your Windows or Mac desktop or notebook PC with green monitors, printers, and other earth-conscious add-ons can help you round out your effort to minimize your computer's carbon footprint.

The products in this chapter were selected for noteworthy sensitivity to the environment, and though you may wind up selecting a different model, knowing what makes these products green can help you choose the one that's right for you.

PC TrickleSaver

http://tricklestar.com

Powering off all the peripherals connected to your computer is the magic act the PC TrickleSaver performs when you turn off your machine. Abracadabra, instant death to the energy vampires!

Turn your PC on, and the undead come back to life. Lather, rinse, repeat.

Ecobutton

www.eco-button.com

Putting your computer to sleep when you walk away is a heck of a lot easier when you have a glowing green ecobutton nearby to remind you.

Plug the ecobutton into your PC's USB port, set it next to your keyboard or notebook, give it a tap, and within seconds your computer switches to energy-saving mode.

Tap again to wake your PC and an included program displays how many carbon units (and how much power and money) you've saved by doing the button thang.

Bamboo Laptop Stand Workstation

http://kangaroomstorage.com

Okay, I admit this one's a stretch because it isn't a high-tech add-on. But the Kangaroom bamboo laptop stand workstation can bring the warm and inviting texture of bamboo to your notebook and keep it cool at the same time, thanks to a wide vent in the middle that allows your computer's underside fans to breathe freely. Cooler-running computers consume less energy.

What's more — or less, when it comes to clutter — is the space beneath the stand for secreting a power strip, plus two side pocket "docks" for storing and charging your mobile phone, music player, or other portable gadget.

SimpleTech [re]drive R500U 500 GB Turbo

www.simpletech.com

Accented with bamboo, the SimpleTech [re]drive is enclosed in 100 percent recyclable aluminum, which acts as a heat sink, cooling the drive without using additional energy or creating noise.

How green is the [re]drive? SimpleTech says your total power savings could equal up to 90 percent when compared to traditional external drives — which is the equivalent of reducing approximately 475 pounds of carbon dioxide emissions over the life of the drive.

Lenovo ThinkVision L197 Wide 19-inch LCD Display

http://lenovo.com

Earning a coveted Gold Certified label from the Electronic Product Environmental Tool (EPEAT), the Lenovo ThinkVision 197 Wide draws 25 percent less power than its predecessors. Drawing up to 20 watts when turned on and cranked to full brightness, the display barely sips a single watt in standby mode.

Apple 24-inch LED Cinema Display

www.apple.com

Apple's highly recyclable LED Cinema Display has a built-in iSight camera, mic, and speakers, to turn your MacBook into a desktop computer; keyboard and mouse not included.

Like other LED-type displays, this one instantly delivers full-screen brightness when you turn it on. It's also free of environmentally harmful mercury, the glass used in the display is arsenic-free, and the internal cables and components are BFR- and PVC-free.

Ink2image Bulk Ink System

http://ink2image.com

Take your Epson or Canon printer, mix with the Ink2image bulk ink system and what does that equal?

An estimated savings of more than $450 on money you would otherwise spend replacing the equivalent of 64 inkjet cartridges. The Ink2image bulk reservoirs continuously feed the printer with a fresh supply of inks, eliminating the need to change cartridges ever again. Now that's what I call sustainability!

Canon Generation Green Printers

www.canon.com

The new Canon Generation Green printers, including the MP180, draw around 3 watts in stand-by mode, which is considerably less than the 20 watts that non–ecofriendly printers draw.

A 4-in-1 and 2-in-1 printing option for stretching multiple pages across just one — a technique you can do with most printers — cuts your printer's paper consumption by up to 75 percent.

Flipping discarded pages over and printing on the other side can double the potential paper savings. Every last scrap counts!

D-Link DGL-4500 Xtreme N Gaming Router

`http://dlink.com`

Some devices, such as broadband modems and home Wi-Fi routers, may need to stay on most of the time if other folks in your house are tapping into them when you're not.

The D-Link DGL-4500 wireless router can sense whether a computer or video game console plugged into one of its Ethernet ports is off, and then put that port into a reduced-power sleep mode. It also gauges the length of the Ethernet cable, trimming power consumption for shorter lengths.

A Wi-Fi scheduling feature lets you program when the radio turns on and off, which can further increase energy savings. Sorry, Junior, when the DGL-4500 cuts the connection to Xbox Live at bedtime, it's game over — no ifs, ands, or buts.

Netgear 3G Broadband Wireless Router

`www.netgear.com`

Paying your mobile carrier for a 3G wireless plan for anywhere-you-go Internet access can be less of a pinch on your wallet when you tap into the Netgear 3G mobile broadband wireless router.

With it, you can create instant Wi-Fi hotspots at events, campsites, home offices, or most any other remote location where you can pick up your carrier or service provider's 3G signal. Like other Netgear Green models, an on/off switch lets you cut the juice when it's not in use. 3G modem, data plan, and mosquito repellant sold separately.

Chapter 18

Ten Green Gadget Designs

· ·

At this year's Greener Gadgets 2009 Conference in Manhattan, judges presented the top ten finalists in its Greener Gadgets Design Competition. The ten finalists were winnowed from 50 entries by visitors who voted for their favorite on the conference's Web site, `http://greener gadgets.com`. In this chapter, I describe the ten finalists (can you guess which design took the top prize?) and then reveal the winners.

The prizes awarded were as green as it gets: cash!

Bware Water Meter

Knowing how much water is flowing from the faucet or shower is the driving purpose of the imaginary Bware water meter. The meter's digital display draws power from the running water (so batteries are unnecessary), and a more advanced version with WiFi taps into your home network so that you can log how much water you're drawing from the well.

Laundry Pod

After learning about resourceful women who used salad spinners to wash their delicates, the designer of the Laundry Pod decided it was time to build a better, well, panties spinner. Giving new meaning to "Don't get your panties in a twist," the human-powered pod washes, rinses, and spins small loads without wasting the energy or water normally used by traditional washing machines. Croutons and Thousand Island dressing sold separately.

Social-Environmental Station: The Environmental Traffic Light

Designed to communicate environmentally threatening information, such as carbon emissions and other difficult to perceive eco-altering factors, such as air pressure and humidity. Inspired by the ubiquitous traffic light, it remains to be seen — should the concept ever see the light of day — whether Green Police will ticket drivers of gas-guzzlers caught running a CO_2 red light.

Indoor Drying Rack

Citing 96 million apartment dwellers in the United States who live without access to a clothesline, and nearly half as many who live without clothes dryers, the indoor drying rack comes to their rescue. No, it isn't a gadget, but the recycled aluminum and bamboo laminated design concept would be the perfect gift for that special Laundry Pod undergarment-spinner someone in your life.

Thermal Touch

Combining the heat-seeking smarts of a thermal camera with a portable projector, the thermal touch would instantly reveal energy-escaping cracks or insulation inefficiencies by simply waving it over walls, window frames, and other surfaces. Scanning bundled-up little ones before sending them off to school on a winter's day wasn't mentioned, but there's no reason why it wouldn't work, right? Isn't playing let's-pretend fun!

Fastronauts

Childhood obesity? Disposable batteries that poison the ground beneath landfills? Look, up in the sky! It's Fastronauts to the rescue! Playing with the ecofriendly action figures juices up the built-in batteries, and a handlebar-mounted "rocket" would convert peddling into power for a headlight or speedometer. If you're tired of the toy, break apart the shell and recycle it into a new one. It's a toy that keeps on giving!

Tweet-a-Watt

Modifying a Kill A Watt power meter with "off the shelf" components, the Tweet-a-Watt taps into your Twitter social network account to "tweet," at the end of the day, the number of kilowatts of power you've used. The designers suggest multiple units for monitoring an entire household. The ultimate goal? Fellow tweeters will compete to see who can go the lowest. And they just may, because this one-upon-a-time concept was a working gizmo when the conference took place.

Standby Monsters

Growing up, the designer of Standby Monsters said she always thought there was something sinister about standby lights. According to the International Energy Agency, there is: An estimated 5 to 15 percent of the world's domestic electricity is wasted by electronic devices idling their time in standby mode. Slap adhesive-backed Standby Monsters over gadgets and devices in your house and glowing red eyes stare back, scaring you into action. Pull the plug!

Power-Hog

Plug the Power-Hog tail into an outlet, then plug a TV, video game console or other powered device into its snout, and feed the little porker a coin for 30 minutes of play time. When the Power-Hog blinks red, it's time to fork over more allowance or else it's game over. How parents prevent kids from bypassing the energy-savings-starved piglet and plugging directly into the wall was not disclosed.

WattBlocks

Bending over to turn off or unplug power strips to stop energy vampires plugged into them can be a pain the neck. Or back, which is why the designer of WattBlocks envisioned a switch that cuts the proverbial cord with a tap of your foot. Talk about *really* putting your foot down once and for all!

And the Winners Are

To see pictures of all 50 Greener Gadgets Design Competition finalists, or watch video of the live competition, visit http://greenergadgets.com.

These three products took the top three spots:

- **First place, $3,000:** Tweet-a-Watt (see Figure 18-1).
- **Second place, $2,000:** Power-Hog (see Figure 18-2).
- **Third place, $1,000:** Indoor drying rack (see Figure 18-3).

Figure 18-1: Tweet-tweeting public displays of consumption.

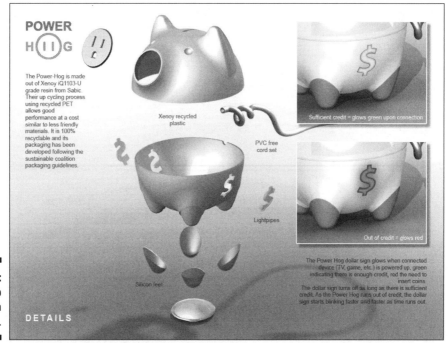

POWER
H (I I) G

The Power-Hog is made out of Xenoy iQ1103-U grade resin from Sabic. Their up cycling process using recycled PET allows good performance at a cost similar to less friendly materials. It is 100% recyclable and its packaging has been developed following the sustainable coalition packaging guidelines.

Xenoy recycled plastic

PVC free cord set

Lightpipes

Silicon feet

DETAILS

Sufficient credit = glows green upon connection

Out of credit = glows red

The Power Hog dollar sign glows when connected device (TV, game, etc.) is powered up, green indicating there is enough credit, red the need to insert coins.
The dollar sign turns off as long as there is sufficient credit. As the Power Hog runs out of credit, the dollar sign starts blinking faster and faster as time runs out

Figure 18-2:
Calling up playtime on your nickel.

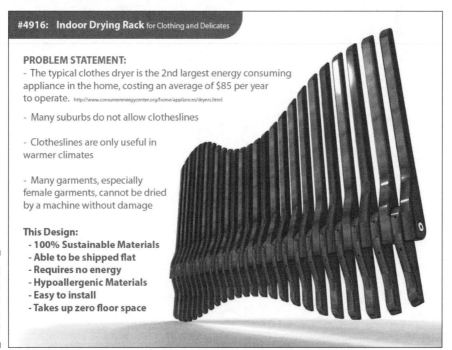

#4916: Indoor Drying Rack for Clothing and Delicates

PROBLEM STATEMENT:
- The typical clothes dryer is the 2nd largest energy consuming appliance in the home, costing an average of $85 per year to operate. http://www.consumerenergycenter.org/home/appliances/dryers.html

- Many suburbs do not allow clotheslines

- Clotheslines are only useful in warmer climates

- Many garments, especially female garments, cannot be dried by a machine without damage

This Design:
- **100% Sustainable Materials**
- **Able to be shipped flat**
- **Requires no energy**
- **Hypoallergenic Materials**
- **Easy to install**
- **Takes up zero floor space**

Figure 18-3:
A design whose drying time has come?

Chapter 19

Ten Green Gadget Buying Tips

● ●

*B*efore plunking down your hard-earned green on new (and not so new) gadgets, the ten buying tips in this chapter can help reduce your negative impact on the planet — and on your bank account.

Don't Buy!

It might sound crazy to start a list of green gadget buying tips with the advice not to buy them, but there's a rhyme to my seeming lack of reason. Throughout this book, I talk about the three Rs — reduce, reuse, recycle — and the bonus R, rethink. So I urge you to rethink whether you truly need that new desktop computer. Upgrading what you already own is an excellent way to reduce and reuse a gadget while also putting off its recycle date.

If the gadget you're thinking about replacing is still working, or if it can be repaired or upgraded so that it can continue to serve you, maybe you don't even need the new gadget.

See Chapters 4, 7, and 8 to read more about getting the most out of gadgets you already own.

Do Your Homework

Figuring out whether a company's green claims are true, false or somewhere in the middle can be next to impossible. Fortunately, many companies are pulling back the veil and making public their environmental impact on many or all levels, including internal practices and policies for reducing consumption. In addition, many companies are detailing the resources and processes involved in producing, packaging, and distributing the electronic products they sell.

Even so, sorting through what's real and what's *greenwashing* (making misleading or false claims regarding a company's green practices and its products) can be dizzying. According to the Consumer Electronics Association (CEA) at MyGreenElectronics.org, the good news is that many more consumer electronics being produced have these qualities:

- ✔ They contain fewer or no harmful chemicals or toxins.
- ✔ They're more energy efficient.
- ✔ They're easier to upgrade, repair, and recycle.

To find out whether gadgets you're thinking about buying are green, visit the following Web sites that evaluate, rate, and list greener electronics by category, brand, or other criteria:

- ✔ **MyGreenElectronics.org:** http://mygreenelectronics.org
- ✔ **Greener Choices:** http://greenerchoices.org
- ✔ **Energy Star:** www.energystar.gov
- ✔ **Electronic Product Environmental Assessment Tool (EPEAT):** www.epeat.net

Chapter 9 has more pointers on making your way through greenwash hype. The other chapters in Part IV can also help you buy smarter when shopping for green gadgets.

Buy Recycled and Highly Recyclable

When doing your homework, pay attention to whether the gadgets you're thinking about buying are made from recycled materials. For example, the Apple MacBook notebook computers are built around a recycled, and highly recyclable, aluminum chassis. Additionally, the Motorola MOTO W233 Renew mobile phone is encased in housing made entirely from recycled water bottles.

When it comes to printing supplies, the Web site Verdant Computing (www.verdantcomputing.com) sells green printer inks and toners in remanufactured cartridges. Printing on recycled paper — and using both sides of the page — can instantly cut your consumption and waste output in half.

See Chapter 16 to find out more about how to properly dispose of or recycle gadgets that have reached the end of their lifecycles.

Buy Reconditioned or Preowned

Buying reconditioned or preowned gadgets is a greener choice than buying new ones, for two reasons:

- ✔ Fewer resources and energy are wasted.
- ✔ You save money.

Many major computer manufacturers — including Apple, HP, and Dell — sell refurbished desktops and notebooks. Other outlets for purchasing refurbished or used but still useful gadgets include

- ✔ The auction Web site eBay
- ✔ Your local newspaper's classified ads
- ✔ Craigslist.org, the regional community classifieds Web site

The buyback Web site EZTradein.com buys unwanted gadgets and then resells them at a reasonable discount. The giveaway Web site Freecycle.org proves that there is such a thing as a free lunch (or gadget); you just might find what you're looking for there without subtracting cash from your wallet.

Buy Small, Think Big Picture

As my grandmother used to say, "Don't fill your plate unless you're going to eat it all." In green gadget–speak, if a notebook computer can serve your computing needs, buy a notebook rather than a desktop model. Doing so is kinder to the environment because notebooks require fewer resources to manufacture, package, ship, operate, and eventually recycle than desktops, their bigger carbon footprint brethren.

The same ecoconscious principle applies to high-definition TVs (HDTVs). Buying an HDTV that's sized ju-u-u-ust right for the room is the greener way to go rather than choosing the biggest (and most energy draining) HDTV money can buy.

Match your green gadget purchases to the purposes they serve as efficiently as possible. Think less is more, and you'll make a smaller negative impact on the planet while achieving positive energy efficiency and savings gains for the life of your appropriately sized gadgets.

Take a Bite Out of Energy Vampires

To know them is to unplug them. I'm talking about energy vampires (the horror-movie way of saying *standby power*). Energy vampires are products that continue to draw power even when they're turned off. Big-time offenders (such as TVs) appear to be off when you press Off; in truth, they're still sipping power to put the picture on the screen more quickly the next time you turn them on.

Smaller-scale energy vampires (such as cellphone chargers, video game consoles, and DVD players) are no less guilty as charged, so to speak, when it comes to wasting energy and costing you extra bucks on your energy bill.

The good news: More and more new electronics are designed to use the smallest amount of energy when they're in Standby mode or fully charged. Two examples: The Sony Bravia VE5 high-definition TV (HDTV) draws almost zero power when it's in Standby mode, and the Samsung E200 Eco mobile phone features a built-in alarm that reminds you to unplug the charger when the battery is fully charged.

To take a bite out of the energy your gadgets waste, I recommend that you invest in a power strip. Then you can plug several gadgets into it and cut the power at one time with the flick of a switch. It's a supercheap way to minimize energy consumption while increasing the savings on your electric bill.

See Chapters 1 and 2 to find out more about energy vampires and smart power strips.

Make the Most of Multifunction Gadgets

In the *really* old days, I might have, at any given moment, carried a cellphone, Nintendo Game Boy handheld video game player, CD player, and Palm Pilot personal digital assistant (PDA). When cellphones grew smarter and turned into smartphones by integrating the PDA with the phone, and CDs gave way to iPods that can also play simple arcade games, such as Pac-Man, four gadgets were reduced to two. And by buying my iPhone, two gadgets have been reduced to just one.

When buying new gadgets, choose ones with multifunction attributes, such as the iPhone and Palm Pre smartphones. This strategy helps you help the environment by reducing the materials and energy necessary to manufacture, ship, and operate multiple devices, and by reducing the number of chargers

Chapter 20

Ten Frequently Asked Questions about Green Gadgets

• •

*W*hat's a green gadget? Who is EPEAT, and why does he spell his name that way? Should I recycle my ancient but still working cellphone? And, are Energy Star and OnStar still dating, or am I confusing them with another celebrity couple?

Ask and ye shall receive.

And now, for my final number, answers to ten of the most frequently asked questions about green gadgets.

What Is a Green Gadget?

In Chapter 1, I pay homage to that ol' Brenda Lee hit "Break It to Me Gently," by explaining ever so delicately what a green gadget is and what it is not. Because of space considerations, I have no choice other than to take the tough love approach and give it to you straight: There's no such thing as a green gadget.

Yes, gadgets come in different colors, including green, like the Apple iPod nano. And yes, as I mention in Chapter 11, the environmental activism organization Greenpeace lavished praise on Apple for eliminating the toxic substances brominated flame retardant (BFR) and polyvinyl chloride (PVC) from its newest iPods. But even a green iPod absent of toxic substances is *not* a green gadget. That's because gadgets contain electronics, and as such, they can never be 100 percent environmentally friendly, or *green*.

The materials and energy used to manufacture, package, ship, operate, and dispose of gadgets makes them, by nature, contributors to the carbon dioxide (CO_2) gases that cause global warming. When improperly disposed of, incinerated gadgets can release poisons into the atmosphere; when buried, they can break down and cause hazardous substances to seep into the Earth's soil and water sources. Both affect the environment and can cause illness and even death to the people living in regions polluted by electronic waste, also known as *e-waste*.

Even so, a gadget — a particular cellphone model, for example — can be greener than another model, and I discuss those models throughout this book. A gadget's greenness is gauged by numerous factors, including:

- ✔ Environmental friendliness of the building-materials collection process
- ✔ Manufacturing process
- ✔ Packaging and shipping process
- ✔ Operating efficiency when you're using it — and when you're not using it
- ✔ Ease of upgrading (so that you don't have to buy a new one to replace it)
- ✔ Ease of breakdown into recoverable parts and substances to be used to create new gadgets

In other words, when I say, "green gadgets," I'm referring to the big-picture subject of "greener" electronic products. Those designed and built with a greater sensitivity to the environment by companies that strive to decrease their carbon footprints by using environmentally friendlier manufacturing processes, packaging and distribution systems, greater energy efficiency, and more thorough recyclability when products reach the end of their life cycles.

Why Should I Care about Buying Green Gadgets?

Buying green gadgets helps to lessen the multitude of negative effects that electronic products have on the environment. Put another way: By buying green gadgets, and using them responsibly, you're making an effort to reduce your carbon footprint.

To use a gadget *responsibly* involves, for example, turning it off when you aren't using it, using it to its fullest capacity (see Chapter 19 for more about this topic), and donating or properly recycling it when you no longer need the thing.

See Part IV for information about smart green gadget shopping.

What Is EPEAT?

The lengthily named Electronic Product Environmental Assessment Tool, also known as EPEAT, is a *procurement tool* — it aims to help you find out whether desktop computers, notebooks, and monitors are environmentally friendly, and if so, to what level, based on various environmental criteria.

Here's my Average Joe translation: Visit the EPEAT Web site (www.epeat.net) to find out whether a product you're thinking of buying earned an EPEAT rating, and if so, whether it's Bronze, Silver, or Gold. (See the EPEAT Web site or Chapter 1 for more about the Bronze, Silver, and Gold ratings.)

Which Electronic Products Does EPEAT Cover?

EPEAT evaluates desktop computers, notebooks, and monitors. As I write this chapter, two groups of the Institute of Electrical and Electronics Engineers (IEEE) are working on a system to evaluate printers, imaging devices, and televisions.

What Is Energy Star?

Energy Star is a two-partner program made up of the U.S. Environmental Protection Agency (EPA) and the U.S. Department of Energy (DOE). Its aim is to help folks buy and use energy-efficient appliances and electronics products; Energy Star-supported products help consumers lessen their negative impact on the environment.

Manufacturers voluntarily participate in the Energy Star labeling program, introduced by the EPA in 1992. The program was originally designed to help reduce greenhouse gas emissions by making it easy for buyers to identify and recognize more energy-efficient computers and monitors.

You can now find the Energy Star label on more than 60 product categories, including TVs, DVD players, refrigerators, fax machines, light fixtures, windows, cordless phones, even commercial fryers and ice machines.

According to the EPA, buying and using products and appliances that bear the Energy Star logo helps save as much as 30 percent on a typical household energy bill of $2,000 per year. That's $700 in greenbacks that would otherwise fly out of your wallet if you didn't choose Energy Star products.

How Does a Product Earn the Energy Star Seal of Approval?

In simple terms, a product must adhere to strict energy-efficiency guidelines established by the EPA and the U.S. Department of Energy. Check out the following link to find out more about those guidelines:

```
www.energystar.gov/index.cfm?c=product_specs.pt_product_
          specs
```

Two examples of criteria that computers and monitors must meet to qualify for Energy Star certification include:

- ✔ **Energy use:** The device must use as little energy as possible when it's in operation.
- ✔ **Auto shutoff or standby:** The device must have automatic shut-off or standby capabilities.

What Is the "Change the World, Start with Energy Star" Campaign?

Aiming to get you aboard the "go green" express, the "Change the World, Start with Energy Star" campaign encourages you to take small steps to reduce your energy consumption. You can find the campaign's Web site at

```
www.energystar.gov/index.cfm?fuseaction=globalwarming.
          showPledgeHome
```

Some of the small steps you can pledge to take include entering the number of lights in your home you'll replace with Energy Star qualified lights, promising to activate your computer's Sleep mode, and committing to setting or programming your thermostat to use less or no energy when you're away from home or sleeping.

Should I Donate or Recycle My Old Computer?

This FAQ requires a two-part answer:

- ✔ *Donate* **if your computer is less than five years old and still functions.** Chances are good that someone can benefit from your giveaway. Even if your computer's Windows or Macintosh operating system (OS) is no longer running like it should, most donation programs wipe the hard drive and reinstall the OS before finding a new home for your unwanted computer.

- ✔ *Recycle* **if your notebook or desktop PC is beyond repair and is "hopelessly useless."** Be sure to take it or send it to a reputable electronic waste (e-waste) recycler, or have it picked up; it's the green thing to do, as I explain in Chapter 16.

If you're donating your computer, include the keyboard, mouse, monitor (if it's a desktop computer rather than a notebook), and any manuals and installation discs. Speaking of those discs, you can always use them to reformat the computer's hard drive and reinstall the OS and any bundled applications that may have come preinstalled on the computer when you purchased it.

Whether you donate or recycle your computer, be sure to check out Chapter 15 to find out how to deauthorize applications and the ability to play purchased content (such as music or movies you purchased from the iTunes Store) on the machine you're disposing of. Doing so enables you to install and run the programs and play the media on your new machine.

Chapter 15 also describes how to erase your hard drive securely before getting rid of your gadgets and computers to prevent potential snoops from accessing your personal information.

Should I Donate or Recycle My Old Cellphone?

The same two-part answer from the preceding section applies to old cellphones, too. If your cellphone stills works, you can find a program that puts the device in the hands of abuse victims, the elderly, or people who cannot afford one. If your phone is broken, on the other hand, and impossible (or too expensive) to repair, check out Chapter 14 to find take-back and recycling programs for smartphones and other handheld gadgets.

Believe it or not, you may even be able to pocket a little cash for your discard — even if you accidentally smashed the screen, as was the case with my original iPhone.

Should I Recycle My Old Rechargeable Batteries?

Yes. To find out how, turn to Chapter 3.

• Z •